Azure Cloud Projects

Learn Microsoft Azure through hands-on, real-world projects

Hamid Sadeghpour Saleh

‹packt›

Azure Cloud Projects

Portfolio Director: Kartikey Pandey
Relationship Lead: Prachi Rana
Project Manager: Sonam Pandey
Content Engineer: Arun Nadar
Technical Editor: Simran Ali
Copy Editor: Safis Editing
Proofreader: Arun Nadar
Indexer: Tejal Soni
Production Designer: Aparna Bhagat
Growth Lead: Shreyans Singh

First published: May 2025

Production reference: 2051125

Published by Packt Publishing Ltd.
Grosvenor House
11 St Paul's Square
Birmingham
B3 1RB, UK.

ISBN 978-1-83620-423-7

www.packtpub.com

I want to thank the people who have been close to me and supported me in the process of writing this book.

Never stop dreaming and taking action to bring your dreams to life.

- Hamid

Forewords

Don't rush up, rocket flying to the clouds!

Rushing up to the cloud unprepared is not wise. *Don't rush up, rocket flying to the clouds* is a phrase I often share when I speak about my cloud migration journey as a developer and cloud architect who had a mission to migrate and lift a .NET legacy application to a cloud platform – Microsoft Azure. The experience and the lessons learned (both technical and non-technical) from that cloud migration motivated me to write my first technical book. As someone who had never written a book then, that was one of the bravest things I did in my career and life.

As an internationally published technical book author, a known expert and Microsoft certified trainer in Microsoft Azure, a developer focused on cloud development in .NET, and a lead cloud infrastructure engineer, I've had the experience and privilege of growing my technical expertise in building and debugging applications on this cloud platform for the past decade.

Microsoft Azure has evolved into a powerhouse of innovation that is limitless and unstoppable, to which I relate, as I am such a person – both personally and in my own career journey. My experience solving problems and building solutions with the cloud platform Microsoft Azure – from planning, architecture, development, and deployment through DevOps to monitoring and security on the cloud infrastructure – has been a proven testament that learning the fundamentals is essential and vital (including being brave enough to accept that mistakes become lessons learned) to everyone who wants to be limitless and unstoppable in learning new technologies and innovation all day.

When I was creating my O'Reilly on-demand video course, *Breaking into Cloud Engineering: A Career Roadmap for Absolute Beginners*, I realized and truly believed in the importance and value of continuous learning – regardless of whatever level you are at right now in your career path. If you are someone new to IT or cloud engineering, or perhaps someone who is breaking into the field, keeping yourself up to date with the technologies we have today is a great investment of your time and effort – especially the recent AI.

Innovation is essential for us to move forward, and it is important to educate ourselves on the responsible use of AI and modern tools, as well as build applications that solve problems and help us with our productivity. We need to use innovative technologies, and design and build them to help us, not work against us – and we should not be scared to learn from it, teach it, and adapt from it. I believe that if the people building the tech are inspired and driven to build something great, great things are the result. Productivity using tech and AI tools helps us save time. Time is precious – and it is all we need.

Hamid Sadeghpour Saleh, the author of this fantastic book, is a fellow Microsoft MVP, MCT, Microsoft Learn Expert, and a community leader like me. His experience and expertise in Microsoft Azure, which are written about in this book, are golden.

As someone with many years of experience in problem-solving and developing applications, I believe in learning by doing. As an author who spent almost 18 months writing my first published book, *Learning Microsoft Azure*, which is currently translated into at least six languages, I can testify that the effort that Hamid invested in each chapter, page, and word in this book, based on my own experience as an author, was invested and created from the time, heart, effort and experience he has had working with this platform.

This book provides knowledge of general concepts, projects, use cases, and all the essential things you need to know about Microsoft Azure, which will hopefully help you with your day-to-day tasks and work as a developer, cloud architect, or whatever role you get within the cloud today. When I was a kid, I learned that knowledge is power, and that's how I succeed. Not because I have so much knowledge about Azure in my head but because I am a learner who shares knowledge and helps others. If you continue to learn about cloud computing and modern technologies as it evolves, you will never be left behind. You will be limitless, along with technology innovation.

As a fellow expert in the Microsoft Azure arena, I am genuinely delighted to recommend Hamid's work in this book, as it discusses Azure's essential principles and practical uses. It is also a great complementary book to mine, *Learning Microsoft Azure*.

Whether you're someone who is just getting started on your cloud journey or someone who wants to refresh your technical skills on Azure, this book will inspire and equip you to empower the potential that Azure provides, which will help you grow in your career. So, dive in, explore, and don't be scared to make mistakes. Learn by doing and pass it forward to others. You never know how it transforms and builds a lot of things!

Enjoy learning, and make sure you and your team are ready when you want to fly your rocket of amazing applications to the cloud!

Jonah C. Andersson

Senior Azure Consultant, Microsoft Certified Trainer, Microsoft MVP, Author

I have known Hamid Sadeghpour as someone who is always eager to share what he learns. Over the years, he has built a strong track record of delivering real-world cloud solutions, and this book is a great reflection of that experience.

Each of the ten projects in this book is based on real scenarios that Hamid has worked on, combined with Microsoft's recommended practices. Whether you're just starting with Azure or already working on cloud-based systems, this book offers practical, hands-on examples that will help you learn and build better solutions.

What I appreciate about Hamid's approach is how he focuses on what actually works in real environments, something that is often missing in theory-heavy resources. From setting up your first Azure project to building secure, scalable architectures and optimizing for cost, this book gives you the tools to succeed.

As someone with over two decades of experience in this industry, I know how valuable it is to have resources that go beyond the basics and bring together practical experience with best practices. This book does exactly that.

I hope you enjoy reading and learning from it as much as I did.

Sherry List

Senior Program Manager, Microsoft

Co-Founder & CEO, SyntheticAIdata

As the Chief Technology Officer for Data & AI at Sogeti Sweden, I've been working hands-on with Azure for almost a decade. Hamid's expertise in this field is truly impressive, and his work consistently demonstrates the vast potential of Azure for businesses looking to streamline their digital processes.

I remember a session where Hamid broke down the complexities of automation and integration in Azure. He pointed out that 25% of the challenges come from picking the wrong platform or service. This is a key insight for anyone wanting to make the most of Azure.

Hamid's approach is both practical and insightful. He focuses on providing clear, actionable strategies that help businesses create secure, reliable, and scalable solutions. His real-world applications make his insights incredibly valuable for professionals at any stage of their Azure journey.

I'm confident that readers will find Hamid's insights both enlightening and empowering. His ability to simplify complex concepts and provide actionable strategies is what makes his work helpful for anyone involved in running projects in Azure.

Get your bookmark ready and learn what Azure offers and take the first step towards transforming your digital processes. Hamid's expertise is your guide to unlocking the full potential of Azure, and I'm excited to introduce his work to you.

Kim Berg

Chief Technology Officer, Data & AI

Sogeti Sweden

Recommendations

Hamid and I share a common passion for technology, programming, and the entire ecosystem of tools that make up what we call "the cloud." We've been colleagues and have spoken at the same technology events multiple times. I have had the privilege of attending several of his sessions, and it doesn't take long to realize that Hamid possesses deep knowledge and hands-on experience in Microsoft Azure architecture of the highest caliber.

Microsoft Azure is a vast platform offering a wide array of tools for building all kinds of solutions, with multiple ways to achieve the same goal. Knowing what to use, when, and why is anything but trivial—and that's where Hamid's expertise truly shines. He has been actively involved in designing many solutions used by millions of users and exposed to public audiences. Security, performance, and cost-efficiency are critical requirements, and it takes someone with Hamid's competence to strike the right balance among them.

Thankfully, Hamid is also someone who shares his knowledge generously—and the book you're about to read is a testament to that. Within these pages, you'll find distilled insights drawn from real-world projects Hamid has contributed to. This is a far cry from reading raw documentation, which often requires additional research and interpretation before it can be applied to real-life scenarios.

The book covers the full breadth of cloud project development—from the earliest considerations, such as identity and access management with Microsoft Entra and networking, to deploying workloads in a containerized, cloud-native manner. Whether your project is large or small, this book provides the guidance you need to get started, get unstuck, or wrap up the final details of your Azure cloud journey.

Nikolaos Delis

Founder & CEO, Aristevin Consulting AB

Microsoft MVP for Microsoft Azure & IoT

Microsoft Certified Trainer

I have known and worked with Hamid Sadeghpour for more than 10 years. He is one of the most talented and knowledgeable technical experts I have ever met. Hamid is not just a great problem solver – he is also passionate about helping others grow and learn new technologies.

In his book, *Azure Cloud Projects*, Hamid shares his deep understanding of Microsoft Azure, one of the top cloud service providers in the world. He has always been a big fan of Microsoft technologies and never stops learning. His dedication to technology and teaching makes this book a valuable resource for anyone who wants to gain real-world knowledge about Azure cloud projects.

This book is filled with practical insights, useful examples, and hands-on experience. Whether you are starting your journey with Azure or looking to expand your skills, you will find great topics that can help you in your career path. Understanding how Azure resources work together is key to mastering the cloud, and this book will guide you through that journey.

I highly recommend reading this book. It will help you build a strong foundation in Azure and open new opportunities in cloud computing.

Mohsen Akhavan

Cloud Security Architect

I have known and worked with Hamid for more than 15 years. I can confidently say he is a dedicated professional and an authority in the realm of cloud technologies.

In this comprehensive book, Hamid takes you on a learning journey through 10 dynamic chapters that cover various Azure project use cases, including identity and access management, automation, DevOps, and security on Azure. Tailored specifically for cloud engineers and architects, this book is an essential resource for those looking to deepen their understanding of Azure's powerful capabilities.

Through *Azure Cloud Projects*, Hamid demonstrates how easy it is to implement a wide range of solutions using Azure. His practical examples and best practices enable organizations to optimize their cloud services, enhancing productivity and security in their development processes.

As you navigate through this book, you'll gain insights into the essential tools and methodologies required to build robust cloud architecture. Hamid's hands-on approach ensures that you not only grasp theoretical concepts but also learn how to apply them effectively in real-world scenarios.

With *Azure Cloud Projects*, you will explore the latest techniques that empower cloud engineers and architects to build scalable and secure applications on Azure. Hamid encapsulates years of experience and knowledge, offering step-by-step instructions, detailed examples, and links to further resources, enabling you to continuously enhance both your skills and your projects.

Embrace the power of Azure and unlock your potential as a cloud professional with Hamid's expert guidance through this valuable book.

Masoud Sabouri

Network Services Manager at Telcoset

Contributors

About the author

Hamid Sadeghpour Saleh is a Microsoft Cloud Technologies Architect with over a decade of experience turning visionary ideas into enterprise-ready cloud solutions. His passion for technology began early and has evolved into a career centered around designing innovative, secure, and scalable systems within the Microsoft Technologies ecosystem.

He specializes in streamlining complex business processes, optimizing workflows, and guiding organizations through digital transformation. In addition to his technical work, Hamid is a dedicated community leader within the Microsoft MVP Program communities. He actively contributes through event organization, mentorship, workshops, and open source collaboration.

Driven by curiosity and a deep belief in the power of technology to inspire and uplift, Hamid is committed to empowering others and building meaningful connections within the global tech community. His work reflects not only technical excellence but also a lifelong dedication to innovation and impact.

About the reviewers

Anuj Tyagi is a senior site reliability engineer with more than a decade of experience in building, scaling, automating, and managing production cloud infrastructure. He is an active open source contributor in the cloud-native community. He is co-founder of AITechNav, a non-profit community that provides mentorship to tech professionals in growing their careers.

Saeid Dahl is the Azure tech lead at Upheads, with over 17 years of distinguished experience driving innovation and transformation across the IT landscape. As a Microsoft Azure MVP, Microsoft Certified Trainer, and Microsoft Learn Learning Expert, he is widely recognized for his deep expertise, visionary leadership, and unwavering commitment to empowering others through technology.

As an Azure tech leader, Saeid shapes strategic cloud journeys, architects enterprise-grade solutions, and mentors technical teams to excellence. His work bridges the gap between cutting-edge cloud capabilities and practical business outcomes, making him a trusted advisor at the highest levels of enterprise IT.

Saeid is the co-founder of two influential communities, Microsoft Zero to Hero and MSFarsi, which have inspired and supported thousands of professionals across the globe, from early learners to seasoned engineers. His community leadership is not only impactful but also transformative, opening new doors and creating inclusive spaces for learning and growth.

As a Global Azure Board Member, international speaker, and authority on hybrid and multi-cloud strategies, automation and integration, AI and enterprise Azure service design, and PowerShell, Saeid is a driving force in shaping the future of cloud technology. His voice carries weight across conferences, leadership round tables, and technical forums, where innovation meets experience.

Table of Contents

1

Introduction to Azure and Cloud Computing   1

2

Implementing Entra ID and Hybrid Connectivity   17

3

Implementing Azure Storage Solutions   43

4

Understanding the Azure Network Topology, Design Principles, and Best Practices   59

5

Implementing a Serverless Solution   85

6

Principles and Practices of Scalable Data Management   111

7

Building a Continuous Integration and Continuous Delivery Pipeline   137

8

Designing and Building a Containerized Solution on Azure   161

9

Enhancing Security and Compliance in an Azure Project   181

10

Developing a Cloud Cost Optimization Strategy   195

11

Preface

Welcome to *Azure Cloud Projects*, a concise guide to real-world scenarios and best practices for navigating Microsoft's Azure platform. From building reliable virtual machines to architecting complex microservices, this book dives into hands-on examples that will help you tackle a variety of challenges in the cloud. Whether you're a seasoned professional or just starting your Azure journey, you'll discover practical strategies for developing secure, scalable, and cost-effective projects. Each chapter presents a unique project scenario, highlighting key decision points and showcasing proven techniques to streamline implementation. Along the way, you'll learn about critical topics such as security, performance, and DevOps processes, all tailored to help you excel in today's fast-paced cloud environment. By the end of the book, you'll have the knowledge and confidence needed to leverage Azure's ecosystem for transformative results, ensuring your projects meet both current and future demands.

Who this book is for

This book is designed for technology professionals who aim to leverage Microsoft Azure to deliver secure, scalable, and efficient cloud solutions. Whether you're a system administrator, solution architect, DevOps engineer, or project manager, the hands-on projects and best practices in these pages will empower you to plan, deploy, and optimize real-world scenarios in Azure. Even if you're relatively new to cloud computing or transitioning from another cloud platform, you'll find the examples accessible and the guidance practical. A basic understanding of cloud concepts and familiarity with common IT infrastructure tools is recommended, but comprehensive explanations will help you bridge any gaps. Ultimately, if your goal is to confidently integrate Azure services into your organization's workflow and unlock the full potential of the platform, this book is for you.

What this book covers

Chapter 1, Introduction to Azure and Cloud Computing, introduces fundamental cloud computing concepts and shows how Azure fits into the broader ecosystem. You'll learn about core Azure services, cloud deployment models, and key considerations for starting your journey in the cloud.

Chapter 2, Implementing Entra ID and Hybrid Connectivity, helps you set up Microsoft Entra ID for identity management and explore hybrid connectivity options that securely bridge your on-premises environments with Azure, ensuring seamless identity and access control.

Chapter 3, Implementing the Azure Storage Solutions, covers the core storage services in Azure—Blob, Files, Table, and Queue—and demonstrates how to configure, optimize, and secure them for various enterprise workloads.

Chapter 4, Understanding the Azure Network Topology, Design Principles, and Best Practices, delves into Azure's networking fundamentals, exploring how to design resilient and secure network architectures. You'll learn about VNet peering, network security groups, and proven strategies to optimize performance.

Chapter 5, Implementing a Serverless Solution, covers how to build and deploy applications without managing servers using Azure Functions and Logic Apps. This chapter illustrates serverless design patterns, cost optimization, and scaling.

Chapter 6, Principles and Practices of Scalable Data Management, teaches you how to handle data at scale in Azure, examining services such as Azure SQL Database, Cosmos DB, and Data Lake. You'll explore best practices for ensuring performance, reliability, and compliance.

Chapter 7, Build a Continuous Integration and Continuous Delivery Pipeline, sets up a robust CI/CD pipeline using Azure DevOps or GitHub Actions. This chapter guides you through automating build, test, and deployment processes to accelerate delivery cycles.

Chapter 8, Designing and Building a Containerized Solution on Azure, covers how to package applications with Docker and orchestrate them using **Azure Kubernetes Service (AKS)**. You will learn strategies for scalability, high availability, and efficient resource utilization.

Chapter 9, Enhancing Security and Compliance in an Azure Project, focuses on protecting your cloud resources by implementing Azure best practices for identity, governance, and threat protection. This chapter also addresses compliance requirements and security monitoring.

Chapter 10, Developing a Cloud Cost Optimization Strategy, explores methods to monitor and optimize your cloud spending. You'll learn how to right-size resources, leverage Azure cost management tools, and establish long-term financial best practices.

To get the most out of this book

To fully benefit from *Azure Cloud Projects*, you should have a working knowledge of fundamental cloud computing concepts, networking principles, and at least one programming or scripting language (such as C#, PowerShell, or Python). You'll also need access to an active Azure subscription and a computer with internet connectivity where you can install or access the necessary tools.

Hands-on exercises and practical examples are a key part of this book, so being comfortable with setting up local development environments and using command-line tools will help you follow along more effectively.

Software/hardware covered in the book	OS requirement
Azure CLI	Windows, Linux, or macOS
Azure PowerShell	Windows, Linux, or macOS
Visual Studio Code	Windows, Linux, or macOS
Docker/Docker Desktop	Windows, Linux, or macOS
Git	Windows, Linux, or macOS
.NET SDK/Node.js/Python	Windows, Linux, or macOS (optional)
Web browser	Windows, Linux, or macOS

The required software is listed in the *Technical requirements* section of the applicable chapter.

Conventions used

There are a number of text conventions used throughout this book.

`Code in text`: Indicates code words in text, database table names, folder names, filenames, file extensions, pathnames, dummy URLs, user input, and Twitter handles. Here is an example: "In this YAML file, the `dotnet publish` command creates a release build of the application, which is then stored as an artifact using the `PublishBuildArtifacts` task"

A block of code is set as follows:

```
jobs:
  e2e:
    runs-on ubuntu-latest
    steps:
    - name Checkout code
      uses actions/checkout@v2
    - name Set up Node.js
      uses actions/setup-node@v2
      with:
        node-version 14
    - name Install Cypress
      run npm install cypress
    - name Run E2E Tests
      run npx cypress run
```

Any command-line input or output is written as follows:

```
kubectl set image deployment/web-app web-app=mycontainerregistry.
azurecr.io/web-app:v2
```

Bold: Indicates a new term, an important word, or words that you see onscreen. For instance, words in menus or dialog boxes appear in **bold**. Here is an example: "Once all settings are configured, click **Review + create** and then **Create** to provision the function app."

> **Tips or important notes**
> Appear like this.

Get in touch

Feedback from our readers is always welcome.

General feedback: If you have questions about any aspect of this book, email us at customercare@packtpub.com and mention the book title in the subject of your message.

Errata: Although we have taken every care to ensure the accuracy of our content, mistakes do happen. If you have found a mistake in this book, we would be grateful if you would report this to us. Please visit www.packtpub.com/support/errata and fill in the form.

Piracy: If you come across any illegal copies of our works in any form on the internet, we would be grateful if you would provide us with the location address or website name. Please contact us at copyright@packt.com with a link to the material.

If you are interested in becoming an author: If there is a topic that you have expertise in and you are interested in either writing or contributing to a book, please visit authors.packtpub.com.

Reviews

Please leave a review. Once you have read and used this book, why not leave a review on the site that you purchased it from? Potential readers can then see and use your unbiased opinion to make purchase decisions, we at Packt can understand what you think about our products, and our authors can see your feedback on their book. Thank you!

For more information about Packt, please visit packt.com

Free Benefits with Your Book

This book comes with free benefits to support your learning. Activate them now for instant access (see the "*How to Unlock*" section for instructions).

Here's a quick overview of what you can instantly unlock with your purchase:

PDF and ePub Copies

Next-Gen Web-Based Reader

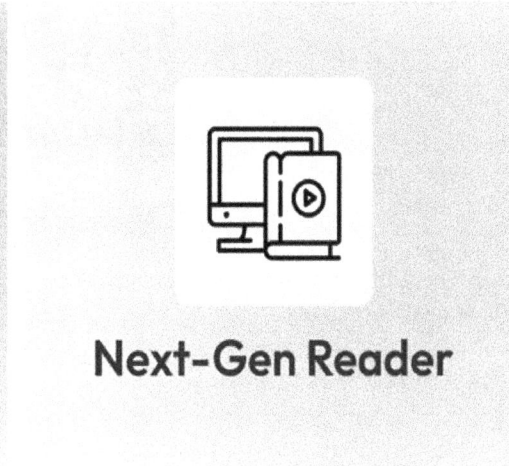

Access a DRM-free PDF copy of this book to read anywhere, on any device.

Multi-device progress sync: Pick up where you left off, on any device.

Use a DRM-free ePub version with your favorite e-reader.

Highlighting and notetaking: Capture ideas and turn reading into lasting knowledge.

Bookmarking: Save and revisit key sections whenever you need them.

Dark mode: Reduce eye strain by switching to dark or sepia themes

How to Unlock

UNLOCK NOW

Scan the QR code (or go to `packtpub.com/unlock`). Search for this book by name, confirm the edition, and then follow the steps on the page.

Note: Keep your invoice handly. Purchase made directly from packt don't require one.

Share Your Thoughts

Once you've read *Azure Cloud Projects*, we'd love to hear your thoughts! Scan the QR code below to go straight to the Amazon review page for this book and share your feedback.

https://packt.link/r/1-836-20423-X

Your review is important to us and the tech community and will help us make sure we're delivering excellent quality content.

Stay Sharp in Cloud and DevOps – Join 44,000+ Subscribers of CloudPro

CloudPro is a weekly newsletter for cloud professionals who want to stay current on the fast-evolving world of cloud computing, DevOps, and infrastructure engineering.

Every issue delivers focused, high-signal content on topics like:

- AWS, GCP & multi-cloud architecture
- Containers, Kubernetes & orchestration
- Infrastructure as Code (IaC) with Terraform, Pulumi, etc.
- Platform engineering & automation workflows
- Observability, performance tuning, and reliability best practices

Whether you're a cloud engineer, SRE, DevOps practitioner, or platform lead, CloudPro helps you stay on top of what matters, without the noise.

Scan the QR code to join for free and get weekly insights straight to your inboxswsw:

https://packt.link/cloudpro

Introduction to Azure and Cloud Computing

You land here! The world of Azure and cloud computing with real life scenarios and hands on experience! In this chapter, we will lay the foundation for your journey into cloud technologies by learning about the essential concepts of cloud computing and the Microsoft Azure platform, because I truly believe in a strong foundation and specially since in this book we will be covering different projects in an advance level. As businesses increasingly move to the cloud, understanding these basics is critical for anyone looking to work with modern IT infrastructure and services.

We will start by exploring the fundamentals of Microsoft Azure, one of the leading cloud platforms in the market, in brief We'll learn about the features of Microsoft Azure, such as scalability, cost efficiency, and flexibility, which are driving its adoption across industries.

Next, we will dive into an overview of Microsoft Azure portal and learn about its core services and solutions, including computing, storage, networking, and databases. We'll also discuss the global network of Azure data centers and the importance of regions and availability zones in ensuring high availability and resilience.

By the end of this chapter, we will have a solid understanding of cloud computing principles and the Azure ecosystem. This knowledge will serve as the foundation for the hands-on projects and advanced topics we'll cover in the subsequent chapters. We'll be ready to start building, deploying, and managing cloud solutions on Azure, harnessing the power of the cloud to meet modern business needs.

This chapter will cover the following topics:

- What is Microsoft Azure?
- Exploring the Azure Portal
- Overview of Azure Core Services and Solutions
- Understanding Azure Regions and Availability

> **Free Benefits with Your Book**
>
> Your purchase includes a free PDF copy of this book along with other exclusive benefits. Check the *Free Benefits with Your Book* section in the Preface to unlock them instantly and maximize your learning experience.

What is Microsoft Azure?

Microsoft Azure is a comprehensive suite of cloud services designed to help organizations build, deploy, and manage applications through Microsoft-managed data centers. Launched in 2010, Azure has rapidly grown to become a leading cloud platform, offering a wide range of services including computing, analytics, storage, and networking (`https://www.forbes.com/sites/janakirammsv/2020/02/03/a-look-back-at-ten-years-of-microsoft-azure/`).

Azure provides a highly flexible, scalable and open platform, supporting a broad selection of operating systems, programming languages, frameworks, databases, and devices. This versatility allows businesses to use their preferred tools and technologies while leveraging the benefits of cloud computing. You can find more about Azure Fundamentals and Core Cloud Concepts on `https://learn.microsoft.com/en-us/training/paths/microsoft-azure-fundamentals-describe-cloud-concepts/`.

Features

Let's look at some of its features:

- **Global reach**: Microsoft operates data centers in numerous regions worldwide, ensuring that Azure services are available wherever you need them. This extensive network of data centers allows businesses to deploy applications closer to their customers, reducing latency and improving performance. For example, a global e-commerce company can use Azure's data centers in different regions to ensure that their website loads quickly for users in Europe, Asia, and North America.

- **Scalability**: Whether you're running a small web application or a large-scale enterprise solution, Azure can scale to meet your needs. You can easily adjust resources up or down based on demand, ensuring that you only pay for what you use. This elasticity is particularly beneficial for businesses with fluctuating workloads, such as retail companies that experience spikes during holiday shopping seasons.

- **Security and compliance**: Azure provides built-in security controls, identity management, and threat detection services. Additionally, Microsoft invests heavily in securing its infrastructure, ensuring compliance with numerous industry standards and regulations.

  For example, Azure's **identity and access management** (**IAM**) tools, such as Azure Active Directory, allow businesses to manage user identities and control access to resources securely. This is particularly useful for organizations with stringent security requirements, such as financial institutions or healthcare providers.

- **Integration**: Azure seamlessly integrates with other Microsoft products and services, such as Office 365, Dynamics 365, and Active Directory. This integration simplifies the management of cloud and on-premises environments, providing a unified and cohesive experience. For instance, a business using Office 365 for productivity can easily integrate it with Azure Active Directory to manage user access and enhance security.

- **Flexibility**: Moreover, Azure supports a wide range of third-party tools and platforms, allowing businesses to use their preferred technologies while leveraging Azure's powerful cloud capabilities. For example, developers can use popular development frameworks like .NET, Java, or Node.js, and integrate them with Azure's services to build robust and scalable applications.

Next, we will explore Azure's core services and solutions in greater detail, providing you with the knowledge and tools needed to harness the full potential of Microsoft Azure. This foundational understanding will prepare you for the hands-on projects and advanced topics covered in the subsequent chapters.

Core Azure Services and Solutions

Microsoft Azure offers a vast array of services that cater to various business needs, ranging from computing power and storage to advanced analytics and machine learning. In this section, we will explore some of the core services provided by Azure, giving you a comprehensive understanding of the platform's capabilities and how you can leverage them for your projects.

Virtual Machines

Azure Virtual Machines (VMs) offer a flexible and scalable way to run applications in the cloud. You can create VMs with various operating systems, including Windows and Linux, and configure them with the resources needed for your applications. For instance, a development team can use VMs to create isolated environments for testing different software versions without impacting production systems.

Creating a VM in Azure is straightforward. You can select the desired operating system, VM size, and configuration through the Azure Portal or use an ARM template for automated deployment. Once deployed, you can manage your VM through the portal, including starting, stopping, and resizing as needed.

Azure App Services

Azure App Services is a fully managed platform for building, deploying, and scaling web apps, mobile backends, and RESTful APIs. With App Services, you can host applications written in various languages, such as .NET, Java, Node.js, PHP, and Python. The platform handles infrastructure management, allowing you to focus on developing your application.

For example, if you are developing a web application, you can use Azure App Services to deploy your app quickly, ensuring high availability and automatic scaling based on demand. The platform also integrates with popular development tools, such as Visual Studio and GitHub, to streamline your development workflow.

Azure Functions

Azure Functions is a serverless compute service that enables you to run code on-demand without managing the underlying infrastructure. This service is ideal for tasks that require short-lived processing, such as responding to HTTP requests, processing data from a queue, or running scheduled tasks.

Using Azure Functions, you can focus on writing code while Azure handles the infrastructure. For instance, an e-commerce website can use Azure Functions to process orders as they are placed, automatically scaling to handle varying loads without any manual intervention.

Storage Services

Azure's storage services provide secure, scalable, and durable storage solutions for a wide range of data types and applications. You can learn more about Azure Storage Services and option on `https://learn.microsoft.com/en-us/azure/storage/common/storage-introduction`

Here's a few examples of Azure Storage Services:

- **Azure Blob Storage**: Azure Blob Storage is designed for storing large amounts of unstructured data, such as documents, images, videos, and backups. It is highly scalable and cost-effective, making it suitable for applications that require extensive data storage.

  For example, a media company can use Blob Storage to store and stream video content to users worldwide. Blob Storage supports various access tiers, allowing you to balance cost and performance based on your needs. You can also integrate Blob Storage with other Azure services, such as Azure CDN, to enhance content delivery performance.

- **Azure File Storage**: Azure File Storage provides fully managed file shares in the cloud, accessible via the Server Message Block (SMB) protocol. This service is useful for scenarios where you need shared storage accessible from multiple virtual machines or applications.

  For instance, a global team working on a software project can use Azure File Storage to collaborate on code and documents, ensuring all team members have access to the latest versions. Azure File Storage supports both standard and premium performance tiers, allowing you to choose the appropriate level of performance for your workloads.

- **Azure Disk Storage**: Azure Disk Storage offers high-performance, durable block storage for use with Azure VMs. It is ideal for applications that require low-latency access to data, such as databases and enterprise applications.

  When you create a VM in Azure, you can attach managed disks to provide persistent storage. Azure Disk Storage offers various disk types, including Standard HDD, Standard SSD, and Premium SSD, to meet different performance and cost requirements.

Networking services

Networking is a critical component of cloud infrastructure, and Azure provides a comprehensive suite of networking services to connect and manage your resources.

- **Azure Virtual Network (VNet)**: Azure Virtual Network (VNet) enables you to create isolated networks within the Azure cloud. You have full control over IP address ranges, subnets, routing, and security settings, allowing you to design and manage your network infrastructure.

  For example, you can use VNet to segment your applications into different subnets for better security and management. You can also establish secure connections between your on-premises network and Azure VNet using VPN Gateway or ExpressRoute.

- **Azure Load Balancer**: Azure Load Balancer distributes incoming network traffic across multiple resources, ensuring high availability and reliability. It is essential for applications that require high uptime and can scale to handle varying loads.

  For instance, an online retail website can use Azure Load Balancer to distribute traffic across multiple web servers, ensuring that no single server becomes a bottleneck during peak shopping periods. This setup improves performance and provides fault tolerance.

- **Azure Content Delivery Network (CDN)**: Azure CDN is designed to deliver high-bandwidth content to users globally with low latency. It caches content at strategically located edge nodes around the world, ensuring fast delivery to users regardless of their geographic location.

  A media streaming service can use Azure CDN to distribute video content efficiently, reducing load times and improving the user experience. The CDN integrates seamlessly with Azure Blob Storage, making it easy to set up and manage.

- **Azure VPN Gateway and Azure ExpressRoute**: For secure and scalable connectivity between on-premises networks and Azure, Azure VPN Gateway and Azure ExpressRoute offer robust solutions. These services provide encrypted tunnels and dedicated private connections, ensuring secure data transfer between your on-premises infrastructure and Azure.

Database Services

Azure provides a variety of managed database services to support different types of data and workloads.

- **Azure SQL Database**: Azure SQL Database is a fully managed relational database service built on SQL Server. It offers high availability, security, and performance, making it suitable for a wide range of applications, from small web apps to large enterprise solutions.

  For example, a financial services company can use SQL Database to manage transaction data securely and efficiently. The service supports advanced features like automatic tuning, threat detection, and geo-replication to ensure optimal performance and security.

- **Azure Cosmos DB**: Azure Cosmos DB is a globally distributed, multi-model database service that provides turnkey global distribution and horizontal scaling. It is designed for applications that require low-latency access to data across multiple regions.

  For instance, a social media platform can use Cosmos DB to store user profiles and activity logs, ensuring fast access regardless of the user's location. Cosmos DB supports multiple data models, including document, key-value, graph, and column-family, making it a versatile choice for various use cases.

- **Azure Database for MySQL and PostgreSQL**: Azure offers managed database services for MySQL and PostgreSQL, providing scalable and secure database solutions for open-source database engines. These services are ideal for businesses that prefer using open-source databases but want to benefit from Azure's management and scaling capabilities.

For example, a tech startup can use Azure Database for MySQL to manage their application's backend database, leveraging built-in high availability and automated backups to ensure data integrity and uptime.

Understanding Azure's core services and solutions is crucial for effectively leveraging the platform to meet your business needs. Whether you need compute power, storage solutions, networking capabilities, or managed databases, Azure provides a comprehensive suite of services to support your applications.

Now that we have covered Azure Fundamentals and have a bit of context from basics, we now know how Azure can help with the services and features and how we can benefit from it. Let's explore Azure portal to see how we work with the dashboard.

Exploring the Azure Portal

Navigating and utilizing the Azure Portal is an essential skill for anyone working with Microsoft Azure. The Azure Portal is a web-based application that provides a **graphical user interface** (**GUI**) to manage your Azure resources efficiently. In this section, we will explore the features of the Azure Portal, how to navigate it, and how to create and manage resources.

It's best to always check for Azure Updates and Portal changes since there are frequent updates to the dashboard and configurations. A good resource for doing so is `https://learn.microsoft.com/en-us/azure/azure-portal/`.

The following image shows how the first landing page in Azure Portal looks like with the default resources, seen in the dashboard.

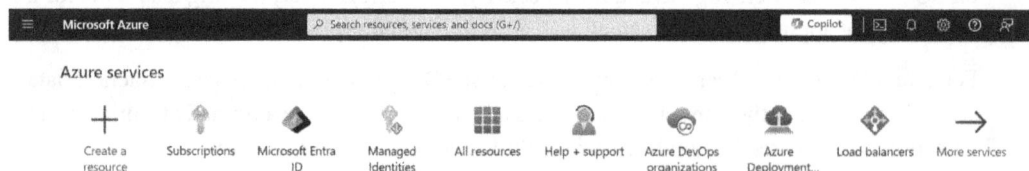

Figure 1.1 – Azure Portal dashboard landing page

Getting Started

To get started with the Azure Portal, you first need to access it through your web browser. Visit `https://portal.azure.com` and log in with your Azure account credentials. If you don't have an Azure account yet, you can sign up for a free account at `https://azure.microsoft.com/`, which provides access to a range of Azure services and a credit to explore them.

Upon logging in, you will be greeted by the Azure Portal's home screen, as shown in *Figure 1.2*.

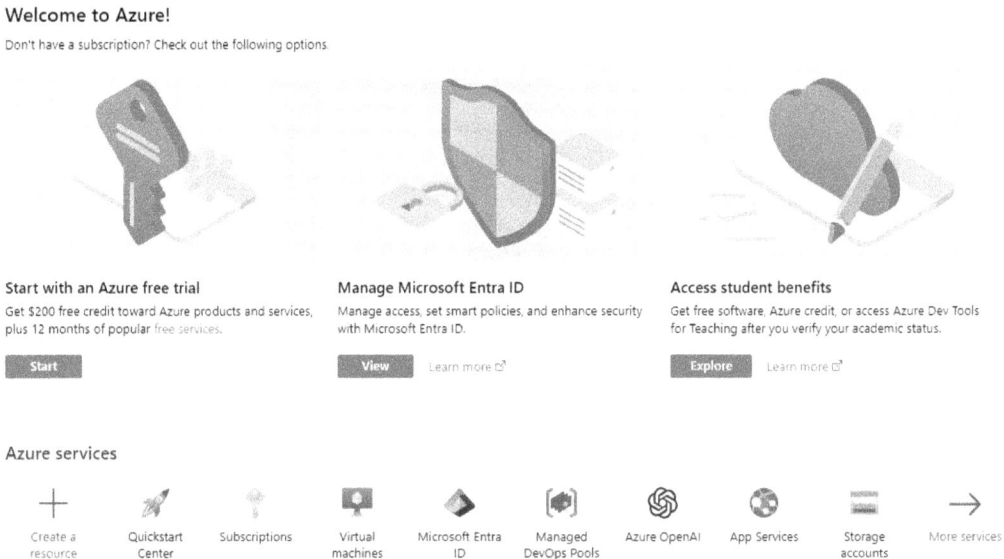

Figure 1.2 – Azure Portal Welcome Page

This home screen features a customizable dashboard that provides an overview of your resources and services. The dashboard is designed to help you quickly access and manage the Azure services you use most frequently.

Customizing Your Dashboard

The Azure Portal dashboard is highly customizable, allowing you to tailor it to your specific needs. You can add, remove, and rearrange tiles to create a personalized workspace. For example, you might add tiles for virtual machines, storage accounts, and resource groups that you frequently manage. This customization helps you stay organized and improves your workflow by keeping important information and tools at your fingertips.

To customize your dashboard, click on the **Dashboard** button in the left-hand navigation pane, then click **Edit** on the top menu. From here, you can drag and drop tiles, resize them, and add new ones by clicking on the **Add tile** button. The following figure demonstrates these features:

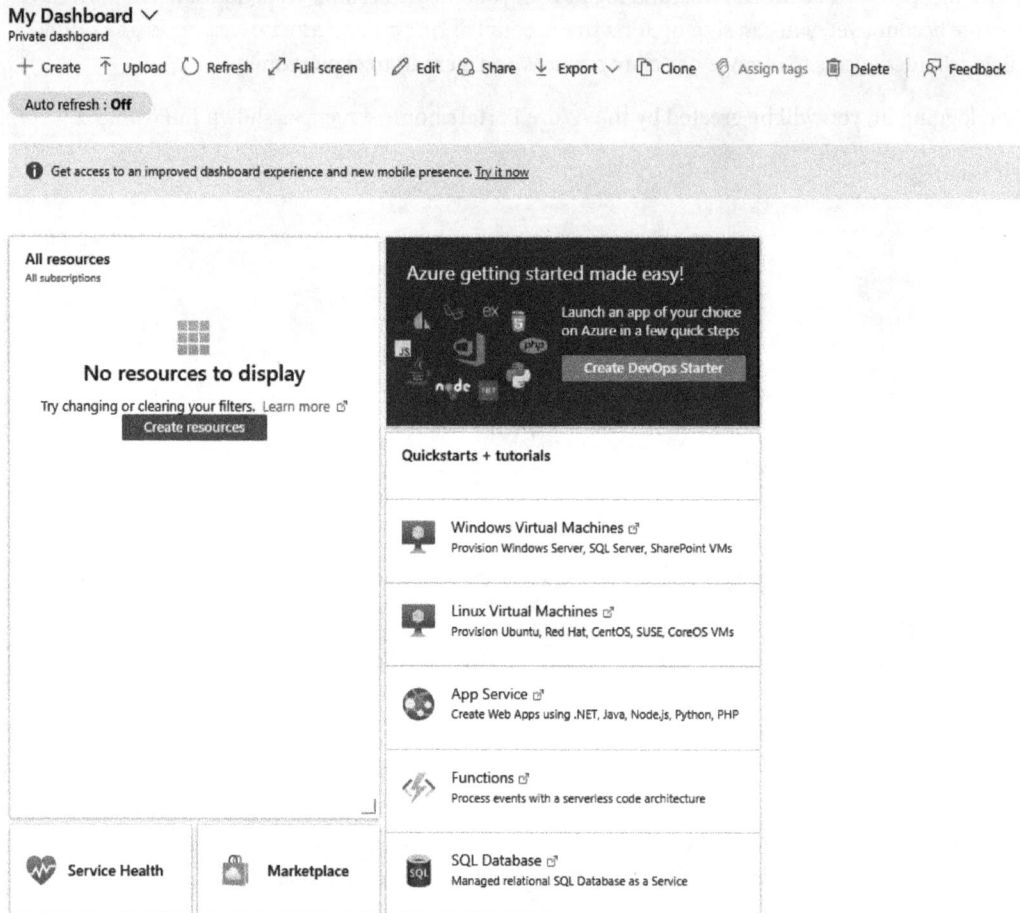

Figure 1.3 – Azure Dashboards where you can Edit tiles, add new tiles depending on need

Navigating the Azure Portal

The Azure Portal is designed to be intuitive and user-friendly. The main navigation pane on the left side of the screen provides access to all Azure services, organized by category. As seen in *Figure 1.3*, this navigation pane includes options such as **Home**, **Dashboard**, **All services**, **Resource groups**, and **Subscriptions**.

Let's learn more about these options:

- **Home**: The home screen provides a high-level overview of your Azure environment, including recent resources, common tasks, and quick access to essential tools.

- **Dashboard**: The dashboard is your customizable workspace where you can pin frequently used resources and services.

- **All services**: This section lists all available Azure services, categorized for easy browsing. You can use the search bar to quickly find specific services.

- **Resource groups**: Resource groups are logical containers that help you manage and organize your Azure resources. They are essential for grouping related resources together for better management.

- **Subscriptions**: This section provides information about your Azure subscriptions, including billing details, usage, and quotas.

Using the Search Bar

The search bar at the top of the Azure Portal is a powerful tool that allows you to quickly find resources, services, and documentation. *Figure 1.4* shows how it looks like:

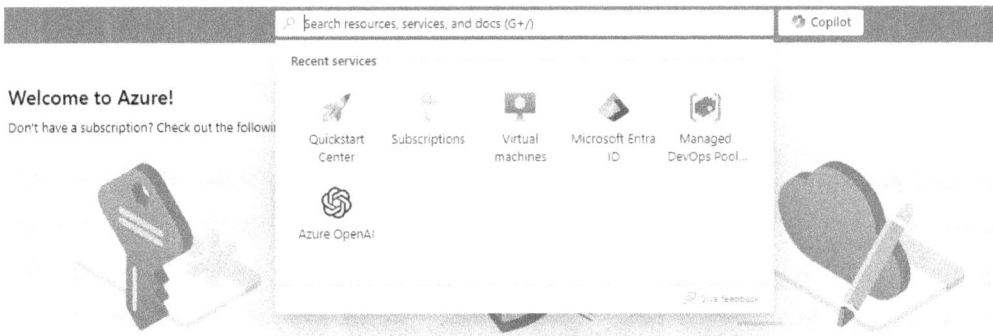

Figure 1.4 – Azure Portal – Using Search Bar

As you may see in the preceding figure, all you need to do is type in the name of the resource or service you are looking for, and the search bar will provide relevant suggestions. For example, if you type `virtual machine`, the search bar will display options to create a new virtual machine, view existing virtual machines, and access related documentation.

Creating and Managing Resources

Creating and managing resources in the Azure Portal is straightforward. Azure provides a wide range of services and resources that you can deploy to meet your specific needs. Whether you are setting up a virtual machine, a database, or a web app, the Azure Portal makes it easy to get started.

Creating a Resource

To create a new resource, click on the **Create a resource** button located in the left-hand navigation pane, as shown in *Figure 1.5*. This will take you to the Azure Marketplace, where you can browse and select from a vast array of services and applications. The Marketplace offers everything from virtual machines and databases to artificial intelligence and machine learning services.

Figure 1.5 – Example of Creating a Resource in Azure Portal

For example, let's say you want to create a new virtual machine. You'd follow these steps to do so:

1. Click on **Create a resource** in the left-hand navigation pane.

2. In the search bar, type `Virtual Machine` and select the appropriate option from the results.

3. Click on **Create** to start the virtual machine creation process.

4. Follow the guided steps to configure your virtual machine, including selecting the operating system, size, and region, as well as configuring networking and storage options.

5. Once you have configured all the settings, click on **Review + create** to review your configurations and then click **Create** to deploy the virtual machine.

The Azure Portal will provide real-time status updates as your virtual machine is being created. Once the deployment is complete, you can manage your virtual machine from the Azure Portal.

Managing Resources

The Azure Portal provides comprehensive tools for managing your resources. After creating a resource, you can monitor its performance, configure settings, and set up alerts to stay informed about its status. For example, if you created a virtual machine, you can view its metrics, start or stop the VM, and adjust its size or configuration as needed.

Additionally, the Azure Portal integrates with Azure Monitor and Azure Security Center, providing advanced monitoring and security capabilities. **Azure Monitor** helps you collect, analyze, and act on telemetry data from your cloud and on-premises environments. You can create dashboards, set up alerts, and create automated actions based on your monitoring data.

Azure Security Center provides unified security management and advanced threat protection for your Azure resources. It offers security recommendations, threat detection, and compliance management to help you safeguard your resources and data.

Using Azure Resource Manager Templates

For consistent and efficient resource deployment, **Azure Resource Manager** (**ARM**) templates are invaluable. ARM templates are JSON files that define the infrastructure and configuration for your Azure deployment. By using ARM templates, you can automate the deployment process, ensuring that your environments are set up consistently across different stages of development and production.

To deploy resources using an ARM template, follow these steps:

1. In the Azure Portal, click on **Create a resource**.
2. Search for **Template deployment** and select **Deploy a custom template**.
3. Click on **Build your own template in the editor** to create or paste your ARM template.
4. Once the template is defined, click on **Save** and proceed to fill out the required parameters for the deployment.
5. Click on **Review + create** to review the template configurations, and then click **Create** to deploy the resources.

ARM templates enable you to define complex deployments, including dependencies between resources, and ensure that your infrastructure is consistently deployed every time.

The Azure Portal is a powerful and user-friendly interface for managing your Azure resources. By customizing your dashboard, navigating the portal, and utilizing its comprehensive tools, you can efficiently manage your cloud infrastructure. Creating and managing resources is straightforward, and advanced features like Azure Monitor, Azure Security Center, and ARM templates provide robust capabilities for monitoring, security, and automation.

In the next section, we will explore the concept of Azure regions and availability zones, which are essential for designing highly available and resilient cloud architectures. This knowledge will further enhance your ability to build robust and scalable solutions on Microsoft Azure, preparing you for the hands-on projects and advanced topics covered in the subsequent chapters.

Understanding Azure Regions and Availability Zones

To fully harness the power of Microsoft Azure, it's crucial to understand the concepts of regions and availability zones. These foundational elements play a significant role in how you design, deploy, and manage your applications and services in the cloud. In this section, we will delve into what Azure regions and availability zones are, how they work, and why they are essential for building resilient, high-availability solutions.

Azure Regions

Azure regions are geographic locations around the world where Microsoft has established data centers. Each region contains multiple data centers that are logically grouped together to provide redundancy and high availability. These regions are interconnected through a dedicated low-latency network, ensuring seamless connectivity and data transfer. As shown in the following figure, there are different **Regions** with **Availability Zones** and **Datacenters**.

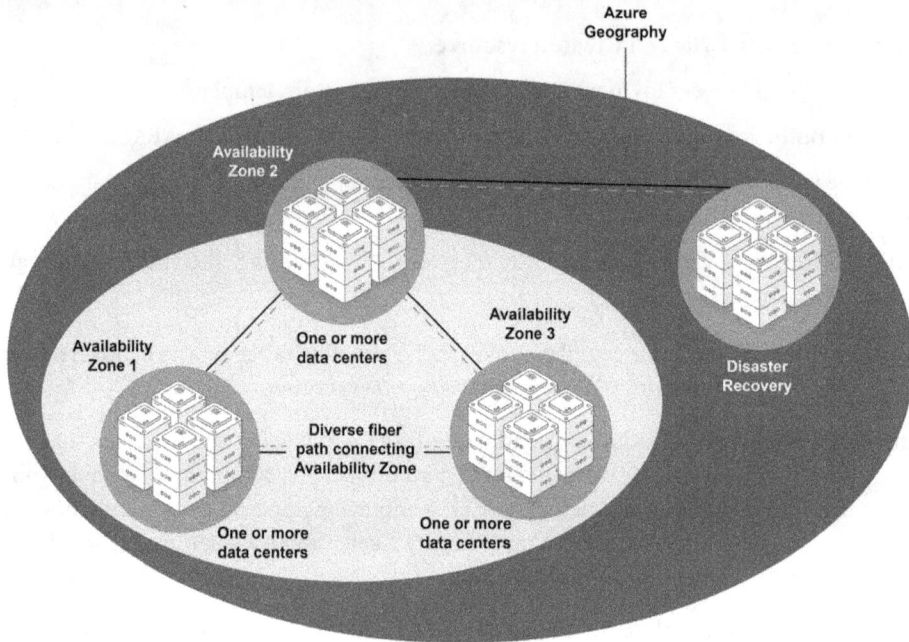

Figure 1.6 – Azure Availability Zones in Different Regions

Why Regions Matter

Regions are critical for several reasons:

- **Latency and Performance**: By selecting a region close to your end-users, you can minimize latency and improve application performance. For example, if your primary user base is in Europe, deploying your application in an Azure region in Europe will provide faster response times compared to a region in North America.

- **Compliance and Data Sovereignty**: Different regions may have specific regulatory and compliance requirements. Choosing a region that complies with local laws and regulations is essential for meeting data sovereignty requirements. For instance, a financial services company operating in Germany might choose the Germany West Central region to ensure compliance with local data protection laws.

- **Redundancy and Disaster Recovery**: Using multiple regions can enhance the resilience of your applications. By replicating data and services across regions, you can ensure continuity in the event of a regional outage. This approach is critical for disaster recovery planning.

Examples of Azure Regions

Azure has a broad global footprint with regions in various parts of the world, including:

- **North America:** East US, West US, Central US, Canada Central

- **Europe:** North Europe, West Europe, UK South, Germany West Central

- **Asia Pacific**: East Asia, Southeast Asia, Australia East, Japan East

- **South America**: Brazil South

- **Middle East and Africa**: UAE North, South Africa North

Each region offers a range of services, although availability can vary. When planning your deployment, it's essential to check the specific services available in your chosen region. For more information about Azure Regions and Availability Zones you can also visit `https://learn.microsoft.com/en-us/azure/reliability/availability-zones-overview?tabs=azure-cli`.

Availability Zones

Within Azure regions, there are availability zones. An **availability zone** is a physically separate location within a region. Each availability zone consists of one or more data centers equipped with independent power, cooling, and networking. The isolation provided by availability zones ensures that if one zone experiences an outage, the others continue operating, thus enhancing the overall availability of your applications.

How do Availability Zones Work?

Availability zones are designed to provide high availability and fault tolerance. Azure guarantees 99.99% uptime for virtual machines deployed across availability zones. This is achieved by distributing resources across multiple zones within a region.

How can Availability Zones be implemented?

When creating resources in Azure, you can specify the availability zone in which to deploy them. For example, when creating a VM, you can choose to deploy it in Zone 1, Zone 2, or Zone 3 within a specific region. By strategically distributing your resources, you can enhance the resilience and availability of your applications.

Benefits of Using Availability Zones

Some key benefits of using availability zones are as follows:

- **High Availability**: By deploying resources across multiple availability zones, you can ensure that your applications remain available even if one zone fails. This approach is particularly important for mission-critical applications that require constant uptime.

- **Fault Isolation**: Each availability zone is isolated from the others, so issues like power outages or network disruptions in one zone do not affect the others. This isolation helps contain faults and minimize their impact on your applications.

- **Disaster Recovery**: Availability zones are ideal for setting up disaster recovery solutions. You can replicate data and services across zones to ensure quick recovery in the event of a failure. For example, an e-commerce website can deploy its web servers in one zone and its database servers in another, ensuring that both tiers remain operational during an outage.

Examples of Services Supporting Availability Zones

Not all Azure services support availability zones, but many critical services do, including:

- **VMs**: Deploy VMs across zones to ensure high availability.

- **Managed Disks**: These store VM disks in different zones to prevent data loss.

- **Load Balancers**: These distribute traffic across zones for balanced and resilient application delivery.

- **Azure Kubernetes Service (AKS)**: These deploy AKS nodes across zones for resilient container orchestration.

- **SQL Databases**: These use zone-redundant databases to protect against zone failures.

Designing for High Availability and Resilience

To design high-availability applications on Azure, it's essential to leverage both regions and availability zones effectively. Here are some strategies:

- **Multi-Region Deployment**: This ensures application availability by deploying across multiple regions.

- **Zone-Redundant Architecture**: This increases fault tolerance by distributing components across availability zones.

- **Automated Failover and Recovery**: This minimizes downtime with automated failover mechanisms.

- **Regular Testing and Monitoring**: This ensures readiness with regular disaster recovery testing and monitoring.

Understanding Azure regions and availability zones is fundamental for designing resilient and highly available applications. By strategically selecting regions and distributing resources across availability zones, you can enhance the performance, availability, and fault tolerance of your applications. Leveraging these concepts effectively will prepare you for the hands-on projects and advanced topics covered in the subsequent chapters, ensuring that you can build robust and scalable solutions on Microsoft Azure.

Summary

In this chapter, we have covered Microsoft Azure in an Engineering perspective, we've tried to cover the benefits that Microsoft Azure can add to your environment by exploring Azure in general and checking what you can do with the Portal, dashboards for a better monitoring and observability and then diving into Core Services and Solutions that we can benefit from, also, we've covered Azure Regions and Availability since having a better understanding of Availability will help you more with the next chapters and in your overall Architectural journey.

Now that you know about Microsoft Azure Services and Cloud Computing, it's time for the next chapter. We will jump into real world scenarios where we will learn how to put together these services from design to implementation to achieve most of the needs within your organization.

Get This Book's PDF Version and Exclusive Extras

UNLOCK NOW

Scan the QR code (or go to `packtpub.com/unlock`). Search for this book by name, confirm the edition, and then follow the steps on the page.

Note: Keep your invoice handly. Purchase made directly from packt don't require one.

2

Implementing Entra ID and Hybrid Connectivity

Starting with the very first project in this book, you'll notice that the projects are somewhat connected to each other. This connection makes the book and its chapters more engaging, as you'll experience not just the technology, but also the soft skills and communication throughout the book, which I think are very important factors in today's world – especially within the IT industry!

So, let's get started!

In this chapter, we will focus on a scenario-based project where you'll implement Microsoft Entra ID (formerly known as Azure Active Directory) for identity management and establish hybrid connectivity between on-premises infrastructure and Azure. This hands-on approach will help you understand the practical applications of these technologies and their best practices.

We will cover the following topics:

- Why use Entra ID?
- Working with Microsoft Entra ID
- Understanding the necessary soft skills

Technical requirements

To follow along with this chapter, you will need the following:

- A Microsoft Azure account
- An on-premises Active Directory setup
- Internet access
- Basic knowledge of networking and identity management

Why use Entra ID?

Microsoft Entra ID is a cloud-based IAM service from Microsoft. It helps organizations manage and secure identities and control access to applications, both on-premises and in the cloud. The next few sub-sections will cover the advantages of using Entra ID. In *Figure 2.1*, a Microsoft Entra ID connectivity map showing how it can connect your identity solutions is presented.

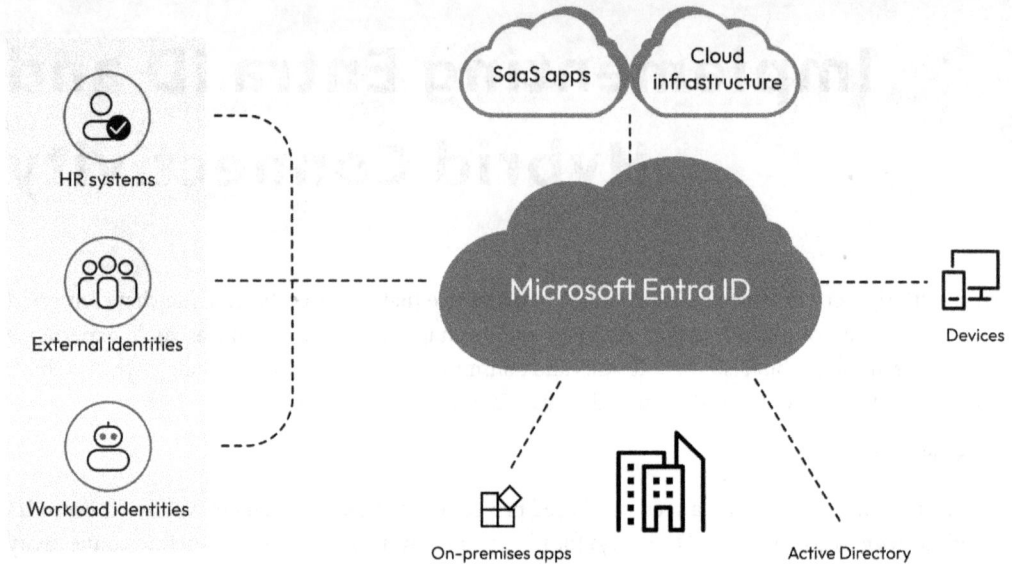

Figure 2.1 – Microsoft Entra ID connectivity map

Centralized identity management

One of the most significant advantages of using Microsoft Entra ID is its ability to centralize identity management. In traditional IT environments, managing user identities and accessing permissions often involves multiple systems and processes, which can lead to inconsistencies and increased administrative workload. Entra ID simplifies this by providing a single platform to manage all user identities and their access rights.

Simply put, centralized identity management means that all user accounts, groups, and roles are managed from a single location. This centralization offers several benefits:

- **Simplified administration**: Administrators can manage user identities, assign roles, and set access permissions from one interface. This reduces the complexity and time required to manage these tasks.

- **Consistency**: Centralized management ensures that security policies and access controls are applied uniformly across the organization. This reduces the risk of security gaps that can occur when policies are inconsistently applied.

- **Efficiency**: With a single source of truth for identity management, processes such as onboarding new employees, managing access requests, and auditing user activity become more streamlined and efficient.

For instance, consider a scenario where an organization has multiple departments, each using different applications and systems. Without centralized identity management, each department might manage its own set of user accounts and access controls, leading to redundant efforts and potential security issues. By implementing Entra ID, the organization can manage all user identities centrally, ensuring that access policies are consistently enforced and reducing the administrative burden on IT staff.

Enhanced security

Security is a top priority for any organization, and Microsoft Entra ID offers advanced security features to protect user identities and access to resources. These features include **Multi-Factor Authentication** (**MFA**), Conditional Access policies, and identity protection mechanisms. Let's learn more about these:

- **MFA**: MFA adds an extra layer of security by requiring users to provide two or more verification factors to gain access. This could include something the user knows (password), something the user has (a mobile device), or something the user is (fingerprint or facial recognition). By implementing MFA, organizations can significantly reduce the risk of unauthorized access due to compromised passwords.

- **Conditional Access policies**: These policies allow administrators to control how users access resources based on specific conditions such as the user's location, device compliance, or risk level. For example, access can be restricted to certain geographical regions or devices that meet specific security criteria. Conditional Access policies help ensure that only authorized and secure devices can access sensitive information.

- **Identity protection**: Entra ID includes features to detect and respond to suspicious activities related to user identities. It uses machine learning algorithms to identify potential risks, such as unusual login attempts or compromised accounts. Administrators can set up automated responses to mitigate these risks, such as requiring additional verification or blocking access until the risk is resolved.

Microsoft Entra ID Internet Access versus Private Access

Microsoft Entra ID offers two main ways for users and applications to connect: Internet Access and Private Access. Each serves different needs, depending on the requirements for security, scalability, and connectivity.

Entra ID Internet Access

Internet Access allows users and applications to authenticate through public internet endpoints. This is the standard method for connecting users and services that are geographically distributed, particularly those accessing resources from diverse locations:

Internet Access is commonly used for connecting remote employees, customers, and partners through public applications such as Office 365, where users can log in from anywhere.

It provides high scalability and easy access globally, making it ideal for B2C services or any application that requires widespread access without strict network boundaries.

Entra ID Private Access

Private Access provides a secure, internal method for authenticating users and applications, bypassing the public internet. This is typically achieved through a **Virtual Network** (**VNet**) or other secure connectivity, such as VPNs or ExpressRoute.

Private Access is used for applications that require enhanced security, such as internal tools or sensitive data environments that must be isolated from the public internet.

Keeping traffic off the public internet reduces exposure to external threats and ensures tighter security control, making it suitable for environments requiring a high degree of data protection and regulatory compliance.

For instance, imagine a company that allows employees to work remotely. Without advanced security measures, remote access could expose the company to various security threats. By using Entra ID's MFA, remote employees are required to verify their identity through their mobile devices in addition to entering their passwords. Conditional Access policies ensure that only compliant devices and secure locations are allowed to access the company's resources. If suspicious activity is detected, such as an attempted login from an unusual location, identity protection features can block the attempt and notify the administrators.

Seamless integration options

Microsoft Entra ID is designed to integrate seamlessly with other Microsoft services, including Office 365, Dynamics 365, and various Azure services. This integration enhances productivity and simplifies user management by providing **Single Sign-On** (**SSO**) capabilities. The details of these benefits are as follows:

- SSO: SSO allows users to access multiple applications with a single set of credentials. Once logged in to Entra ID, users can access other integrated Microsoft services without needing to re-enter their credentials. This reduces the complexity of managing multiple passwords and improves user convenience.

- Unified management: Integration with Microsoft services means that administrators can manage user identities, access permissions, and security policies across all Microsoft applications from a single interface. This unified management approach simplifies administration and ensures consistent application of security measures.

- Enhanced collaboration: Seamless integration with Office 365 and other collaboration tools facilitates better teamwork and productivity. Users can easily access email, documents, and collaboration platforms without worrying about multiple logins.

Non-Microsoft services integration support

While Microsoft Entra ID is optimized for seamless integration with Microsoft products, it also supports authentication and authorization for third-party and non-Microsoft services. This flexibility allows organizations to extend Entra ID's capabilities to various external platforms using industry-standard identity protocols, such as OpenID Connect and OAuth 2.0:

- **OpenID Connect integration**: OpenID Connect is an identity layer on top of the OAuth 2.0 protocol, used for verifying users' identity and obtaining their profile information. It is widely supported by many non-Microsoft services and allows users to sign in using their Microsoft Entra ID credentials.

- **OAuth 2.0 integration**: OAuth 2.0 is a protocol primarily used for authorization, allowing applications to obtain limited access to user accounts without exposing their credentials. It's used to enable secure and granular permissions to non-Microsoft services.

Let's consider an example. A typical organization might use a suite of Microsoft products, including Office 365 for email and document management, Dynamics 365 for customer relationship management, and Azure services for cloud infrastructure. With Entra ID, employees can log in once and gain access to all these services without needing to enter their credentials multiple times. This seamless integration not only improves the user experience but also simplifies IT management by providing a unified platform for identity and access management.

Improved user experience

User experience is a critical factor in the adoption and success of IT systems. Microsoft Entra ID enhances the user experience by providing SSO capabilities and simplifying the login process. Here is how:

- **SSO**: With SSO, users only need to remember one set of credentials to access multiple applications and services. This reduces the cognitive load on users and minimizes the frustration associated with managing multiple passwords.

- **Consistent access**: Users experience consistent access across different devices and locations. Whether they are accessing resources from their office computer, home laptop, or mobile device, the login experience remains the same, enhancing convenience and productivity.

- **Reduced login frustration**: By streamlining the authentication process, Entra ID reduces the time and effort required to log in to different systems. This not only improves user satisfaction but also encourages the use of secure practices, as users are less likely to seek workarounds such as writing down passwords.

Let's imagine a scenario. Consider an employee who needs to access various applications throughout the day, including email, file storage, CRM systems, and collaboration tools. Without SSO, the employee would need to log in to each application separately, remembering different passwords and potentially experiencing login errors. With Entra ID, the employee logs in once and gains access to all required applications seamlessly, enhancing their productivity and reducing frustration.

Scalability and reliability

Scalability and reliability are crucial for any identity management system, especially as organizations grow and their needs evolve. Microsoft Entra ID is built on a highly scalable and reliable cloud infrastructure, ensuring it can handle millions of users and provide continuous availability. Let's learn more:

- **Scalability**: Entra ID can scale to accommodate the identity management needs of organizations of any size, from small businesses to large enterprises. The cloud infrastructure allows for dynamic scaling, ensuring that performance remains consistent even as the number of users increases.

- **High availability**: Entra ID is designed for high availability, with redundant systems and failover mechanisms in place to ensure continuous operation. This reliability means that users can access resources without interruption, even during maintenance or unexpected outages.

- **Global reach**: With data centers located around the world, Entra ID provides low-latency access to users regardless of their geographic location. This global presence ensures that all users experience fast and reliable access to the services they need.

- **Access reviews**: Periodically review user access to resources to ensure only the right people have the appropriate permissions.

- **Life cycle workflows**: Automate access changes as users join, switch roles, or leave, ensuring appropriate access management throughout their life cycle.

- **Conditional Access policies**: Apply specific rules based on the user context, such as location or device, to manage how resources are accessed securely.

- **Privileged Identity Management (PIM)**: Entra ID provides just-in-time elevated permissions to minimize security risks by only granting privileged access when needed.

Let's consider an example. A rapidly growing tech start-up starts with a small team but quickly expands to hundreds of employees across multiple locations. As the team grows, so does the need for a robust identity management system that can handle the increased load without compromising performance. With Entra ID, the start-up can scale its identity management seamlessly, ensuring that all employees have reliable access to the necessary applications and resources, regardless of their location. The high availability and global reach of Entra ID ensure that the start-up's operations run smoothly, supporting its growth and success.

Now that we have a better understanding of Microsoft Entra ID and its benefits, as well as how we can use it within a real-case scenario, let's implement it together in the next section.

Understanding Microsoft Entra ID B2C and B2B capabilities

Microsoft Entra ID offers comprehensive solutions to manage identity and access for both **Business-to-Consumer** (**B2C**) and **Business-to-Business** (**B2B**) scenarios. These services are essential for enabling secure, scalable identity management for diverse user groups—whether they are your external customers or partner organizations. Let's explore each service in detail and understand how Microsoft Entra ID helps you seamlessly manage access and identity across a variety of business models.

Microsoft Entra ID B2C

Microsoft Entra ID B2C is a cloud identity management service specifically designed to enable organizations to provide secure access to external users, including customers, partners, and citizens. It offers a customer-focused solution that allows users to sign in to applications using social accounts or local credentials, providing seamless, secure, and personalized experiences.

B2C features and capabilities

Microsoft Entra ID B2C provides organizations with a robust set of features to manage customer identities securely and efficiently. These capabilities help businesses offer a seamless authentication experience while ensuring security and compliance. Here are some of the key features:

- **Identity and access management for customers**: Microsoft Entra ID B2C allows organizations to handle the registration and authentication of millions of consumers. It is used for applications that require a custom-branded, secure, and easy-to-use identity management solution.

- **Sign-in options**: B2C supports multiple sign-in methods, such as email, phone number, or social logins such as Google, Facebook, and LinkedIn. This flexibility enhances the user experience by allowing customers to use existing identities they are comfortable with.

    Always try to offer multiple sign-in options to increase conversion rates and minimize user frustration during the sign-up process.

- **Customization and branding**: With B2C, you can completely customize the user experience by adding your company's branding, adjusting the layout, and configuring the look and feel of the sign-in and registration pages. You can even use HTML and JavaScript to create a user journey that matches your application's needs.

- **Security and compliance**: B2C uses the same security infrastructure as Microsoft Entra ID, which means that customers benefit from the enterprise-level security and compliance features that Microsoft provides. This includes features such as MFA and Conditional Access policies that add layers of security to protect sensitive data.

- **Conditional Access**: You can enforce Conditional Access policies, such as requiring MFA when users log in from unfamiliar locations. This helps to prevent unauthorized access while keeping the user experience simple.

- **Data compliance**: The data stored by Microsoft Entra ID B2C adheres to strict data protection regulations such as GDPR, ensuring that user information is managed securely.

How B2C helps your business

Implementing Microsoft Entra ID B2C can significantly benefit businesses by improving user engagement and reducing operational complexity. Here's how:

- **Improved user experience**: B2C helps enhance user engagement by allowing easy registration and sign-in. By supporting social logins, users are less likely to face friction during onboarding.

- **Reduced management overhead**: With B2C, you don't need to build and maintain your own identity management solution. Instead, you can use a secure, managed platform, freeing your development team to focus on your core product or service.

How B2B helps your business

While B2C focuses on customer identity, Microsoft Entra ID B2B is designed for organizations that need to collaborate with external partners. It simplifies identity management for business collaborations by offering secure access control. Here's how B2B can support your organization:

- **Simplified collaboration**: B2B makes it easy to invite external partners and manage their access to your resources, whether it's a SharePoint document, Teams chat, or an internal application.

- **Enhanced security**: External users must adhere to your organization's security policies. This ensures that partners and suppliers accessing your sensitive data meet the same standards of security as your internal employees.

- **Scalability**: Since B2B users can use their existing credentials, you don't have to worry about onboarding and managing countless external accounts, simplifying identity management as your partnerships expand.

B2C versus B2B use cases

Understanding when to use B2C versus B2B is crucial for selecting the right identity solution. While both solutions enhance identity management, their use cases differ significantly:

- **B2C** is ideal for customer-facing applications, such as an online retail store or a government portal that provides services directly to citizens. It helps simplify the authentication process by providing multiple sign-in options and easy access.

- **B2B** is designed for organizations that collaborate closely with external partners, such as suppliers or contractors. It allows for seamless integration of external users into your internal systems while providing control over what data they can access.

Working with Microsoft Entra ID

Imagine you are an IT administrator for a growing organization that has recently decided to move part of its IT infrastructure to the cloud. The primary goals are to enhance flexibility, improve scalability, and reduce operational costs. The organization wants to ensure seamless integration between its existing on-premises environment and the new cloud infrastructure.

To achieve these objectives, your task is to implement Microsoft Entra ID to manage user identities and establish hybrid connectivity between the on-premises network and Azure. This setup will enable centralized identity management, secure access to cloud resources, and reliable communication between on-premises and cloud environments.

In this section, we will achieve the following objectives:

- Setting up Microsoft Entra ID
- Synchronizing on-premises Active Directory with Microsoft Entra ID
- Implementing SSO and MFA
- Establishing hybrid connectivity using a VPN gateway
- Testing and validating the hybrid connectivity setup

Before moving on to the implementation, let's get acquainted with the associated costs.

Plans and pricing

Like any other Microsoft cloud services, Microsoft Entra also comes with different plans and pricing options and it's an important step to choose the right plan according to the needs of your organization. *Figure 2.2* shows the available plans.

Microsoft Entra ID Free	Microsoft Entra ID P1	Most comprehensive Microsoft Entra ID P2	Promotional offer available[2] Microsoft Entra ID Governance
Free	$6.00 user/month	$9.00 user/month	$7.00 user/month
Included with Microsoft cloud subscriptions such as Microsoft Azure, Microsoft 365, and others.[1]	Microsoft Entra ID P1 (formerly Azure Active Directory P1) is available as a standalone or included with Microsoft 365 E3 for enterprise customers and Microsoft 365 Business Premium for small to medium businesses, including versions of these suites that do not include Microsoft Teams.	Microsoft Entra ID P2 (formerly Azure Active Directory P2) is available as a standalone or included with Microsoft 365 E5 for enterprise customers, including versions of this suite that do not include Microsoft Teams.	Entra ID Governance is an advanced set of identity governance capabilities for Microsoft Entra ID P1 and P2 customers. Special pricing is available for Microsoft Entra P2 customers.
Sign in with your Microsoft account	Try free for 30 days	Try free for 30 days	Try free
Create a free Azure account >	Contact sales >	Contact sales >	Contact sales >

Figure 2.2 – Entra ID plans and pricing (June 2024)

If you would like to learn more about the exact features included in each plan and compare the various plans' offerings with one another, you can go to `https://www.microsoft.com/en-us/security/business/microsoft-entra-pricing`. Now, let's get started with the first objective.

Setting up an Entra ID tenant

Setting up Microsoft Entra ID is the foundation of our project – not just this specific project but also an important step for every project in the future. This involves creating a new Entra ID tenant, which acts as the container for your organization's users, groups, and applications. Think of it as setting up the main office for your organization in the cloud, where all identity-related activities will be managed.

Scenario

Imagine you are an IT administrator for a mid-sized company that has been rapidly expanding. Managing user accounts, access permissions, and security policies across multiple locations has become increasingly complex. By setting up an Entra ID organization tenant, you can centralize all these tasks, ensuring that everyone in the organization has the right access to the tools they need, no matter where they are located. For this reason, we are going to initialize an Azure account, which will create an Entra ID tenant for us.

Steps

If you already have an Azure account, you also have an Entra ID tenant associated with it and, in the left pane of your Azure dashboard, you'll see Entra ID. However, if you don't have an Azure account yet, you can simply create one for free at `https://azure.microsoft.com/`.

To directly access the Entra ID portal, you can also use the following link:

`https://entra.microsoft.com/`

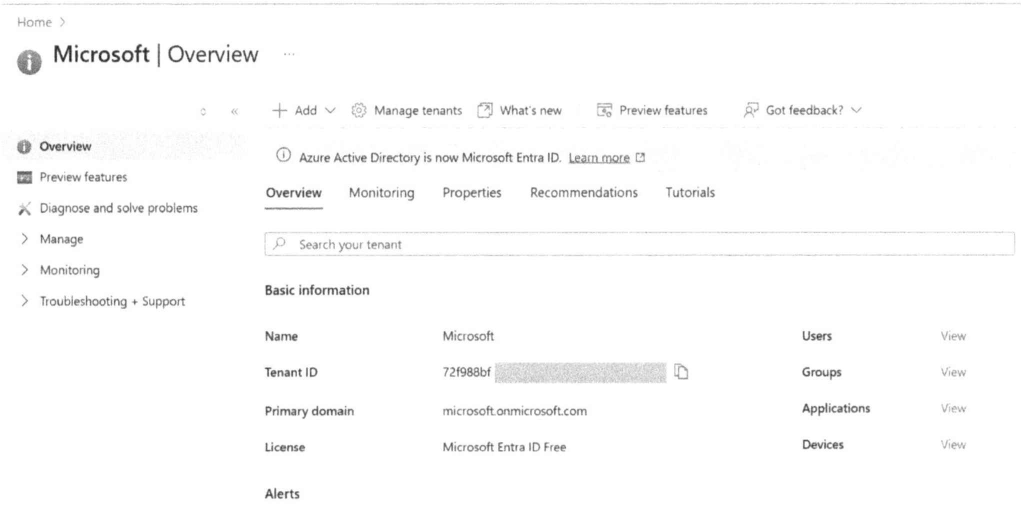

Figure 2.3 – Entra ID properties page

After visiting the mentioned link, you will have to log in and provide your information, as well as your organization's information and payment information to verify your account. Once the Azure account is created, then you'll also have an Azure subscription alongside your Microsoft Entra ID tenant.

Now that we have an Entra ID tenant, it's time to move on to the second objective.

Synchronizing on-premises Active Directory

Synchronizing your on-premises Active Directory with Microsoft Entra ID ensures that all user accounts, groups, and attributes are mirrored in the cloud. This synchronization provides a unified identity management system, allowing users to seamlessly access resources both on-premises and in the cloud.

Scenario

Imagine your company has a traditional on-premises Active Directory setup. As your business expands, you decide to adopt a hybrid cloud approach. By synchronizing your on-premises AD with Microsoft Entra ID, you ensure that your employees can access cloud resources using their existing credentials, without the need to manage multiple accounts.

Steps

Here's how you can achieve synchronization:

1. **Download Microsoft Entra Connect**: Download and install Microsoft Entra Connect on your on-premises server AD domain controller. You can download it from `https://www.microsoft.com/en-us/download/details.aspx?id=47594`.

2. **Express Settings**: As visible in *Figure 2.3*, this option is suitable when you have a single forest environment in your on-premises Active Directory, and you can simply continue with this option to quickly sync your directory.

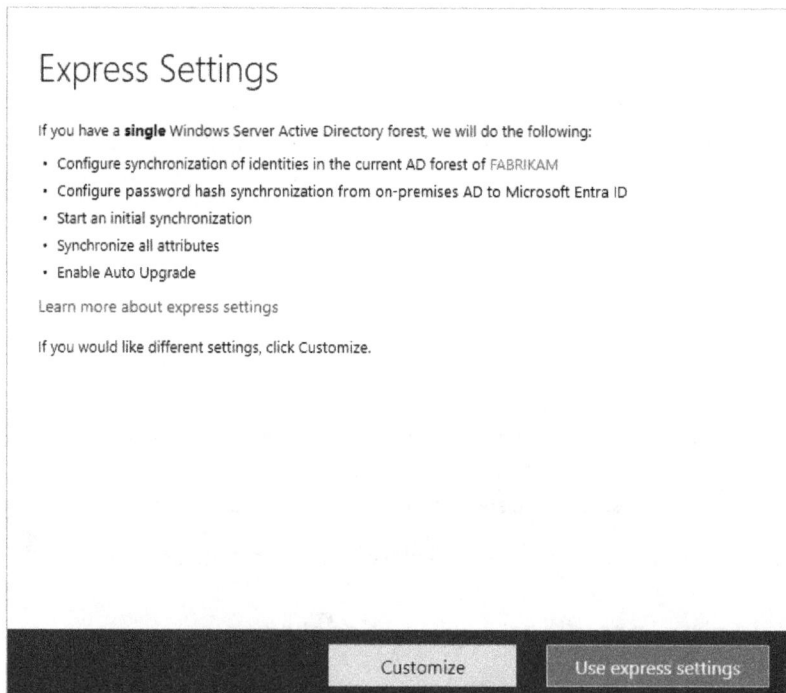

Figure 2.4 – Express Settings dialog box

3. **Launch the setup**: Launch the Microsoft Entra Connect setup and choose **Express Settings** for a quick setup or **Custom Settings** for more control over the configuration.

4. **Connect directories**: Follow the wizard to connect your on-premises AD and Entra ID. You will need to provide administrative credentials for both directories.

   - **On-premises AD admin**: admin@organization.com

   - **Entra ID admin**: admin@organization.onmicrosoft.com

5. **Configure synchronization options**: Choose the synchronization options according to your requirements. For instance, you can select which **Organizational Units (OUs)** to synchronize.

6. **Complete the setup**: Review the configuration and complete the setup. Microsoft Entra Connect will start the initial synchronization process, bringing your on-premises AD objects into Microsoft Entra ID.

In *Figure 2.5*, you see the window for Entra ID Connect configuration settings.

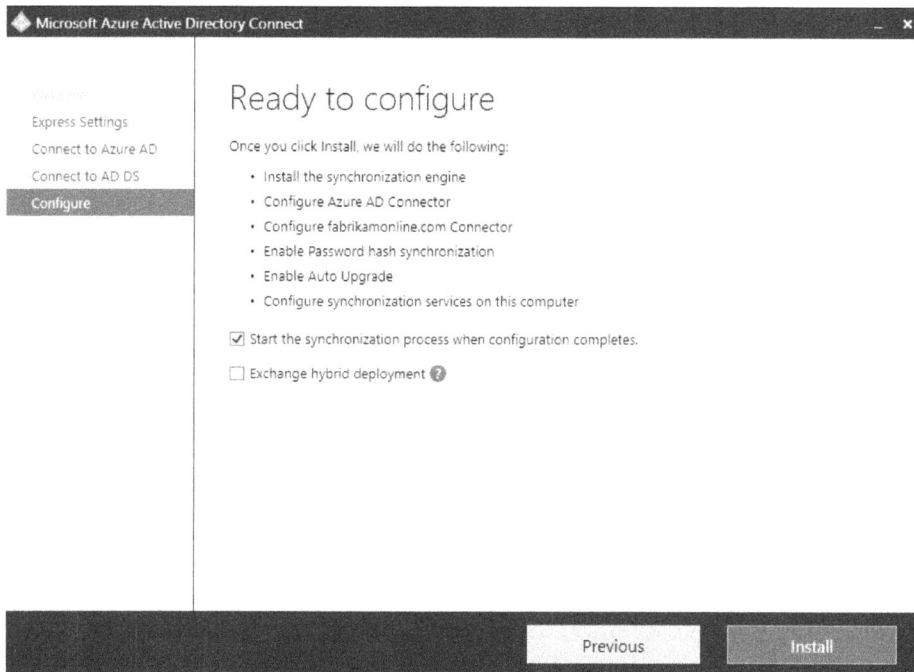

Figure 2.5 – Microsoft Entra ID Connect

Up to this point, we've learned how to create an account with Azure and how to consume the Azure environment and Entra ID Connect to connect our on-premises Active Directory and sync our identities with Entra ID, which brings up the term hybrid connectivity. Since we have covered this important step, now let's explore more options in Entra ID to configure and see how they can make things easier and more secure for our cloud environment.

Implementing SSO and MFA

Implementing SSO and MFA significantly enhances security and the user experience. SSO allows users to access multiple applications with a single set of login credentials, while MFA adds an extra layer of security by requiring additional verification steps. But let's see what the differences are, the benefits, and some examples of SSO and MFA. *Figure 2.6* shows steps and conditions that can apply in MFA.

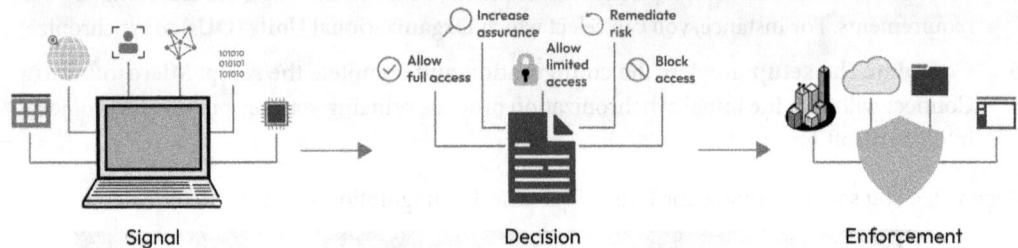

Figure 2.6 – MFA steps and conditions

SSO

SSO is an authentication process that allows a user to access multiple applications or systems with one set of login credentials. This means that, after logging in once, the user can access various services without being prompted to log in again for each one. SSO simplifies the user experience and improves security by reducing the number of passwords users need to remember and manage.

How does SSO work? It relies on a centralized authentication server that performs the authentication process. Once the user is authenticated, the server generates a token that can be used to access other applications and services. This token is typically a small piece of data containing the user's authentication information, which is trusted by the other services.

For example, imagine a company that uses multiple cloud applications, such as Office 365 for email, Salesforce for CRM, and Slack for team communication. Without SSO, employees would need to remember and enter separate login credentials for each application, which can be time-consuming and prone to security risks, such as using weak passwords or writing them down.

With SSO implemented through Microsoft Entra ID, employees log in once using their Entra ID credentials. After successful authentication, they can access all the integrated applications without needing to log in again. This seamless experience not only boosts productivity but also enhances security by centralizing and controlling the authentication process.

Here are some other benefits of SSO:

- **Improved user experience**: Users no longer need to remember multiple usernames and passwords or log in multiple times, making their experience more convenient and efficient.

- **Enhanced security**: SSO reduces the likelihood of password fatigue, where users might choose weak passwords or reuse the same password across multiple services. It also allows for centralized enforcement of security policies.

- **Simplified administration**: IT administrators can manage access to all applications from a single point, simplifying user provisioning and de-provisioning processes.

MFA

MFA is an authentication method that requires users to provide two or more verification factors to gain access to a resource, such as an application, online account, or VPN. This added layer of security makes it significantly harder for unauthorized users to access systems, even if they have obtained the user's password.

How does MFA work? MFA typically combines two or more of the following factors, as briefly mentioned in the *Enhanced security* section:

- **Something you know**: This is usually a password or PIN

- **Something you have**: This could be a mobile device, hardware token, or smart card

- **Something you are**: This involves biometrics, such as a fingerprint, facial recognition, or voice recognition

For example, consider an online banking system where security is paramount. When a user logs in, they enter their username and password (something they know). To further verify their identity, the system sends a one-time code to the user's registered mobile device (something they have). The user must enter this code to complete the login process. Some systems may also include biometric verification, such as scanning a fingerprint or using facial recognition (something they are).

In a corporate environment, implementing MFA with Microsoft Entra ID ensures that even if an employee's password is compromised, unauthorized access is still prevented unless the attacker also has the second factor, such as the employee's mobile phone to receive an authentication code.

Here are some benefits of MFA:

- **Increased security**: MFA significantly reduces the risk of unauthorized access by requiring multiple forms of verification. Even if one factor (such as a password) is compromised, the additional factors provide a strong defense against unauthorized access.

- **Compliance**: Many regulatory standards and frameworks require MFA for sensitive data and critical systems. Implementing MFA helps organizations meet these compliance requirements.

- **User trust**: MFA helps build trust among users and customers by demonstrating that their accounts and data are protected with advanced security measures.

Now, let's see how that works within a project.

Scenario

Your organization uses various cloud applications, such as Office 365, Salesforce, and Dropbox. Each application requires separate login credentials, which is cumbersome for users and poses security risks. By implementing SSO, users can access all these applications using their Entra ID credentials. Adding MFA ensures that even if a password is compromised, unauthorized access is still prevented. Configuring and managing these services enhances security, improves reliability, and simplifies access for both users and the entire organization.

Steps for SSO

To set up SSO, follow these steps:

1. In the Azure portal, go to **Enterprise applications** – you can either search for **Enterprise applications** in the dashboard or access it on the left pane of Entra ID.

2. Choose an application you want to configure for SSO or add a new one from the gallery. In *Figure 2.7*, you can see the page in Entra ID for creating an enterprise application.

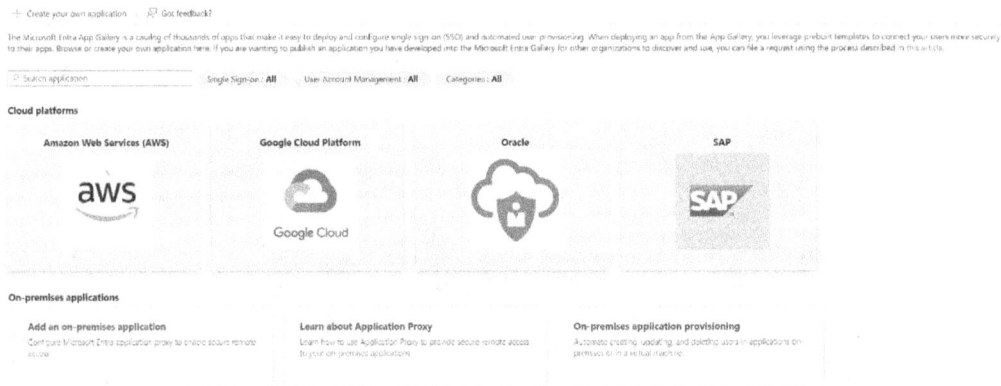

Figure 2.7 – Create an Entra ID enterprise application

3. Go to the **Single sign-on** section and select **SAML** as the SSO method.

Select a single sign-on method   Help me decide

Disabled
Single sign-on is not enabled. The user won't be able to launch the app from My Apps.

SAML
Rich and secure authentication to applications using the SAML (Security Assertion Markup Language) protocol.

Linked
Link to an application in My Apps and/or Office 365 application launcher.

Figure 2.8 – Selecting the SSO method in Entra ID enterprise applications

Here are example inputs we have used to initiate an enterprise application:

- **SSO method**: SAML

- **Configuration URL**: `https://app.organization.com/saml`

- **Certificate**: Upload your SAML certificate

4. Configure the **Attributes & Claims** user as required by the application. For example, you might map the **User Principal Name (UPN)** to the application's expected username format.

Attributes & Claims

⚠ Fill out required fields in Step 1

givenname	user.givenname
surname	user.surname
emailaddress	user.mail
name	user.userprincipalname
Unique User Identifier	user.userprincipalname

Figure 2.9 – Attributes & Claims in enterprise application SSO configuration

5. Save the configuration and test the SSO setup by logging in with an Entra ID user. Ensure that the user can access the application without needing to enter additional credentials.

Steps for MFA

Here is how MFA can be set up:

1. In the Azure portal, go to the **Entra ID Conditional Access** part of Entra ID, by searching in the general search bar.

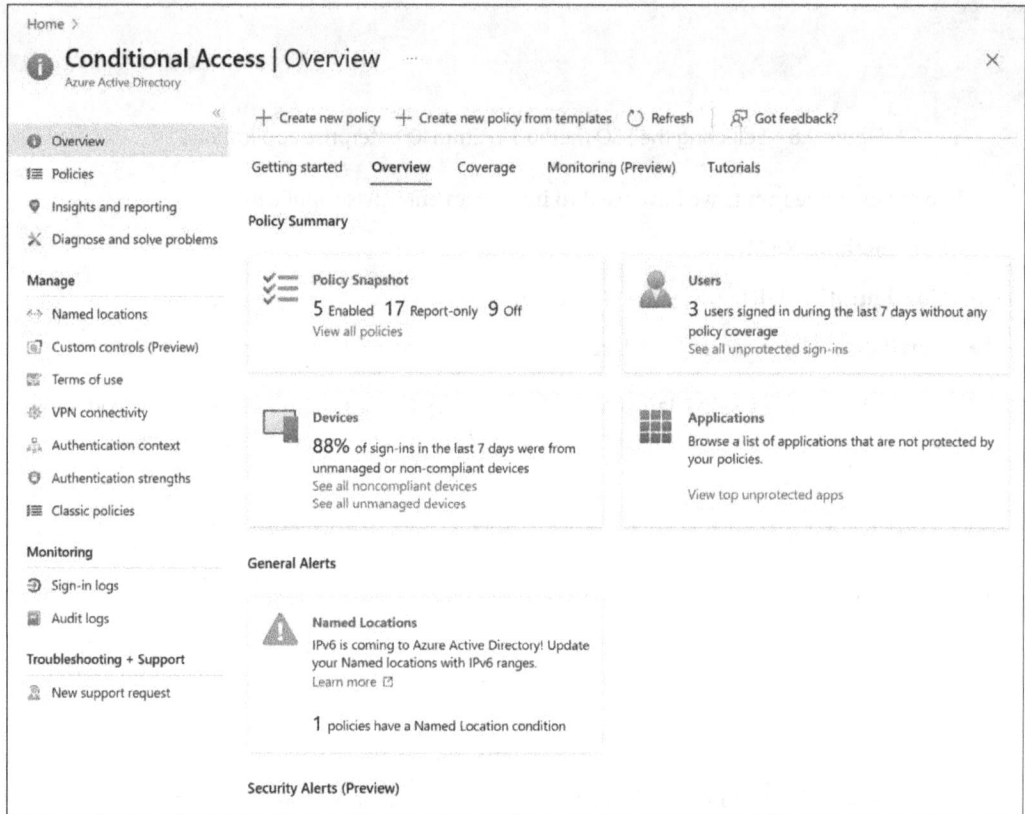

Figure 2.10 – Conditional Access window in Entra ID

2. Click on **New policy** to create a new Conditional Access policy.

    An example policy name is *Require MFA for HR Team*.

3. Select **Users and groups** to specify who the policy applies to. For example, apply the policy to the **HR Team** group.

4. Under **Cloud apps**, choose the apps to which the policy applies. You can select all cloud apps or specific ones.

5. In the **Grant** section, select **Require multi-factor authentication** and create the policy. Here's an example:

Grant Control: **Require multi-factor authentication**

6. Users in the specified group will now be prompted to set up MFA the next time they sign in. Test the policy by logging in as a member of **HR Team** and verifying that MFA is required.

That is how we configure SSO and MFA with Entra ID! It might seem simple through the portal, but this is exactly the purpose of our project in this chapter, to get to know different aspects and features of Entra ID and to make sure we're making the most of it in our environment and staying up to date with the most secure features from Microsoft.

Establishing hybrid connectivity using a VPN gateway

Establishing hybrid connectivity using a VPN gateway enables secure communication between your on-premises network and Azure and is a crucial step in integrating your on-premises infrastructure with the Azure cloud. This setup allows you to extend your on-premises network into the cloud, providing seamless access to resources across both environments.

Why hybrid connectivity?

Hybrid connectivity is essential for organizations that want to leverage cloud resources while maintaining their existing on-premises infrastructure. This approach provides several benefits:

- **Resource optimization**: You can keep critical applications and sensitive data on-premises while taking advantage of Azure's scalability and advanced services for other workloads
- **Project requirements**: Some organizations have legacy applications or specific requirements, such as Kerberos authentication, that must remain on-premises while still integrating with cloud solutions
- **Business continuity**: Hybrid connectivity ensures that your on-premises and cloud environments can operate together smoothly, providing redundancy and failover capabilities
- **Flexibility and scalability**: It allows for dynamic allocation of resources based on demand, enabling you to scale up or down as needed
- **Cost efficiency**: By offloading certain workloads to the cloud, you can reduce the need for expensive on-premises hardware and maintenance

Scenario

Your company has an on-premises data center that hosts critical applications and databases. To take advantage of Azure's scalability and advanced services, you decide to move some workloads to the cloud. By establishing hybrid connectivity using a VPN gateway, you ensure secure and reliable communication between your on-premises network and Azure.

Steps

Follow these steps to achieve the fourth objective:

1. In the Azure portal, go to **Create a resource** and select **Virtual Network**:

    -   **Name**: OrganizationVNet

    -   **Address Space**: 10.0.0.0/16

    -   **Subnet Name**: Default

    -   **Subnet Address Range**: 10.0.0.0/24

2. Configure the required settings as shown in *Figure 2.11*, including the name, resource group, and subnets, then create the VNet.

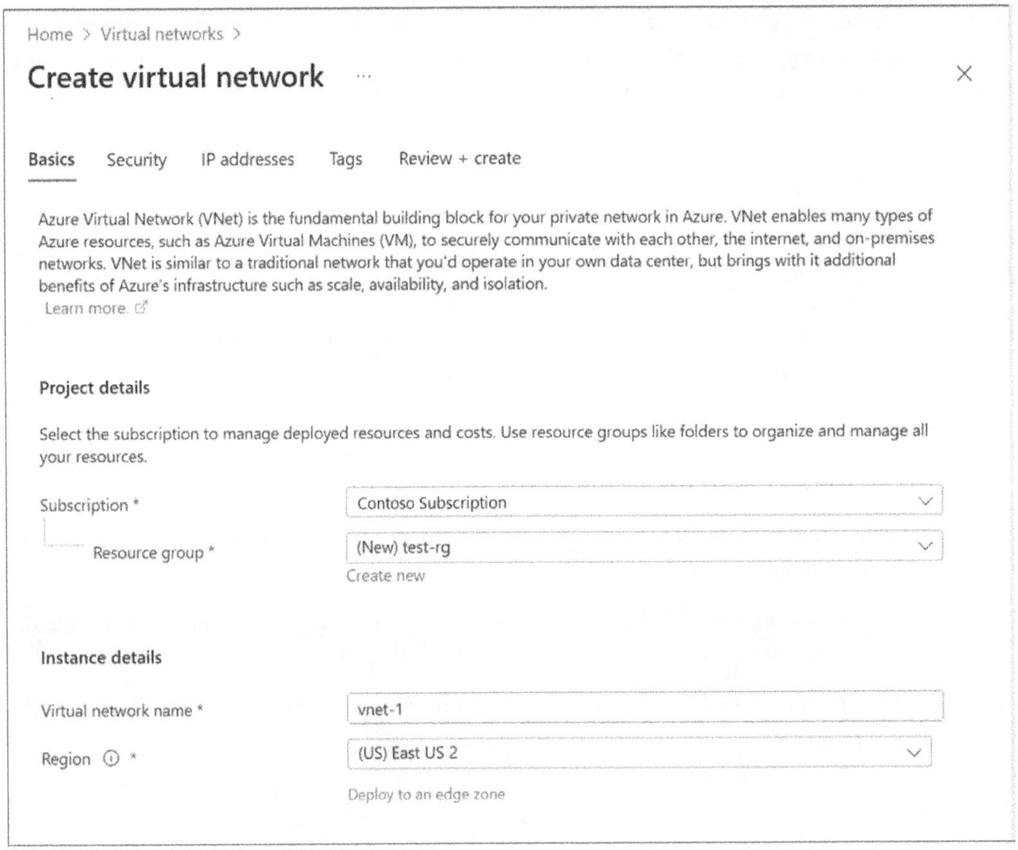

Home > Virtual networks >

Create virtual network   ...   ✕

Basics   Security   IP addresses   Tags   Review + create

Azure Virtual Network (VNet) is the fundamental building block for your private network in Azure. VNet enables many types of Azure resources, such as Azure Virtual Machines (VM), to securely communicate with each other, the internet, and on-premises networks. VNet is similar to a traditional network that you'd operate in your own data center, but brings with it additional benefits of Azure's infrastructure such as scale, availability, and isolation.
Learn more. ☐

Project details

Select the subscription to manage deployed resources and costs. Use resource groups like folders to organize and manage all your resources.

Subscription * | Contoso Subscription   ⌄ |

    Resource group * | (New) test-rg   ⌄ |
                       Create new

Instance details

Virtual network name * | vnet-1 |

Region ⓘ * | (US) East US 2   ⌄ |
                     Deploy to an edge zone

Figure 2.11 – Creating an Azure virtual network

3. After the VNet is created, navigate to **VPN gateways** under **Connections** in the Azure dashboard and click **Create**:

   - **Connection type**: `Site-to-Site(IPsec)`
   - **Name**: `VPNGateway`
   - **Virtual Network**: `Org-Vnet`
   - **Shared Key(PSK)**: `*Secret*`

4. Configure the VPN gateway settings, including the gateway type (VPN) and the VNet created earlier.

5. Once the VPN gateway is deployed, note the public IP address assigned to it since it's the internet-facing part that will be making the connection to your on-premises network.

Configuring an on-premises VPN device

To complete the hybrid connectivity setup, configure your on-premises VPN device to establish a connection to the Azure VPN gateway:

1. Access the configuration settings of your on-premises VPN device (e.g., a Cisco router). Keep in mind that the configuration settings page might be different for each device and service.

2. Create a new VPN connection and configure the settings to match those of the Azure VPN gateway, including the public IP address and shared key:

   - **Azure VPN Gateway Public IP**: [Your VPN gateway public IP]
   - **Shared Key**: [Your shared key]

3. Ensure that the VPN device is set to use the correct routing and encryption protocols.

4. Verify that the VPN connection is established by checking the status on both the on-premises VPN device and the Azure VPN gateway.

In this section, we have covered hybrid connectivity using and configuring an Azure VPN gateway, which will initiate the connection with your on-premises environment and will keep your connection secure and encrypted, and you can make sure that data in transit is totally safe.

Testing and validating the hybrid connectivity setup

Testing and validating the hybrid connectivity setup ensures that the configuration works as expected and that resources on both networks can communicate securely. This step involves verifying the VPN connection, checking the network connectivity, and ensuring that applications and data can be accessed seamlessly across the hybrid environment.

Scenario

After setting up the VPN gateway and configuring the on-premises VPN device, you need to ensure that everything is functioning correctly. Imagine a scenario where your finance team needs to access a cloud-based financial application hosted in Azure, while still using an on-premises database. Validating the hybrid connectivity setup ensures that such interactions happen smoothly without any interruptions.

Steps

Here is how we will test and validate the setup:

1. In the Azure portal, navigate to the VPN gateway and check the connection status. Ensure that the connection is listed as **Connected**.

2. Use network utilities (e.g., `ping` or `tracert`) to verify connectivity between your on-premises network and the Azure VNet. For example, ping a virtual machine in the Azure VNet from an on-premises machine to ensure connectivity:

```
ping 10.0.0.4
tracert 10.0.0.4
```

3. Ensure that resources on both networks can communicate as expected. For example, access a file share on an Azure VM from an on-premises machine.

In the early sections of this chapter, we focused on establishing a secure and reliable connection between your on-premises network and Azure using a VPN gateway. We explored how to configure a VPN gateway to enable secure, encrypted connections over the internet, ensuring that your on-premises infrastructure can seamlessly integrate with Azure. This setup is essential for creating a cohesive hybrid cloud environment where your on-premises resources can communicate efficiently with Azure services.

Now that we've laid the groundwork for hybrid connectivity from a technical perspective, it's crucial to shift our focus to the human elements that can significantly impact the success of such projects. Technical expertise is only part of the equation; effective communication, stakeholder management, and collaboration are equally vital. In the next section, we will explore the necessary soft skills required to manage these aspects, ensuring that the project not only meets its technical goals but also aligns with the expectations and needs of all stakeholders involved.

Understanding the necessary soft skills

Here we go – the most important topic and my favorite one. Implementing a complex IT project such as hybrid connectivity and identity management involves more than just technical skills. Effective communication, stakeholder management, and collaboration are critical to the success of the project.

Communication

Clear and effective communication is essential throughout the project life cycle. As the IT administrator, you need to do the following:

- **Communicate goals and benefits**: Clearly explain the goals and benefits of the project to all stakeholders, including management, end users, and the IT team. Use non-technical language when necessary to ensure everyone understands the project's value.

- **Provide regular updates**: Keep stakeholders informed about the project's progress through regular updates. This can be done through emails, meetings, or project management tools. Regular communication helps manage expectations and ensures that everyone is on the same page.

- **Address concerns and feedback**: Be open to feedback and address any concerns raised by stakeholders promptly. This helps build trust and ensures that potential issues are identified and resolved early.

To learn more about effective communication strategies, you can check out the following:

```
https://www.forbes.com/advisor/business/soft-skills-examples/#what_
are_soft_skills_section
```

Stakeholder management

Managing stakeholders effectively is crucial for the success of the project. Stakeholders can include senior management, department heads, end users, and external partners. Here are some best practices for stakeholder management:

- **Identify stakeholders**: Identify all stakeholders who will be impacted by the project. This includes both internal and external stakeholders.

- **Understand their needs**: Understand the needs, expectations, and concerns of each stakeholder group. This will help you tailor your communication and engagement strategies accordingly.

- **Engage early and often**: Engage with stakeholders early in the project to gather their input and ensure their needs are considered. Regular engagement throughout the project helps maintain their support and buy-in.

- **Manage expectations**: Set realistic expectations about what the project will deliver and the timelines involved. Be transparent about any challenges or delays that may arise.

To learn more about impactful stakeholder management, you can check out the following links:

- `https://www.mindtools.com/at2o1co/what-is-stakeholder-management`
- `https://sg.indeed.com/career-advice/finding-a-job/stakeholder-management-skills`

Collaboration

Collaboration is key to ensuring that the project is executed smoothly. Here are some tips for fostering collaboration:

- **Create a collaborative environment**: Aim for a collaborative environment where team members feel comfortable sharing ideas and working together. Encourage open communication and teamwork.

- **Use collaboration tools**: Leverage collaboration tools such as Microsoft Teams, Slack, or project management platforms to facilitate communication and collaboration among team members.

- **Define roles and responsibilities**: Clearly define the roles and responsibilities of each team member to avoid confusion and ensure accountability.

- **Encourage cross-functional collaboration**: Encourage collaboration between different departments, such as IT, HR, and finance, to ensure that all aspects of the project are considered.

To learn more about effective collaboration techniques, you can check out the following links:

- https://hbr.org/2007/11/eight-ways-to-build-collaborative-teams
- https://www.indeed.com/career-advice/career-development/collaboration-strategy

Best practices for implementing hybrid connectivity

Lastly, here are some best practices to keep in mind when implementing hybrid connectivity:

- **Redundancy**: Implement redundant VPN connections to ensure high availability and failover capabilities. This can involve setting up multiple VPN gateways and configuring failover settings on your on-premises VPN device.

- **Security**: Use strong encryption methods and regularly update VPN device firmware to protect your connections. Ensure that all traffic between your on-premises network and Azure is encrypted and that access controls are in place.

- **Monitoring**: Use Azure Monitor and Network Watcher to keep an eye on the performance and health of your VPN connections. Set up alerts to notify you of any issues, such as connection drops or latency spikes.

- **Documentation**: Maintain detailed documentation of your network configuration and changes to aid in troubleshooting and management. Include information on IP address ranges, VPN settings, and any custom configurations.

In this section, we covered the importance of effective communication, stakeholder management, and collaboration in successfully managing hybrid connectivity projects. These skills are essential for ensuring that all team members and stakeholders are aligned, informed, and engaged throughout the project, which is crucial for achieving the desired outcomes.

Summary

In this chapter, you have learned how to implement Microsoft Entra ID for identity management, set up SSO and MFA, and establish hybrid connectivity between your on-premises network and Azure, as well as how to maintain professional communication in the project, from stakeholder management to collaboration and teamwork. These skills are essential for managing a hybrid cloud environment and ensuring secure, seamless access to resources. In the next chapter, we will explore Azure storage solutions and their implementation in detail, providing you with the knowledge to manage and utilize Azure's storage capabilities effectively.

Exercises

I've prepared several example exercises to give you hands-on experience working directly with the resources in a real environment.

Exercise 1: Creating a user and group in Microsoft Entra ID

1. **Create a new user**: Create a new user in your Entra ID tenant with the role of `User`:

   - User name: `jane.doe@organization.onmicrosoft.com`

   - Name: `Jane Doe`

   - Password: `[Auto-generate or enter a custom password]`

2. **Create a new group**: Create a new group named `Finance Team` and add the user you just created to this group:

   - Group name: `Finance Team`

   - Description: `Group for Finance department`

   - Members: `jane.doe@organization.onmicrosoft.com`

3. **Verify group membership**: Ensure that the user appears in the group members list.

Exercise 2: Configuring SSO for an application

1. **Select an application**: Choose an application from the Entra ID gallery and configure SSO using SAML:

   - Application: `Salesforce`

   - SSO Method: `SAML`

   - Configuration URL: `https://login.salesforce.com`

   - Certificate: `Upload your SAML certificate`

2. **Test SSO configuration**: Test the SSO configuration by logging in with an Entra ID user and verifying access to the application.

Exercise 3: Setting up a VPN connection

1. **Create a virtual network**: Create a new VNet and VPN gateway in Azure:

   - VNet Name: `ProjectVNet`

   - Address Space: `192.168.0.0/16`

   - Subnet Name: `ProjectSubnet`

   - Subnet Address Range: `192.168.1.0/24`

   - VPN Gateway Name: `ProjectVPNGateway`

2. **Configure an on-premises VPN device**: Configure your on-premises VPN device to connect to the Azure VPN gateway:

   - Azure VPN Gateway Public IP: `[Your VPN Gateway Public IP]`

   - Shared Key: `[Your Shared Key]`

3. **Validate connection**: Validate the connection by pinging a resource in the Azure VNet from your on-premises network:

   ```
   ping 192.168.1.4
   ```

3

Implementing Azure Storage Solutions

In this chapter, we will delve into the comprehensive implementation of Azure storage solutions as a project, a critical component of modern cloud computing infrastructure. As with any other chapter in this book, this chapter is an important one during your project phase – also, as mentioned previously, all chapters are related to each other and create a Zero to Hero project at the end. **Azure storage solutions** offer a range of services that cater to diverse data storage needs, from storing large unstructured data such as media files to structured data in tables and queues. Understanding and effectively implementing these storage solutions can significantly enhance your organization's ability to manage data efficiently, securely, and cost-effectively. Before diving into the project, we'll talk about some important facts, features, and benefits of Azure Storage, and then we'll dive into a live project. As usual, since we are focusing on learning Azure services in a project-based scenario, we are now going to learn a bit about soft skills around a project related to Azure storage solutions and how to start a related project from scratch.

The following topics will be covered in this chapter:

- Why use Azure storage solutions?
- Project scenario – implementing a comprehensive Azure storage solution
- Essential best practices and key soft skills for success

Technical requirements

To follow along with this chapter, you will need the following:

- A Microsoft Azure account
- Basic knowledge of cloud storage concepts
- Access to the Azure portal

- The Azure CLI installed on your local machine

- AzCopy installed on your local machine

- Source data for migration (for example, files on an on-premises server)

- Access to Azure Data Factory

Why use Azure storage solutions?

Azure Storage provides scalable, durable, and secure cloud storage for a variety of data objects. Whether you need to store large amounts of unstructured data, such as images and videos, or structured data in the form of tables, Azure Storage has a solution for you.

Benefits and features

Some key benefits and features of Azure storage solutions are as follows:

- **Scalability and performance**: Azure Storage is designed to handle massive amounts of data and can scale seamlessly with your business needs. This is particularly important for businesses that experience rapid growth or have fluctuating data demands. Azure Storage can handle petabytes of data and millions of transactions per second, ensuring that your applications perform reliably even under heavy load.

  As mentioned in practical applications and use cases, imagine a video streaming service that needs to store and stream thousands of videos to millions of users worldwide. Azure Blob Storage can handle the storage and delivery of these large video files efficiently, providing high throughput and low latency, which is critical for ensuring a smooth streaming experience for users.

- **Security**: Security is a top priority for any data storage solution, and Azure Storage excels in this area. Azure provides robust security features, including the following:

  - **Encryption**: Data is encrypted both while stored and during transmission, safeguarding it against unauthorized access. Azure Storage handles encryption automatically and offers tools for managing encryption keys effectively.

  - **Access control**: **Role-based access control** (**RBAC**) and integration with Entra ID allow you to manage who has access to your data and what they can do with it. You can set granular permissions to control access at the account, container, or even file level.

  - **Advanced threat protection** (**ATP**): Azure provides advanced threat detection capabilities, helping to identify and respond to potential security threats. Features such as Azure Security Center and Azure Defender provide continuous security assessment and **threat intelligence** (**TI**).

  - **Backup solution**: Azure Storage provides a scalable, secure solution for data backups, with features such as Azure Blob Storage for storing large volumes, tiered storage to optimize costs, and **geo-redundant storage** (**GRS**) for **disaster recovery** (**DR**). It integrates seamlessly with Azure Backup for automated backups and long-term retention, offering encryption, security controls, and compliance to protect critical data efficiently.

Consider a healthcare organization that needs to store sensitive patient records. Azure Storage ensures that this data is encrypted and only accessible to authorized personnel, meeting regulatory requirements such as the **Health Insurance Portability and Accountability Act** (**HIPAA**) and ensuring patient data privacy and security.

- **Integration with Microsoft services**: Azure Storage integrates seamlessly with other Azure services and third-party applications, making it a versatile and flexible storage solution. This integration allows you to build complex workflows and applications that leverage multiple Azure services, enhancing productivity and enabling innovative solutions.

  Here are a few examples of Azure services that use and integrate with Azure Storage:

  - **Azure Functions**: This uses Azure Blob Storage to trigger serverless functions when new files are uploaded, automating processes such as image processing or data transformation.

  - **Azure Kubernetes Service (AKS)**: This stores container images in Azure Container Registry, backed by Azure Blob Storage, to streamline your container deployment pipeline.

  - **Azure Machine Learning**: This stores training data in Azure Blob Storage and uses it in your **machine learning** (**ML**) workflows to build and train models.

  For instance, a company developing an ML model for predictive maintenance can use Azure Blob Storage to store large datasets collected from IoT sensors. These datasets can then be accessed directly by Azure Machine Learning for training and testing models, creating a seamless workflow from data collection to model deployment.

- **Pricing tiers and storage options**: Azure Storage provides a lot of options in terms of cost efficiency. It offers various pricing tiers and storage options, enabling businesses to choose the most cost-effective solution based on their data access patterns and requirements. This flexibility allows you to optimize costs by storing frequently accessed data in hot storage and less frequently accessed data in cool or archive storage. The following are the options provided by Azure Storage:

  - **Hot tier**: This online tier is designed for data that is frequently accessed or modified. It offers the lowest access costs but comes with the highest storage costs.

  - **Cool tier**: An online tier suitable for data that is accessed or modified less often. It is recommended that data should be stored in this tier for at least 30 days. This tier has lower storage costs but higher access costs compared to the hot tier.

  - **Cold tier**: This online tier is ideal for data that is rarely accessed or modified but still needs to be quickly retrieved. Data should be kept in this tier for a minimum of 90 days. It provides lower storage costs and higher access costs compared to the cool tier.

- **Archive tier**: Designed for data that is infrequently accessed and has flexible latency requirements, typically measured in hours. Data should be stored in this offline tier for at least 180 days.

You can find all the details about Azure Storage tiers at `https://learn.microsoft.com/en-us/azure/storage/blobs/access-tiers-overview`.

Here is an example of how this proves helpful for organizations: A financial institution can store transaction logs and audit data in cool or archive storage to reduce costs while keeping this data accessible for compliance purposes. Frequently accessed operational data can be kept in hot storage to ensure quick access.

- **High availability (HA) and redundancy in Azure Storage**: Azure Storage ensures HA and durability of data through replication and redundancy. Data is replicated across multiple locations within a region or even across regions, ensuring that it is always available and protected against hardware failures, network issues, or natural disasters. The following are some redundancy options offered by Azure Storage:

  - **Locally redundant storage (LRS)**: LRS keeps three copies of your data within the same data center. This redundancy helps protect against hardware failures within the facility, ensuring that your data remains available despite localized issues.

  - **Zone-redundant storage (ZRS)**: ZRS distributes your data across multiple data centers within the same region. This replication across different physical locations within the region enhances data availability and durability by protecting against the failure of an entire data center.

  - **GRS**: GRS replicates your data to a secondary region, often far from the primary location. This setup ensures HA and durability even in the event of a major regional outage, providing a robust DR solution by keeping your data accessible from geographically distant locations.

An e-commerce company can ensure that its product catalog and customer data are always available by using GRS. Even if there is a regional outage, the data remains accessible from the secondary region, ensuring uninterrupted service for customers.

- **Flexibility**: Azure Storage is also very flexible as it supports a wide range of data types and access methods. Whether you need to store unstructured data such as media files, structured data in tables, or manage large-scale data processing workflows, Azure Storage provides the necessary tools and services to meet your needs.

A multimedia company can use Azure Blob Storage to store large volumes of video files, Azure Table Storage to manage metadata and indexing information, and Azure Queue Storage to handle processing tasks in an asynchronous manner. This comprehensive suite of storage solutions allows the company to efficiently manage its diverse data needs.

Figure 3.1 shows different Azure storage types that can be leveraged depending on the needs.

Figure 3.1 – Azure storage types

You can also find more information about Azure storage types at `https://learn.microsoft.com/en-us/azure/storage/common/storage-introduction#azure-storage-data-services`.

Now, let's see some important steps to keep in mind while starting a new project for Azure storage solutions.

When starting a project involving Azure Storage from scratch, it's crucial to carefully plan and consider several factors to ensure successful implementation. Here's a detailed guide covering key aspects from designing, meetings, stakeholder management, and budgeting to deployment and implementation.

Making the most of Azure storage solutions

Regardless of the specific definitions and benefits of each service, and the availability of all essential information about any Azure service in the Microsoft Learn documentation, it's important to have a foundational understanding tailored to our project needs. However, the most important thing here is to keep notes of best practices that come with the experience during each project phase with Azure Storage or best practices that are shared with the community by professionals from all over the world. So, let's explore some of the best practices I've experienced in different situations, and let's see how they can benefit us:

- **Designing the Azure storage solution**: This involves a comprehensive understanding of your organization's data storage needs. Begin by assessing the types and volumes of data you need to store, including whether the data is unstructured (such as images and videos) or structured (such as transactional records). It's essential to consider how this data will be accessed – whether it will be read-heavy, write-heavy, or a balanced mix, and to identify performance requirements such as latency and throughput. Selecting the appropriate Azure storage services is the next step, choosing from options such as Blob Storage for unstructured data, File Storage for shared filesystems, Table Storage for NoSQL structured data, and Queue Storage for message queuing.

- **Security**: This is another critical factor, necessitating encryption for data at rest and in transit, robust access control via RBAC, and integration with Microsoft Entra ID. Scalability and performance should be built into the design, with strategies for data partitioning, sharding, and using **content delivery networks** (**CDNs**) for global access. Finally, cost optimization must be considered, selecting the appropriate storage tiers (hot, cool, archive) based on data access patterns and implementing life cycle management policies to move data between tiers efficiently.

- **Initial meetings and planning**: These are crucial to align all stakeholders and set the project on the right path. Start with a kick-off meeting that gathers all key stakeholders, including IT teams, project managers, and data owners, to define the project scope, objectives, and deliverables. Follow this with detailed requirement-gathering sessions with different departments to understand their specific data storage needs and document these requirements thoroughly to ensure the final design meets all needs. Conduct a technical design review where the proposed storage solution design is presented to stakeholders, feedback is gathered, and necessary adjustments are made to finalize the design with detailed architecture diagrams. These steps ensure comprehensive planning and alignment across all involved parties.

- **Stakeholder management**: This is critical for the success of the project. Begin by identifying all stakeholders, including internal teams such as IT and finance, as well as external partners, and understand their roles, interests, and potential concerns. Develop a robust communication plan to keep stakeholders informed throughout the project life cycle, including regular update meetings and progress reports. Engage stakeholders early and often, involving them in the decision-making process to gather valuable input and maintain their support. Plan comprehensive training sessions to educate stakeholders on the new storage solution and provide ongoing support to address any issues post-deployment, ensuring successful adoption and maximizing the solution's benefits.

- **Budget planning**: This is a crucial aspect of project management. Start by estimating the costs of different storage services based on data volume and access patterns, including costs for data ingress/egress, storage transactions, and additional services such as encryption and backup. Allocate funds not only for the initial setup and configuration but also for ongoing costs such as monitoring, maintenance, and support. Implement cost optimization strategies such as automated tiering and data life cycle management to ensure cost efficiency. Regularly review and adjust the storage strategy using Azure's cost management tools to identify areas for savings and optimize overall expenses.

- **Deployment and implementation**: These involve several key steps. First, set up Azure Storage accounts based on the defined requirements and design, configuring them with necessary settings for performance, replication, and security. Implement robust security measures, including encryption for data at rest and in transit, RBAC, and ATP features. Develop a detailed data migration plan using Azure tools such as Azure Data Factory or AzCopy for efficient data transfer, ensuring data integrity and minimizing downtime. Conduct thorough testing and validation to ensure the storage solution meets performance and security requirements, simulating various scenarios to identify and rectify potential issues. Set up monitoring tools to track storage performance and health, implementing alerts and automated responses for potential issues. Plan the deployment in phases to minimize disruption and execute the go-live plan, ensuring all stakeholders are informed and prepared. Finally, conduct a post-implementation review meeting with stakeholders to assess the implementation process and outcomes, documenting lessons learned and making recommendations for future improvements.

Now that you have an overall idea of what Azure Storage is and what you can achieve with it depending on your needs for the solutions, let's get into the scenario to explore even more!

Project scenario – implementing a comprehensive Azure storage solution

Imagine you are an IT administrator for a mid-sized company experiencing rapid growth. The company's current on-premises storage systems are struggling to keep up with the increasing volume and variety of data. Performance bottlenecks are becoming frequent, and maintenance costs are escalating. The organization has decided to modernize its data storage infrastructure by leveraging Azure storage solutions. The goal is to design and implement a scalable, secure, and cost-effective storage solution in Azure that meets the diverse data storage needs of the company together with using what we have learned from this chapter so far. This includes managing large media files, application logs, and structured datasets while ensuring data security, HA, and seamless integration with existing systems.

Project objectives

Let's start by establishing the objectives of our project:

- **Assess current data storage needs and future growth**: Begin by evaluating the types and volumes of data currently stored within the organization. This includes unstructured data such as documents, images, and videos, as well as structured data such as transactional records and logs. It's essential to analyze access patterns to understand how frequently different types of data are accessed and determine the performance requirements for these accesses. Additionally, consider future growth projections to ensure the solution can scale with the company's expanding data needs.

- **Design a scalable and secure storage architecture**: Based on the assessment, design a storage architecture using Azure's suite of storage services. For unstructured data such as documents and media files, Azure Blob Storage is ideal. Use Azure File Storage for shared filesystems that need to be accessed by multiple users or applications. For structured data, consider Azure Table Storage, and for message queuing, use Azure Queue Storage. Ensure that the storage architecture is designed for scalability, allowing it to handle increasing volumes of data without compromising performance. Implement security measures such as encryption at rest and in transit, RBAC, and integration with Microsoft Entra ID. Consider using ATP features provided by Azure Security Center and Azure Defender.

- **Migrate existing data to Azure**: Develop a detailed data migration plan that outlines the steps and tools needed to move existing data to Azure Storage with minimal disruption to business operations. Use Azure tools such as Azure Data Factory, AzCopy, or Azure Migrate to facilitate the data transfer. Plan the migration in phases to minimize disruption, starting with non-critical data and gradually moving to more critical datasets. Ensure data integrity during the migration process by conducting thorough testing and validation at each stage. Implement strategies for handling potential issues such as data transfer failures or discrepancies.

Figure 3.2 shows a chart where you can find appropriate options for each phase during the data migration planning to Azure.

Assessment phase steps	Options
Choose a target storage service	- Azure Blob Storage and Data Lake Storage - Azure Files - Azure NetApp Files - ISV solutions
Select a migration method	- Online - Offline - Combination of both
Choose the best migration tool for the job	- Commercial tools (Azure and ISV) - Open source

Figure 3.2 – Data migration phases and options

The following link takes you to an Azure migration overview in detail: `https://learn.microsoft.com/en-us/azure/storage/common/storage-migration-overview`

- **Implement security and compliance measures**: Ensure that the storage solution complies with all relevant security standards and regulations. Encrypt data at rest using Azure **Storage Service Encryption** (**SSE**) and encrypt data in transit using secure transfer protocols such as HTTPS. Implement RBAC to control access to data, and integrate with Entra ID for centralized **identity and access management** (**IAM**). Use Azure Policy to enforce compliance with organizational and regulatory standards. Regularly review and update security policies to address emerging threats and ensure ongoing compliance.

- **Set up monitoring and management processes**: Implement tools and processes to monitor the performance and health of the storage solution. Use Azure Monitor and Azure Storage Analytics to track key metrics such as data usage, transaction rates, and latency. Set up alerts to notify administrators of potential issues, such as high latency or unexpected data access patterns. Develop a management plan that includes regular backups, maintenance tasks, and updates to ensure the storage solution remains reliable and secure. Use Azure Cost Management tools to monitor and optimize storage costs, adjusting storage tiers and policies as needed to achieve cost efficiency.

Technical objectives

In this section, you will witness the technical perspective of the scenario that we are going to configure from our project objectives. For this reason, we have divided each objective into a separate technical mission.

The first objective in implementing an Azure storage solution is to design a scalable and secure storage architecture that aligns with the organization's data requirements. This involves selecting the appropriate Azure storage services, ensuring scalability for future growth, and implementing robust security measures to protect data. This section will guide you through the process of designing such an architecture.

Evaluating storage requirements

Start by thoroughly assessing the organization's data storage needs. This involves understanding the types of data to be stored, such as documents, images, videos, application logs, and transactional records. Estimate the current volume of data and project future growth to ensure the architecture can scale as the organization grows. Analyzing access patterns is crucial to determining the read/write ratio and performance requirements.

Here is an example assessment:

- **Data types**: Documents, images, videos, application logs, transactional records
- **Current data volume**: 50 TB, projected to grow to 200 TB in 3 years
- **Access patterns**: 70% read-heavy, 30% write-heavy
- **Performance requirements**: Low-latency access for critical transactional data, high throughput for media files

Setting up Azure Storage infrastructure

Setting up the Azure Storage infrastructure is a critical step in establishing a robust, scalable, and secure data storage environment in the cloud. This process involves creating storage accounts, configuring various Azure storage services, such as Blob Storage, File Storage, Table Storage, and Queue Storage, and applying necessary security settings. Proper setup ensures efficient data management and seamless integration with other Azure services.

The first step in setting up the Azure Storage infrastructure is to create storage accounts. A storage account provides a unique namespace in Azure for your data and allows you to use Azure's storage services. Follow these steps to create a storage account:

1. Go to `https://portal.azure.com/` and sign in with your Azure account credentials.
2. Create a storage account:

   - Navigate to **Storage accounts** and click **Create**. *Figure 3.3* illustrates how to navigate through the Azure portal to create a storage account.

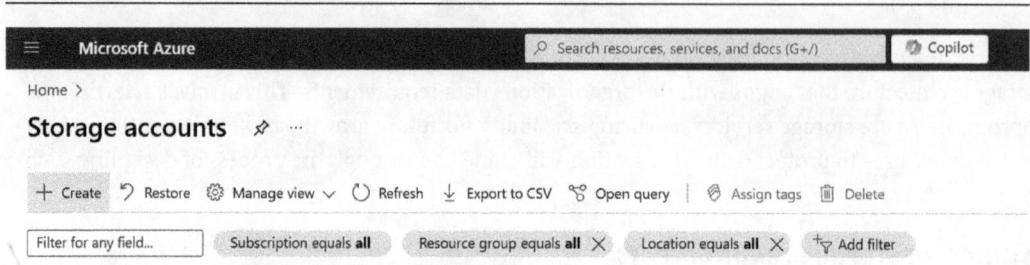

Figure 3.3 – Creating a storage account

- Provide the necessary details:

    - **Subscription**: Select your subscription.

    - **Resource Group**: Create a new resource group or select an existing one. For this example, create a new resource group named `DataTechResourceGroup`.

    - **Storage Account Name**: Enter a unique name, such as `datatechstorageaccount`. The character length should be between 3 and 24 characters.

    - **Region**: Select a region close to your operations (for example, **East US**).

    - **Performance**: Choose **Standard** for cost-effective storage or **Premium** for low-latency storage.

    - **Replication**: Select **Locally-redundant storage (LRS)** for lower cost or **Geo-redundant storage (GRS)** for higher availability.

- Click **Review + create** and then **Create**.

Implementing a data migration plan

The first step for data migration is to plan it. To minimize disruption, develop a phased migration plan that outlines the steps and timeline for moving data to Azure. Phasing the migration allows for incremental progress and makes it easier to manage and troubleshoot issues as they arise.

Here are examples of migration phases:

- **Phase 1**: Migrate non-critical data, such as logs and historical data

- **Phase 2**: Migrate active operational data, such as documents and media files

- **Phase 3**: Migrate critical transactional data and applications

Applying security and compliance measures

Ensuring that your Azure storage solution meets security and compliance requirements is essential for safeguarding sensitive data and adhering to regulatory standards. This involves implementing encryption, configuring access controls, using ATP, and enforcing compliance policies. The next sections outline the detailed steps to achieve these objectives.

Implementing encryption

Securing your data, encrypting, and making sure data is safe during transit and at rest is a critical step, so here we're going to see what the different data encryption options with Azure Storage are.

Data encryption at rest

Azure Storage automatically encrypts data at rest using Microsoft-managed keys. However, for enhanced security, you can opt to use customer-managed keys stored in Azure Key Vault.

The following options are necessary to check and make sure that encryption is configured and enabled:

1. **Enable encryption for data at rest**: By default, data at rest is encrypted in Azure Storage. To verify and manage encryption settings, follow these steps:

    I.   Navigate to your storage account in the Azure portal.

    II.   Under the **Security + networking** section, click on **Encryption**.

    III.   Ensure that **Encryption type** and **Encryption scopes** are configured accordingly.

2. **Configure customer-managed keys**: If you choose to use customer-managed keys, follow these steps:

    I.   Create or select an existing Azure key vault.

    II.   Generate or import the encryption key into Azure Key Vault.

    III.   Configure your storage account to use the customer-managed key from Azure Key Vault.

Data encryption in transit

Encrypting data in transit protects data from interception and tampering as it travels over the network.

A good practice is to ensure that all data transfers to and from the storage account are encrypted by enforcing HTTPS. This can be found under **Settings | Configuration**.

Figure 3.4 shows how and where to configure secure transfer.

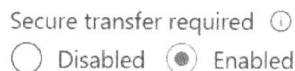

Secure transfer required ⓘ
◯ Disabled   ⦿ Enabled

Figure 3.4 – Enabling secure transfer in Azure Storage settings

Configuring access controls

RBAC allows you to manage who has access to Azure resources and what they can do with those resources. By assigning roles to users, groups, or applications, you can control access to your storage account. Here's how access controls can be configured:

- **Assign roles to users or groups**: Define roles and assign them to users or groups based on their access requirements.

- **Use Entra ID integration**: Integrate your storage account with Entra ID for centralized IAM.

- **Implement a shared access signature (SAS)**: An SAS provides a secure way to grant limited, time-based access to Azure Storage resources without sharing the account keys. This is useful for allowing clients or applications temporary permissions to read, write, or manage resources (such as blobs or queues) while retaining control over the level of access and its expiration.

- **Access keys**: Azure Storage account access keys are credentials that provide full access to all resources in a storage account. They are typically used for administrative purposes or configuring services that need full control. Due to their broad permissions, it is recommended to store and rotate access keys securely to minimize security risks.

Using ATP

ATP helps detect and respond to potential security threats to your storage account. Here's how it can be used:

- **Enable Azure Defender for Storage**: Azure Defender provides advanced threat detection capabilities and continuous monitoring for your storage account

- **Configure security alerts**: Set up alerts to notify you of suspicious activities, such as unusual data access patterns or potential data breaches

  Here is an example configuration in the Azure portal:

  I.   Navigate to your storage account and select **Microsoft Defender for Cloud** under the **Security + networking** section.

  II. Click on **Enable on storage account** and configure alert settings based on your security requirements.

Enforcing compliance policies

Azure Policy helps you manage and enforce compliance with organizational and regulatory standards by creating policies that govern the behavior of your Azure resources. Here's how compliance policies can be enforced:

- **Create and assign policies**: Establish policies to enforce security and compliance standards, such as mandating encryption for all storage accounts or restricting access to certain IP ranges

- **Monitor compliance**: Use Azure Policy to continuously monitor compliance with your defined policies and take corrective actions if necessary

Here's an example of monitoring using Azure Policy:

I.   Navigate to **Policy** in the Azure portal.

II.   Under **Compliance**, view the compliance state of your resources and take action to remediate non-compliant resources.

Setting up monitoring and management processes

Monitoring and managing your Azure storage solution is essential to maintain its reliability, security, and efficiency. This involves tracking performance, configuring alerts for potential issues, and developing a plan for regular maintenance and cost optimization. Let's take a closer look at this:

- **Monitoring Azure Storage performance**: Setting up Azure Monitor is essential for tracking key metrics such as ingress, egress, transactions, capacity, and latency. By monitoring these metrics, you gain valuable insights into how your storage is performing and can identify potential bottlenecks or inefficiencies. Creating a dedicated dashboard for these metrics allows for continuous real-time monitoring, making it easier to spot trends and respond quickly to any issues.

- **Azure storage analytics**: Enabling logging for storage services captures detailed performance data, which is crucial for understanding how your storage accounts are being accessed and utilized. Using tools such as Azure Storage Explorer helps analyze these logs, diagnose problems, and make informed decisions to optimize storage performance. This detailed data is valuable for troubleshooting and improving overall storage efficiency.

- **Configuring alerts for potential issues**: Azure Monitor can be configured to set up alert rules that detect potential issues, such as high egress or latency. These alerts enable proactive management by providing early warnings about potential problems. Configuring action groups helps define how these alerts are handled, whether through notifications to the IT team or automated responses to address issues promptly, minimizing downtime and maintaining optimal performance.

- **Developing a management plan**: Regular maintenance is crucial for data integrity and security. Scheduling regular backups ensures data protection against unexpected loss. Periodically reviewing storage account configurations and permissions helps maintain security by ensuring that only authorized users have access.

- **Cost optimization**: This is another critical aspect of managing storage. Using Azure Cost Management, you can monitor usage and expenses effectively. Adjusting storage tiers based on access patterns and implementing life cycle management policies help manage costs by moving less frequently accessed data to more cost-effective storage options, ensuring efficient use of resources.

Now that we have discovered the best practices for implementing a successful Azure Storage project, let's do a technical exercise with hands-on experience.

Essential best practices and key soft skills for success

Before concluding the chapter, let's look at some best practices and key soft skills that will help you attain success while implementing Azure storage solutions:

- **Hands-on approach to implementation**: This chapter provides practical guidance on setting up and managing Azure storage solutions, offering a foundational understanding of resource creation and basic security configurations. While the focus is on general steps for creating and managing storage accounts, you will also learn how to enable essential security options and apply fundamental access controls. This approach ensures you gain the practical skills needed to get started with Azure storage solutions and prepare for more advanced configurations in real-world scenarios.

- **Practical applications and use cases**: Understanding the practical applications of these services is crucial. For instance, a company developing a web application might use Azure Blob Storage to store and manage user-uploaded images and videos, ensuring these media files are easily accessible and scalable. Another organization might leverage Azure File Storage to create a shared filesystem accessible by employees from various locations, enhancing collaboration and productivity. For applications requiring rapid, high-volume data transactions, Azure Table Storage provides a reliable solution for storing structured data without the overhead of traditional relational databases.

- **Management and optimization**: Managing and optimizing Azure storage solutions involves several best practices. These include implementing proper access controls to secure your data, choosing the appropriate storage tiers based on your data access patterns to optimize costs, and monitoring your storage performance to ensure HA and reliability. This chapter covers these best practices in detail, providing you with the knowledge to manage your Azure storage efficiently and effectively.

- **Exploring various Azure storage services**: Azure provides several types of storage services, each designed to handle specific types of data and workloads. These include Azure Blob Storage, Azure File Storage, Azure Table Storage, and Azure Queue Storage. Each service is optimized for different use cases.

Summary

In this chapter, we focused on implementing Azure storage solutions to build a scalable, secure, and efficient data storage environment. We began by discussing the advantages of Azure Storage, which provides reliable and secure options for storing both unstructured data (such as images) and structured data (such as tables).

We covered designing a scalable and secure storage architecture by choosing the right Azure storage services (Blob, File, Table, Queue Storage) and planning for scalability with data partitioning, replication, and CDN integration. Security was a priority, implementing encryption for data at rest and in transit and using RBAC with Azure Active Directory (Entra ID).

Finally, we set up monitoring and management processes with Azure Monitor and Storage Analytics to track performance and configure alerts. We also explored cost optimization strategies by adjusting storage tiers and implementing life cycle management policies.

With these skills, you can design scalable, secure Azure storage solutions, migrate data effectively, and maintain performance and security. In the next chapter, we'll dive into designing and implementing an Azure network topology, exploring Azure networking, configuring security, implementing hybrid connectivity, and optimizing network performance.

Join the CloudPro Newsletter with 44000+ Subscribers

Want to know what's happening in cloud computing, DevOps, IT administration, networking, and more? Scan the QR code to subscribe to **CloudPro**, our weekly newsletter for 44,000+ tech professionals who want to stay informed and ahead of the curve.

https://packt.link/cloudpro

4

Understanding the Azure Network Topology, Design Principles, and Best Practices

This chapter will cover one of the most important topics and projects in this book, your network topology. Networking is the foundation of every project in general. With every project with Azure, it's one of the first major things you need to consider in your core design and one of the key architectural elements of your design vision that needs to be considered either from the beginning or in the future.

Let's get started with looking at the network topology and its importance!

In this chapter, we will explore the essential elements of designing and implementing a robust network topology in Azure. A **network topology** refers to the arrangement of different elements (links, nodes, etc.) in a computer network. It is the layout pattern of interconnections between the various elements of a network, such as switches, routers, and hosts. In the context of Azure, a network topology is the arrangement of your **virtual networks** (**VNets**), subnets, and other networking components, such as **network security groups** (**NSGs**) and firewalls that ensure secure, reliable, and high-performance communication between your Azure resources and your on-premises network. We will cover the creation and configuration of VNets, subnets, NSGs, Azure Firewall, and hybrid connectivity solutions such as VPN Gateway and ExpressRoute. Additionally, we will discuss how to optimize network performance using Azure Load Balancer and Traffic Manager.

This chapter will cover the following broad topics:

- The importance of the Azure network topology
- Key architectural concepts
- Practical scenario

So, now that you know about the network topology and the focus of this chapter, let's get started with it.

Technical requirements

To follow along with this chapter and carry out the practical exercises, you will need the following:

- A Microsoft Azure account
- Basic knowledge of networking concepts
- Access to the Azure portal
- The Azure CLI installed on your local machine
- On-premises network details for hybrid connectivity

The importance of the Azure network topology

The network topology is a critical aspect of any cloud infrastructure, determining how resources communicate with each other and external systems. A well-designed Azure network topology provides several key benefits that are essential for ensuring a secure, efficient, and scalable cloud environment.

A sample network topology is shown in *Figure 4.1*, just to give you an overview of what a network topology would look like.

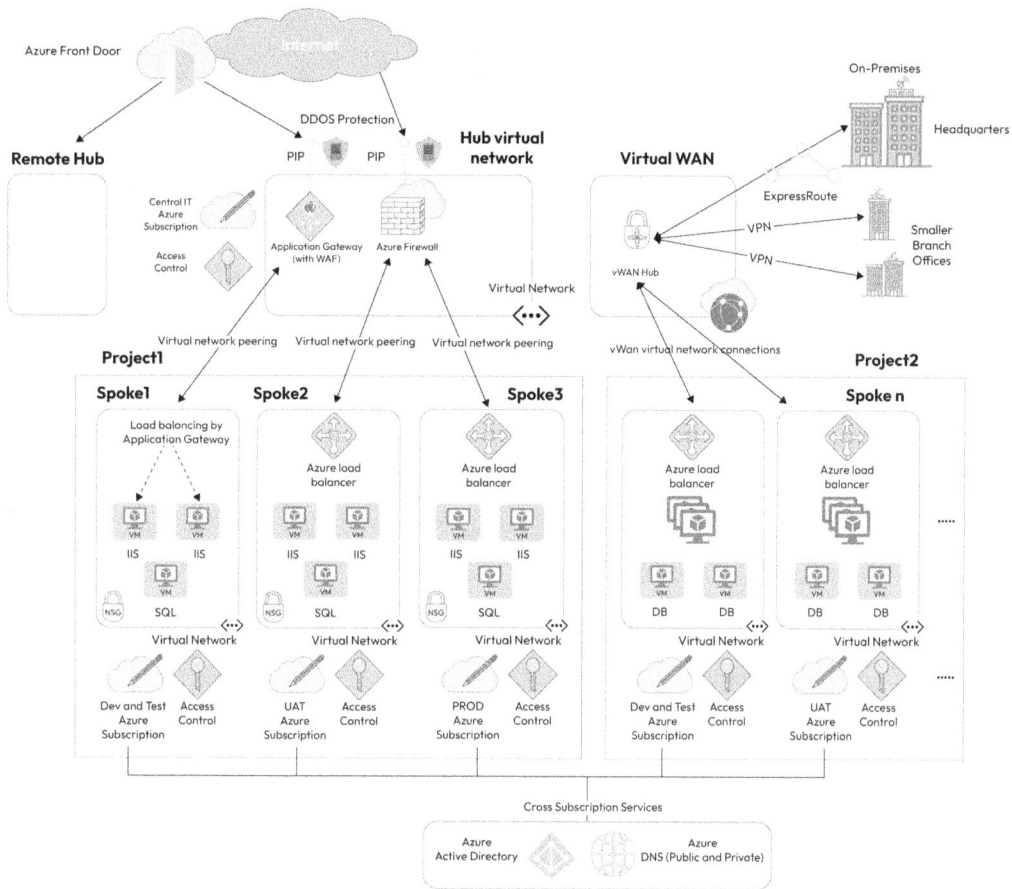

Figure 4.1 – Sample network topology

Let's go over the benefits in detail now:

- **Improved security**: One of the primary advantages of a well-designed network topology is enhanced security. By segmenting your network into VNets and subnets, you can isolate different workloads and control traffic between them. This segmentation reduces the attack surface, making it more difficult for malicious actors to move laterally within the network. Additionally, implementing NSGs and Azure Firewall further enhances security by defining and enforcing security rules that regulate inbound and outbound traffic, protecting your resources from unauthorized access and potential threats.

As illustrated in *Figure 4.2*, different Azure network security components can protect you at different levels and in different situations at the same time in the application and platform layers, which you can also refer to as your infrastructure.

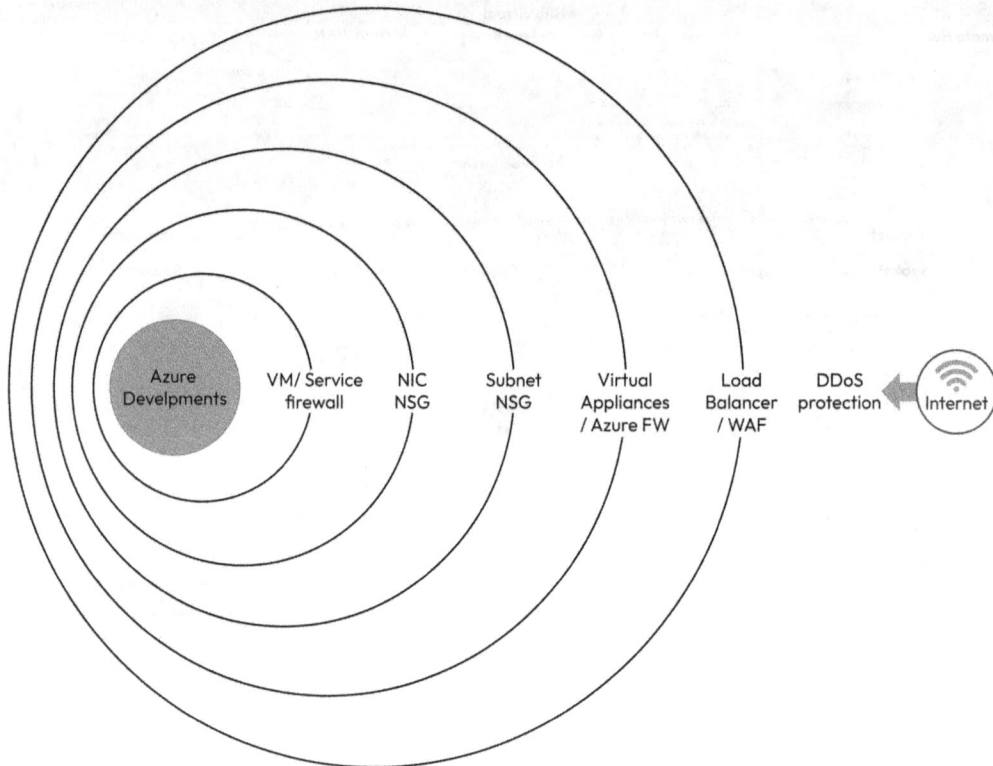

Figure 4.2 – Network security components in Azure

For example, in an e-commerce application, you can create separate subnets for web servers, application servers, and database servers. By doing so, you can apply stricter security rules to the database subnet, limiting access only to the application servers, thereby protecting sensitive customer data. For instance, NSG rules might allow HTTP and HTTPS traffic to the web server subnet from the internet, but only allow SQL traffic to the database subnet from the application server subnet.

- **Enhanced performance**: A well-planned network topology optimizes data flow and minimizes latency, leading to improved performance of your applications. By strategically placing resources within VNets and subnets, you can ensure efficient communication between components. Using tools such as Azure Load Balancer and Traffic Manager, you can distribute traffic evenly across multiple resources and direct user requests to the nearest or most responsive endpoints, enhancing the overall performance and user experience.

For example, for a global application, Azure Traffic Manager can route user requests to the closest Azure region, reducing latency and providing a faster response time. If a user from Europe accesses your application, Traffic Manager directs the request to the Azure data center in Europe, rather than one in the US, ensuring quicker response times and a better user experience.

- **Increased reliability**: Network redundancy and failover mechanisms are crucial for maintaining high availability and reliability. By designing your network topology with redundancy in mind, you can ensure that your applications remain available even in the event of hardware failures or other disruptions. Azure provides various features, such as VNet peering and VPN Gateway, to create resilient network connections. Additionally, using Azure ExpressRoute provides a more reliable and consistent network performance compared to public internet connections.

    For example, by setting up VPN Gateway with Azure ExpressRoute, you can establish a private and resilient connection between your on-premises network and Azure, ensuring continuous access to critical applications and data. For instance, if your company's headquarters have a dedicated ExpressRoute connection to Azure, it ensures that critical business applications hosted in Azure remain accessible even if the public internet connection experiences issues.

- **Seamless integration with on-premises networks**: Hybrid cloud deployments are becoming increasingly common, allowing organizations to leverage the benefits of both on-premises and cloud environments. A well-designed Azure network topology facilitates seamless integration between on-premises networks and Azure. Solutions such as VPN Gateway and Azure ExpressRoute enable secure and reliable connectivity, allowing you to extend your on-premises infrastructure to the cloud and create a cohesive hybrid environment.

As shown in *Figure 4.3*, different Azure networking components help you to connect to your on-premises securely and seamlessly.

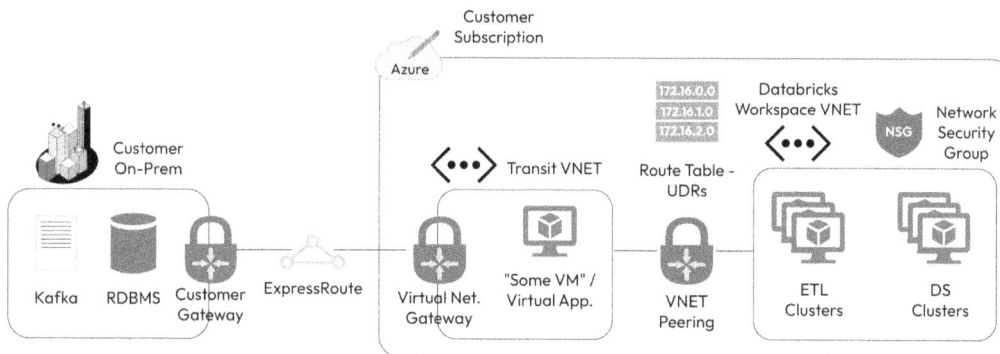

Figure 4.3 – Azure networking components for integration with on-premises

For example, a company with an on-premises data center can use Azure ExpressRoute to establish a private connection to Azure, enabling secure data transfer and integration of on-premises applications with cloud services. This setup allows an organization to run applications that span both environments seamlessly. For example, an on-premises **Enterprise Resource Planning (ERP)** system might integrate with Azure-hosted analytics services to provide real-time business insights without exposing sensitive data to the public internet.

* **Scalability and flexibility**: As your organization grows, your network topology needs to scale accordingly. Azure's flexible network architecture allows you to easily expand your VNets and subnets, add new resources, and reconfigure your network as needed. This scalability ensures that your infrastructure can accommodate increasing workloads and evolving business requirements without compromising performance or security.

  For example, when launching a new service, you can quickly create additional VNets and subnets to support the new workload, ensuring that your network can handle increased traffic and resource demands. For example, if your company develops a new mobile app, you can set up a dedicated VNet with subnets for web servers, application servers, and databases, configured with appropriate NSG rules and load balancing to handle the expected increase in user traffic efficiently.

So far, we have learned about network topology in general, as well as about different Azure networking components, how and where you should use them depending on your needs, and staying on the edge of technology with Azure. We have also covered how you can make your environment secure with Azure network security components, as well as how you can connect to your on-premises network. Now, before diving into a real-world scenario, we will go through some key architectural and design concepts about Azure networking in the next section.

Key architectural concepts for designing and implementing networking in Azure

When designing and implementing networking in Azure, several architectural concepts are fundamental to creating a secure, scalable, and efficient infrastructure. These concepts are interrelated and often come together in specific design patterns, such as the hub-and-spoke model, which is particularly effective for large, complex environments. Now, let's explore the key components and design areas in Azure that you need to keep in mind during a high-level design.

VNets form the foundation of Azure's networking architecture. A VNet is an isolated, logical network within Azure that allows your resources to communicate securely with each other, with the internet, and with on-premises networks. When setting up a VNet, it is crucial to plan the IP address space carefully to avoid conflicts with on-premises networks, especially in hybrid cloud environments. VNets act as containers for your networked resources, where you can control traffic flow, apply security policies, and manage connectivity.

Figure 4.4 shows Azure VNet components and connectivity.

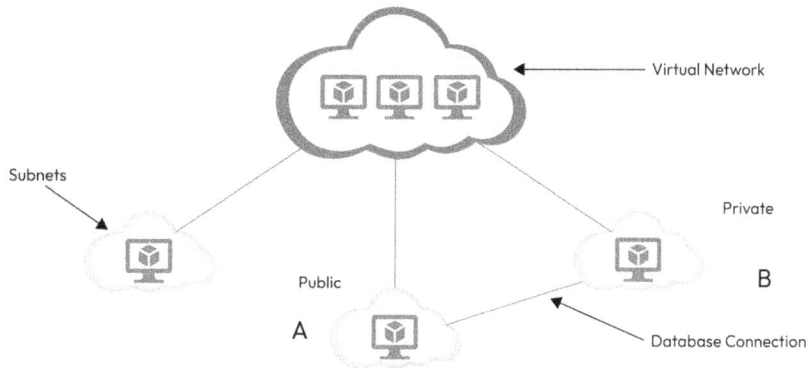

Figure 4.4 – Azure VNet diagram

Within a VNet, **subnetting** is used to further segment the network into smaller, more manageable segments, as shown in *Figure 4.4*. Subnets help organize resources by function, security level, or application needs. For example, you might create separate subnets for web servers, application servers, and databases. Subnetting is critical for both resource management and security, as it allows for the isolation of different workloads. By placing different workloads in separate subnets, you can enforce distinct security rules, reducing the risk of unauthorized access and improving overall security.

This is where the **hub-and-spoke** design model becomes particularly useful. In this model, the hub is a central VNet that acts as the core point of connectivity for all spoke VNets. The spoke VNets are connected to the hub via VNet peering, allowing them to communicate with the hub and, if necessary, with each other. The hub typically contains shared services, such as DNS, Active Directory, and security appliances, as well as connectivity services such as VPN gateways or Azure Firewall. This centralization simplifies management, security enforcement, and monitoring, making it easier to scale and control the network as it grows. *Figure 4.5* illustrates it in more detail and you can see how the design concept helps you to design your environment.

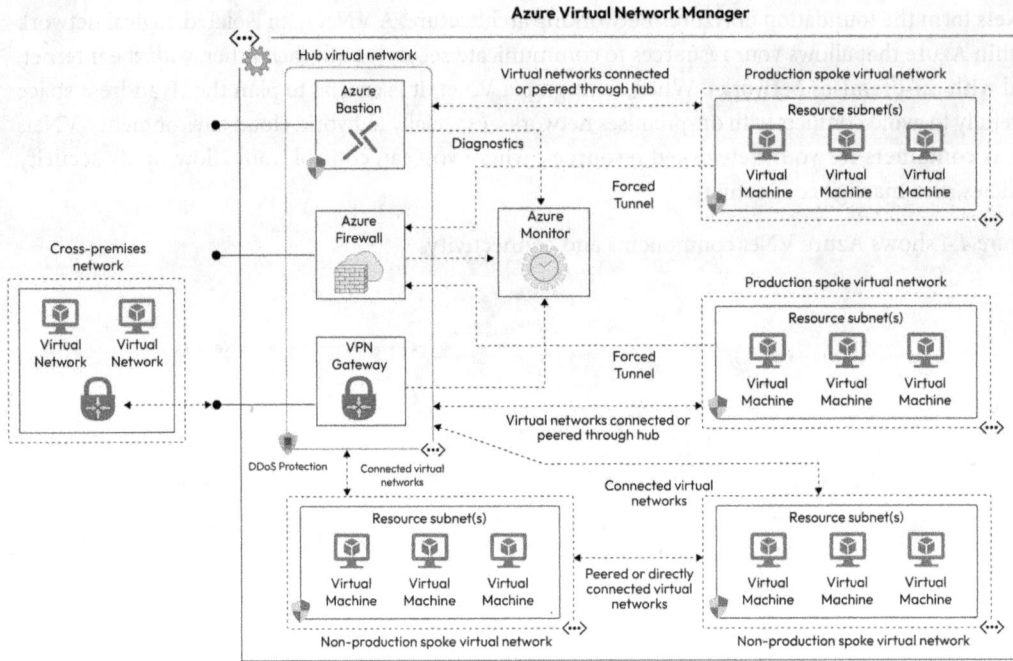

Figure 4.5 – Hub-and-spoke network topology in Azure

The hub-and-spoke model is particularly beneficial for network security. The hub acts as the central point for applying security policies, which can be enforced across all connected spokes. NSGs play a critical role here, as they control the flow of traffic in and out of the VNets. NSGs allow you to define security rules that determine which types of traffic are allowed or denied based on source and destination IP addresses, ports, and protocols. This is essential for maintaining a secure environment, especially in complex architectures where different workloads require different levels of access.

Figure 4.6 shows how the hub-and-spoke model can help to design your connectivity between spokes using different Azure networking components.

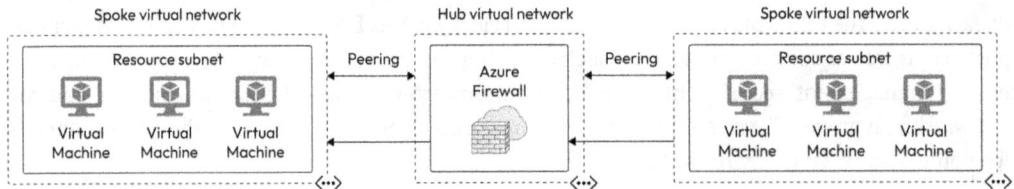

Figure 4.6 – Hub-and-spoke connectivity concept

For environments that demand even higher levels of security, Azure Firewall can be deployed in the hub. **Azure Firewall** is a managed, cloud-native network security service that provides centralized protection for all your VNets. It filters both inbound and outbound traffic, allowing you to create and enforce comprehensive security policies across the entire network. In the hub-and-spoke model, Azure Firewall can act as the main security gateway, controlling and monitoring all traffic between the spokes and the hub, as well as traffic entering and leaving the Azure environment.

Another critical aspect of the hub-and-spoke model is **load balancing**, which ensures that network traffic is distributed efficiently across multiple resources, such as **virtual machines** (**VMs**). Azure Load Balancer and Azure Application Gateway are key tools for this purpose. **Azure Load Balancer**, which operates at the transport layer (*Layer 4*), is typically used to distribute traffic across VMs within a VNet. **Azure Application Gateway**, which operates at the application layer (*Layer 7*), provides additional features, such as SSL termination and a **web application firewall** (**WAF**), making it ideal for web applications. In the hub-and-spoke model, these load-balancing services can be centrally managed in the hub, ensuring that traffic is efficiently routed across all spokes.

In *Figure 5.5*, the Azure Load Balancer concept is illustrated to show how it handles the traffic between two VMs in a backend pool.

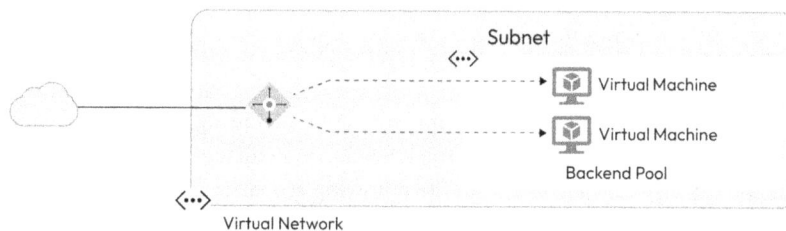

Figure 4.7 – Azure Load Balancer concept

Hybrid connectivity is another area where the hub-and-spoke model excels. For organizations that need to connect their on-premises networks with Azure, solutions such as VPN Gateway and Azure ExpressRoute are essential. In the hub-and-spoke model, these connectivity services are typically located in the hub, acting as the single point of ingress and egress for all on-premises traffic. VPN Gateway provides secure, encrypted connections over the internet, while ExpressRoute offers a private connection that bypasses the public internet, providing more reliable and consistent performance. This setup simplifies the management of hybrid connectivity and ensures that all on-premises communication is routed through a secure, controlled environment.

Identity and access management (**IAM**) is also crucial in the hub-and-spoke design. Entra ID is used to manage identities and enforce access controls across the entire network. By integrating Entra ID with **role-based access control** (**RBAC**), you can ensure that users and applications have the appropriate permissions to access resources, whether they are in the hub or one of the spokes. This centralized management of identities and permissions simplifies administration and enhances security by ensuring that access is tightly controlled and monitored.

Monitoring and diagnostics are essential for maintaining the health and performance of a network designed around the hub-and-spoke model. Azure Monitor and **Network Watcher** provide the tools needed to collect and analyze metrics, logs, and diagnostic data from all parts of the network. These services enable real-time monitoring and troubleshooting, helping to identify and resolve issues before they impact performance or security. In the hub-and-spoke model, monitoring can be centralized in the hub, providing a single pane of glass for observing the entire network.

Finally, DNS and name resolution are critical components of Azure networking that ensure resources can communicate effectively within and across VNets. **Azure DNS** allows you to manage DNS records for your domains, ensuring fast and reliable name resolution. In the hub-and-spoke model, the hub often hosts the DNS services, allowing all spokes to use a common DNS infrastructure. Private DNS zones can be used within the VNets to facilitate internal name resolution, enabling resources in different spokes to communicate using hostnames rather than IP addresses.

The hub-and-spoke design model brings together various architectural concepts to create a robust, secure, and scalable network infrastructure in Azure. By carefully considering VNets, subnetting, security measures, connectivity, identity management, and monitoring within this model, you can build a network that meets your organization's needs today and is flexible enough to adapt to future demands. The hub-and-spoke model provides the structure and control necessary to manage complex environments efficiently, making it an ideal choice for organizations looking to leverage the full potential of Azure's networking capabilities.

Now that we've covered the essential architectural concepts, including the hub-and-spoke design model, and their importance in building a secure, scalable, and efficient Azure network, it's time to apply these principles in a practical context. In the following scenario, we will take you through the steps of designing and implementing a network topology in Azure for a fictional company, CloudNet Solutions. This scenario will help you understand how to put these concepts into practice, ensuring that your network infrastructure not only meets current requirements but is also prepared for future growth and complexity. Let's dive into the scenario and see how these concepts come to life in a real-world setting.

Project scenario for Azure networking

As the IT network engineer at CloudNet Solutions, you are responsible for designing and implementing an Azure network topology that supports the company's new cloud infrastructure. CloudNet Solutions is transitioning to Azure to leverage the cloud's scalability, flexibility, and cost efficiency. Your goal is to create a network architecture that ensures secure communication between Azure resources and seamless integration with the on-premises network in this project.

The company's current infrastructure includes several on-premises applications and databases critical to business operations. These applications must communicate securely with the new cloud-based services deployed in Azure. The network topology must also support future growth, handle increased traffic, and provide high-availability and disaster recovery capabilities.

Company background

CloudNet Solutions is a mid-sized technology firm that develops software solutions for various industries. The company has decided to migrate its existing applications and data to Azure to take advantage of cloud computing benefits. The IT department is tasked with ensuring that the transition is smooth, secure, and minimally disruptive to business operations.

Current infrastructure

The existing infrastructure at CloudNet Solutions includes the following components:

- **On-premises data center**: The on-premises data center hosts several applications, including an ERP system, customer databases, and internal collaboration tools

- **Network configuration**: The on-premises network uses a traditional hub-and-spoke model, with centralized security and access controls

- **Security requirements**: The company has strict security policies to protect sensitive customer data and ensure regulatory compliance

Migration goals

The migration goals of the organization are as follows:

- **Security**: Implement robust security measures to protect data and resources during and after migration

- **Seamless integration**: Ensure that on-premises and Azure resources can communicate securely and efficiently

- **Scalability**: Design the network to accommodate future growth and increased workloads

- **High availability**: Implement redundancy and failover mechanisms to ensure the continuous availability of critical applications

Objectives

Here are the objectives we're going to follow in this section to achieve our migration goals:

- **Design a VNet topology**: Create and configure VNets and subnets to segment your network

- **Implement network security**: Set up NSGs and Azure Firewall to control traffic and enhance security

- **Establish hybrid connectivity**: Implement VPN Gateway and Azure ExpressRoute to connect the on-premises network to Azure

- **Optimize network performance**: Utilize Azure Load Balancer and Traffic Manager to ensure high availability and performance

Let's start by exploring the current infrastructure.

On-premises data center

CloudNet Solutions operates a well-established on-premises data center that serves as the backbone for all of its critical IT infrastructure. This data center is home to a variety of systems and applications that support the company's operations across different departments. The data center hosts essential business applications, databases, and services that are integral to the daily functioning of the organization. Some more details are as follows:

- **Applications and databases**: The on-premises data center houses several critical applications, including an ERP system that manages the company's core business processes such as finance, supply chain, and human resources. Additionally, the data center runs a **customer relationship management (CRM)** system that stores and manages all customer interactions and data, enabling sales, marketing, and customer service teams to work effectively. The data center also supports internal collaboration tools such as project management software, email servers, and file storage systems, all of which are crucial for employee productivity.

- **Servers and storage**: The infrastructure within the data center consists of a mix of physical servers and VMs that host these applications. These servers are connected to a centralized **storage area network (SAN)** that provides high-performance, scalable storage solutions for databases and filesystems. The storage architecture is designed to ensure high availability and data redundancy, with regular backups and disaster recovery plans in place to protect against data loss.

Network configuration

The network configuration of the on-premises data center is designed with a traditional hub-and-spoke model. This model centralizes all network traffic through a core network switch, which acts as the hub, while various departmental networks and resources are connected as spokes. This setup allows for efficient management of network traffic and centralized control over security policies:

- **Core network switch**: At the heart of the network is a high-capacity core network switch that manages the routing and switching of all data traffic within the data center. This switch connects to multiple distribution switches that service different parts of the data center, such as the server farms, storage systems, and user workstations. The core switch also manages traffic between the data center and external networks, including the internet and any remote offices.

- **Internal segmentation**: The network is segmented into different **virtual local area networks** (**VLANs**) to separate traffic based on function and security requirements. For example, there are dedicated VLANs for the ERP and CRM systems, another VLAN for internal collaboration tools, and additional VLANs for employee workstations and guest Wi-Fi access. This segmentation helps in controlling traffic flow and applying security policies specific to each segment, ensuring that sensitive data is isolated from less secure areas of the network.

- **Connectivity and redundancy**: The data center is equipped with redundant network connections to ensure continuous availability. This includes multiple **internet service providers** (**ISPs**) for external connectivity and dual power supplies for critical network equipment. In case of a hardware failure, traffic can be rerouted through backup connections, minimizing downtime and maintaining service availability.

Security requirements

Given the sensitive nature of the data and applications housed within the on-premises data center, security is a top priority for CloudNet Solutions. The company has implemented a comprehensive security strategy to protect its assets from both external threats and internal vulnerabilities. This strategy includes the following:

- **Firewalls and intrusion detection systems (IDS)**: The first line of defense is a robust firewall system that controls all inbound and outbound traffic to and from the data center. The firewall is configured with strict rules to allow only necessary traffic while blocking any unauthorized access attempts. In addition to firewalls, the data center employs an IDS that continuously monitors network traffic for suspicious activity. The IDS is designed to detect potential security breaches and alert the IT security team for further investigation.

- **NSGs and access controls**: Within the data center, NSGs are used to control access between different segments of the network. These groups define which resources can communicate with each other and what types of traffic are permitted. For example, the ERP and CRM systems are isolated from the general employee network, with access restricted to authorized users only. Access controls are enforced at multiple levels, including at the network level through NSGs and at the application level through RBAC.

- **Data encryption and compliance**: To protect data at rest and in transit, CloudNet Solutions has implemented encryption across its storage systems and network connections. All sensitive data stored within the data center is encrypted using industry-standard algorithms, and data transmitted over the network is secured using SSL/TLS protocols. Additionally, the company is committed to complying with industry regulations such as GDPR and HIPAA, which mandate strict controls over data protection and privacy. Regular security audits and compliance checks are conducted to ensure that all security measures are up to date and effective.

- **Disaster recovery and backup**: As part of its security strategy, CloudNet Solutions has a comprehensive disaster recovery plan in place. This plan includes regular backups of all critical data, stored both on-site and in secure off-site locations. In the event of a disaster, the company can quickly restore operations using these backups, minimizing data loss and downtime. The disaster recovery plan is tested regularly to ensure its effectiveness and to make any necessary updates.

With this robust on-premises infrastructure, CloudNet Solutions is well prepared to handle its current operational needs. However, as the company expands and moves toward a hybrid cloud model, it is essential to integrate this on-premises setup with Azure in a way that maintains security, reliability, and performance.

Now that we have a good understanding of the current infrastructure, it's time to move on to the development phase and check for the best practices that we learned about in the *Objectives* section.

As CloudNet Solutions transitions from a solely on-premises infrastructure to a hybrid cloud environment using Azure, the network architecture must be meticulously designed to meet several critical objectives. These objectives are aimed at ensuring the security, scalability, and efficiency of the new infrastructure while seamlessly integrating with the existing on-premises setup. Let's explore each of these objectives in greater detail, emphasizing best practices and how they align with our goals:

- **Designing a VNet topology**: This is the foundation of the network architecture. The VNet serves as the backbone for all cloud-based resources, enabling secure communication between these resources, on-premises systems, and the internet. When designing the VNet topology, it is essential to start by planning the IP address space. Careful planning is necessary to ensure that the IP ranges chosen for the VNet do not overlap with those used in the on-premises network. Overlapping IP ranges can cause conflicts when routing traffic between the two environments, leading to connectivity issues.

  Subnetting within the VNet allows us to segment the network based on function, security level, or application needs. For instance, we might create distinct subnets for web servers, application servers, and databases, each with tailored security policies and routing rules. This segmentation is crucial for both organizing resources and enhancing security. By isolating different workloads into separate subnets, we can apply specific security controls and optimize traffic flow within the network.

  Adopting the hub-and-spoke design model for our VNet topology will centralize shared services, such as DNS, Active Directory, and security appliances, in the hub VNet. The spoke VNets, connected to the hub via VNet peering, will host individual workloads or departments. This design not only simplifies management and security enforcement but also supports future scalability as new spokes can be added without disrupting the existing network structure. The goal here is to create a VNet topology that is robust, scalable, and capable of supporting CloudNet Solutions' evolving needs.

- **Implementing network security**: This is another critical objective, given the sensitive nature of the data and applications involved. Robust security measures must be in place to protect the Azure environment from unauthorized access and potential threats while ensuring compliance with industry regulations. NSGs play a pivotal role in this by controlling traffic flow at the subnet level. NSGs allow us to define rules that restrict or allow traffic based on criteria such as source and destination IP addresses, ports, and protocols. By applying NSGs to each subnet, we can enforce the principle of least privilege, ensuring that only the necessary traffic is permitted, thus minimizing the attack surface.

  To further enhance security, Azure Firewall will be deployed in the hub VNet. Azure Firewall provides a centralized security policy management system that filters both inbound and outbound traffic across all connected spokes. This managed, cloud-native firewall service enables us to implement comprehensive security policies that protect the entire Azure environment from external threats and unauthorized access. Additionally, advanced threat protection services such as Azure Security Center will be used to continuously monitor the network for vulnerabilities, offering proactive alerts and recommendations to address potential risks.

  The ultimate goal in this area is to establish a security framework that is both robust and flexible, capable of adapting to new threats and ensuring that all data and applications within the Azure environment are protected to the highest standards.

  For more information about Azure network security, you can also refer to `https://learn.microsoft.com/en-us/azure/security/fundamentals/network-overview`.

- **Establishing hybrid connectivity**: This is essential for maintaining seamless communication between the on-premises data center and Azure. As CloudNet Solutions transitions to a hybrid cloud model, it is critical that both environments work together harmoniously. This involves setting up secure and reliable hybrid connectivity solutions that allow for efficient communication between on-premises resources and those hosted in Azure.

In *Figure 4.8*, a sample Azure secure hybrid network architecture is illustrated.

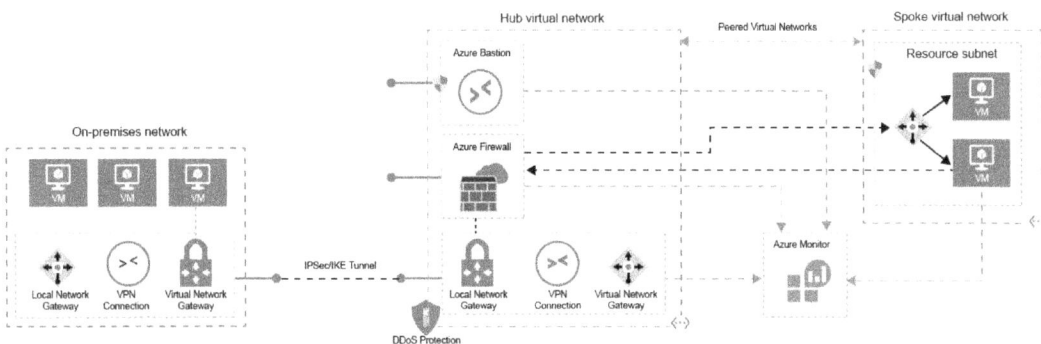

Figure 4.8 – Azure secure hybrid network sample architecture

The initial setup will involve configuring VPN Gateway to create secure, encrypted connections over the internet between the on-premises network and Azure. This VPN Gateway will enable the extension of the on-premises infrastructure into Azure, allowing data and resources to flow securely between the two environments. While VPN Gateway provides a cost-effective and flexible solution for hybrid connectivity, the network architecture will be designed with the potential to upgrade to Azure ExpressRoute in the future. ExpressRoute offers a private connection that bypasses the public internet, providing more reliable, higher-bandwidth, and lower-latency connectivity. This would be particularly beneficial for mission-critical applications that require consistent and dependable performance.

VNet peering will be used to connect the Hub and Spoke VNets within Azure. This peering ensures seamless communication between the spokes and the hub, allowing resources in different spokes to access shared services in the hub without compromising security. The overall goal here is to establish a hybrid connectivity solution that is secure, reliable, and capable of supporting the company's hybrid cloud strategy both now and in the future.

- **Optimizing network performance**: This is crucial to ensure that applications and services perform optimally. The network must be designed to handle traffic efficiently, avoid bottlenecks, and provide high availability. This objective involves implementing solutions that enhance network performance and reliability.

Azure Load Balancer will be employed to distribute incoming traffic across multiple VMs within a VNet. This load balancing ensures that no single VM is overwhelmed with traffic, thereby improving application availability and reliability. The load balancer will also be configured to provide automatic failover, further enhancing the resilience of the applications.

For applications that span multiple regions or need to route users to the closest or most responsive endpoint, Azure Traffic Manager will be implemented. Traffic Manager uses DNS-based load balancing to direct user traffic to the most appropriate Azure region based on factors such as performance, availability, and user location. This capability is particularly useful for global applications that need to minimize latency and provide the best possible user experience.

Continuous monitoring of network performance will be essential to maintain optimal operations. Tools such as Azure Monitor and Network Watcher will be utilized to collect and analyze metrics, logs, and diagnostic data, allowing for proactive identification and resolution of performance issues. The goal is to create a network that not only meets current performance requirements but also provides the infrastructure needed to monitor, maintain, and optimize performance as the network grows and evolves.

- **Applying best practices in network design**: This is the final objective, ensuring that the network architecture adheres to industry standards and Azure's architectural guidelines. Best practices in network design will focus on creating a secure, scalable, and cost-efficient network that is easy to manage and capable of supporting long-term business objectives.

Scalability will be a key consideration, allowing the network to expand as the organization grows. The hub-and-spoke model inherently supports scalability, making it easy to add new spokes, services, or regions as needed. Security best practices, such as the use of NSGs, Azure Firewall, encryption, and identity management, will be rigorously applied to protect the network and ensure compliance with industry regulations.

Cost efficiency is another important factor, as the network will be designed to optimize resource usage, minimize redundancy, and reduce operational costs wherever possible. Comprehensive documentation of the network design, including IP address management, security policies, and connectivity configurations, will be maintained to support ongoing management, troubleshooting, and alignment with organizational goals.

The overall objective is to implement a network design that is robust, secure, scalable, and cost-efficient, capable of supporting CloudNet Solutions' long-term business objectives while remaining flexible enough to adapt to future changes and challenges.

Now that we've established the foundational objectives and thoroughly explored the architectural concepts and best practices required to design a robust Azure network topology, it's time to translate these plans into action. The next phase involves stepping into the technical scenario, where we will implement the network architecture for CloudNet Solutions. This scenario will guide you through the practical configurations and setup processes necessary to bring the Azure environment to life, ensuring that it meets the company's needs for security, scalability, and seamless integration with their existing on-premises infrastructure. Let's dive into the technical details and see how these concepts are applied in a real-world setting.

Implementing a comprehensive Azure network topology

As we now understand, CloudNet Solutions is embarking on a significant transition from a traditional on-premises infrastructure to a hybrid cloud environment using Azure. The objective is to design and implement a robust, scalable, and secure network topology that seamlessly integrates Azure with the existing on-premises data center. In this scenario, we will combine detailed explanations with the technical implementation steps necessary to achieve a functional and secure Azure environment:

1. **Designing the VNet topology**: This is the first step, and it involves setting up the foundational structure of your Azure environment. A well-designed VNet topology is crucial because it forms the backbone of your cloud infrastructure, enabling secure communication between resources, both within Azure and with your on-premises environment:

    I.   The process begins with creating the hub VNet, which will act as the central point of connectivity for your entire Azure deployment. This hub VNet will host shared services and security components that are crucial for the network's overall functionality.

II.   As shown in *Figure 4.9*, in the Azure portal, you start by navigating to **Create a resource | Networking | Virtual networks**. Here, you define your hub VNet's name, such as Hub-VNet, and choose an address space, such as 10.0.0.0/16, ensuring it doesn't overlap with your on-premises network.

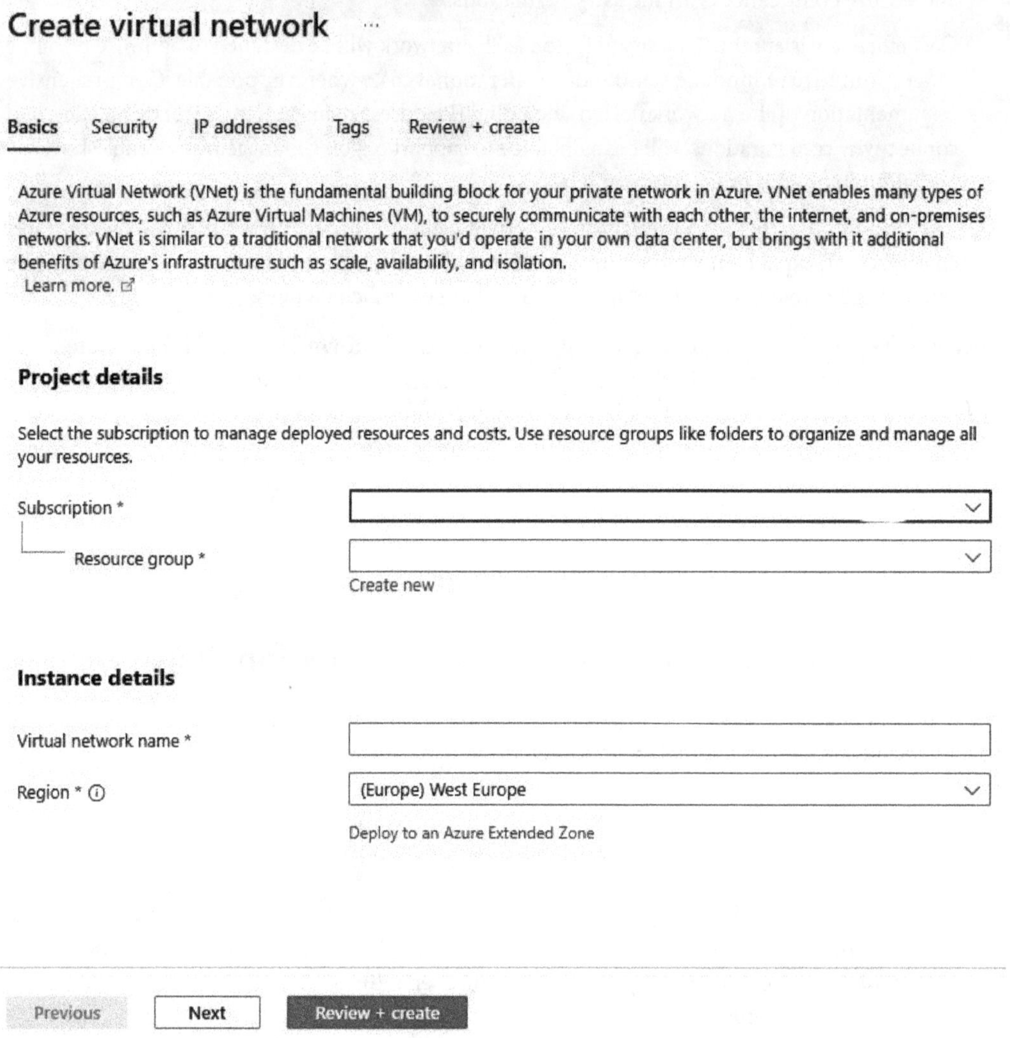

Create virtual network   ...

Basics   Security   IP addresses   Tags   Review + create

Azure Virtual Network (VNet) is the fundamental building block for your private network in Azure. VNet enables many types of Azure resources, such as Azure Virtual Machines (VM), to securely communicate with each other, the internet, and on-premises networks. VNet is similar to a traditional network that you'd operate in your own data center, but brings with it additional benefits of Azure's infrastructure such as scale, availability, and isolation.
Learn more. ⌐

Project details

Select the subscription to manage deployed resources and costs. Use resource groups like folders to organize and manage all your resources.

Subscription *   [∨]

          Resource group *   [∨]
                               Create new

Instance details

Virtual network name *   [   ]

Region * ⓘ   [(Europe) West Europe   ∨]
               Deploy to an Azure Extended Zone

[Previous]   [Next]   [Review + create]

Figure 4.9 – Create an Azure VNet

III. Within this hub VNet, you then create subnets dedicated to specific functions, as shown in *Figure 4.10*. For example, you might create a subnet called `SharedServicesSubnet` with an IP range of `10.0.1.0/24` to host essential services such as DNS and Active Directory. Another subnet, `AzureFirewallSubnet` (`10.0.2.0/24`), will be reserved for security appliances such as Azure Firewall. These subnets allow for better organization and security control over the network traffic within the VNet. You can also refer to this link for detailed steps on Azure VNet creation: `https://learn.microsoft.com/en-us/azure/virtual-network/quick-create-portal`.

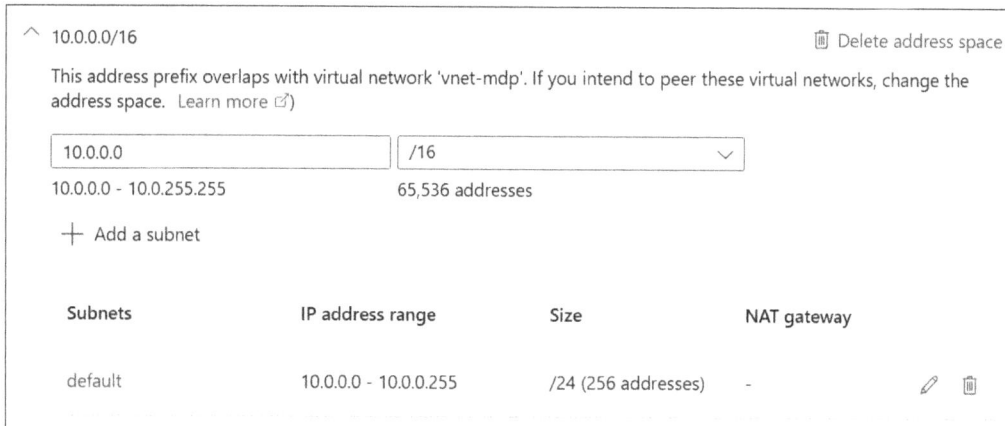

10.0.0.0/16				🗑 Delete address space

This address prefix overlaps with virtual network 'vnet-mdp'. If you intend to peer these virtual networks, change the address space. Learn more ⬦)

10.0.0.0		/16		⌄

10.0.0.0 - 10.0.255.255   65,536 addresses

+ Add a subnet

Subnets	IP address range	Size	NAT gateway		
default	10.0.0.0 - 10.0.0.255	/24 (256 addresses)	-	✎	🗑

Figure 4.10 – Create Azure VNet subnets

IV. Following the setup of the hub VNet, the next task is to create spoke VNets for individual workloads or departments, which will connect back to the hub. Each spoke VNet should be allocated a unique address space, such as `10.1.0.0/16` for `Spoke1-VNet` and `10.2.0.0/16` for `Spoke2-VNet`. These spoke VNets will also be segmented into subnets based on the specific needs of the workloads they support. For instance, in a spoke VNet dedicated to web applications, you might create `WebSubnet` (`10.1.1.0/24`), `AppSubnet` (`10.1.2.0/24`), and `DbSubnet` (`10.1.3.0/24`) subnets, each with its own IP range.

V. To enable communication between the hub-and-spoke VNets, you'll establish VNet peering. VNet peering is configured by navigating to the hub VNet's settings, selecting **Peerings**, and then adding a new peering connection. You'll peer the hub VNet with each spoke VNet, ensuring that traffic can flow seamlessly between them. This step is critical for enabling shared services hosted in the hub to be accessed by resources in the spokes.

You can also follow the steps through this link for VNet peering: `https://learn.microsoft.com/en-us/azure/virtual-network/virtual-network-peering-overview`.

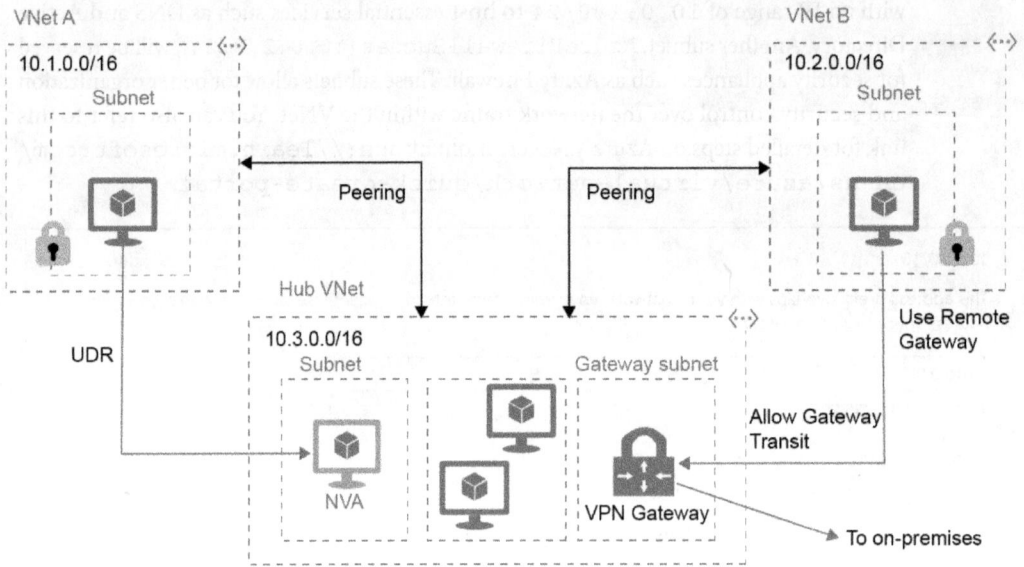

Figure 4.11 – VNet peering topology

2. **Implementing network security**: This is the next critical phase, focusing on securing the Azure environment against unauthorized access and potential threats. This begins with configuring NSGs, which act as virtual firewalls for controlling inbound and outbound traffic at the subnet or network interface level:

I.   In the Azure portal, you can create NSGs by going to **Create a resource | Networking | Network Security Group**. For example, you might create a `WebNSG` NSG to apply to `WebSubnet`, allowing inbound traffic only on ports `80` and `443` for HTTP and HTTPS, while blocking all other ports. Similarly, an `AppNSG` NSG can be configured to allow only traffic from `WebSubnet` on specific ports needed for application communication. Once the NSGs are configured, they should be associated with the respective subnets to enforce the security rules.

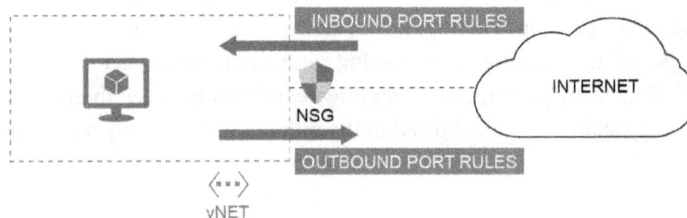

Figure 4.12 – Azure NSG topology

II. To provide a centralized security solution, Azure Firewall will be deployed within the hub VNet. Navigate to **Create a resource | Networking | Azure Firewall** and configure the firewall by assigning it to the previously created `AzureFirewallSubnet`. Azure Firewall will filter both inbound and outbound traffic across all connected VNets, allowing you to enforce comprehensive security policies centrally. You'll configure network rules that control traffic based on IP addresses, protocols, and ports, and application rules that manage traffic based on domain names and URLs.

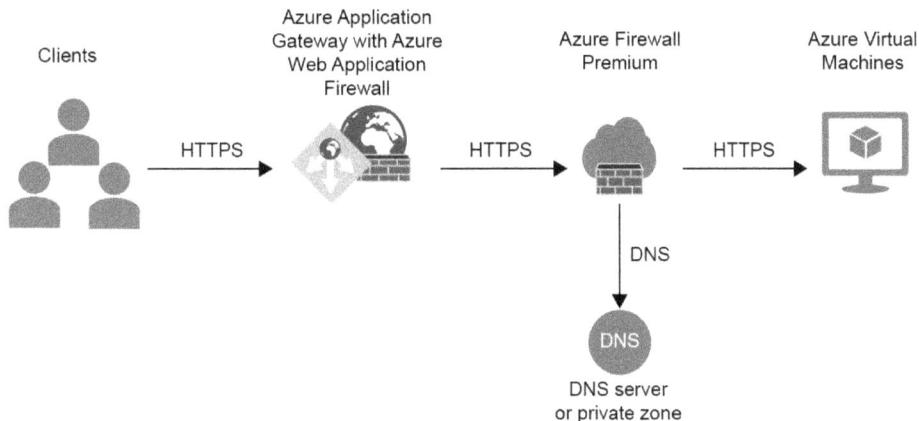

Figure 4.13 – Azure Firewall sample topology

For instance, you might set up a network rule that allows outbound traffic only to certain trusted IP ranges, while blocking all others. Application rules can restrict outbound web traffic to approved domains, providing an additional layer of security.

3. **Establishing hybrid connectivity**: This step is essential for integrating the on-premises data center with the Azure environment, ensuring seamless communication and data flow between the two. The primary method for achieving this is through a VPN gateway, which provides secure, encrypted connectivity.

Here is a full list of different types of VPN SKUs and tiers in which you can make detailed decisions:

`https://learn.microsoft.com/en-us/azure/vpn-gateway/vpn-gateway-about-vpngateways`

Begin by deploying a VPN gateway in the hub VNet. In the Azure portal, go to **Create a resource | Networking | Virtual Network Gateway**. Configure the gateway by selecting **Hub VNet** and assigning it to a dedicated `GatewaySubnet`, such as `10.0.255.0/27`. This gateway will act as the bridge between Azure and your on-premises network. After provisioning the VPN gateway, configure your on-premises VPN device to establish a site-to-site VPN connection with Azure. Azure provides configuration scripts tailored to different VPN devices, which you can download and apply to your on-premises equipment.

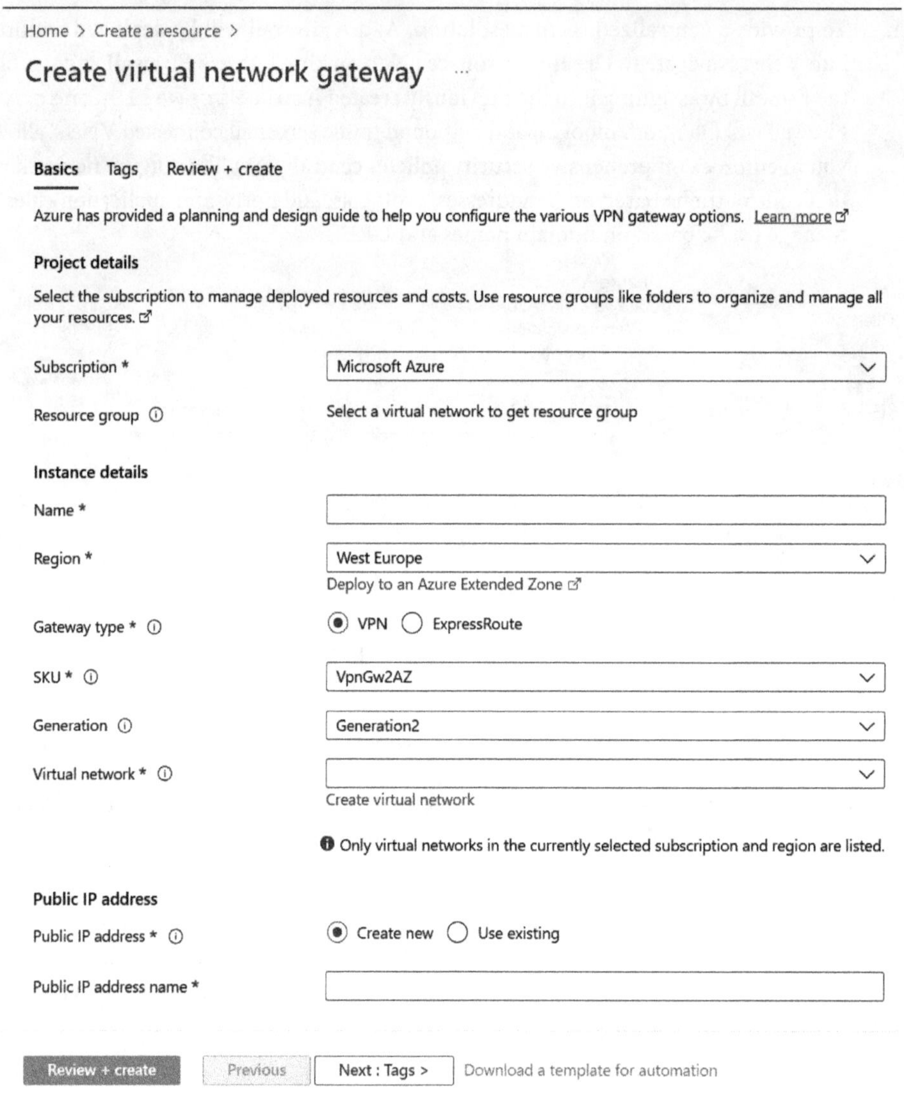

Figure 4.14 – Azure VNet gateway creation page

The connection between the on-premises network and Azure is secured using a **pre-shared key (PSK)**, which is configured on both Azure VPN Gateway and the on-premises VPN device. This ensures that the connection is encrypted and protected from unauthorized access. Once the connection is established, testing is crucial to confirm that data can flow securely between the two environments.

While the initial setup focuses on using VPN Gateway, consider the future potential of upgrading to Azure ExpressRoute. ExpressRoute offers a private, dedicated connection that bypasses the public internet, providing more reliable and consistent performance, especially for mission-critical applications that require low latency and high bandwidth.

4. **Optimizing network performance**: This involves ensuring that applications and services operate efficiently, with minimal latency and maximum availability. This is achieved through the use of load balancing and traffic management solutions.

Azure Load Balancer is a key tool for distributing incoming traffic across multiple VMs within a VNet:

I.   In the Azure portal, go to **Create a resource | Networking | Load Balancer** and set up the load balancer by configuring frontend IP addresses and backend pools. The frontend IP receives incoming traffic, while the backend pool consists of VMs that handle the traffic. You'll also configure health probes to monitor the status of these VMs, ensuring that traffic is only directed to healthy instances. Load balancing rules will dictate how the traffic is distributed based on factors such as IP, port, and protocol.

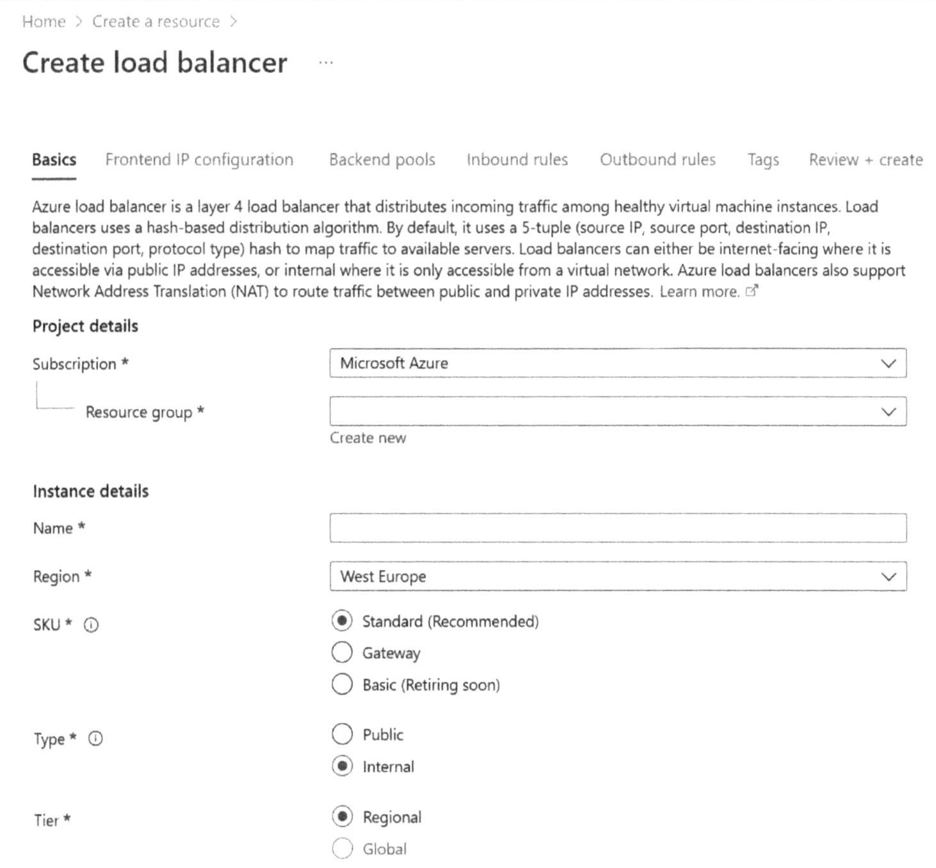

Home > Create a resource >

Create load balancer ...

Basics   Frontend IP configuration   Backend pools   Inbound rules   Outbound rules   Tags   Review + create

Azure load balancer is a layer 4 load balancer that distributes incoming traffic among healthy virtual machine instances. Load balancers uses a hash-based distribution algorithm. By default, it uses a 5-tuple (source IP, source port, destination IP, destination port, protocol type) hash to map traffic to available servers. Load balancers can either be internet-facing where it is accessible via public IP addresses, or internal where it is only accessible from a virtual network. Azure load balancers also support Network Address Translation (NAT) to route traffic between public and private IP addresses. Learn more. ☐

Project details

Subscription *	Microsoft Azure ⌄
Resource group *	⌄
	Create new

Instance details

Name *	
Region *	West Europe ⌄
SKU * ⓘ	⦿ Standard (Recommended)
	○ Gateway
	○ Basic (Retiring soon)
Type * ⓘ	○ Public
	⦿ Internal
Tier *	⦿ Regional
	○ Global

Figure 4.15 – Azure Load Balancer creation page

For applications that need to serve a global audience or require performance-based routing, Azure Traffic Manager, Application Gateway, and Front Door are deployed. Traffic Manager uses DNS-based routing to direct user traffic to the most appropriate Azure region, depending on factors such as latency and availability.

II.   To set up Traffic Manager, navigate to **Create a resource | Networking | Traffic Manager profile**. Add endpoints representing the public IPs of the load balancers in different regions to the Traffic Manager profile. This configuration ensures that users are directed to the nearest or most responsive endpoint, enhancing the overall user experience.

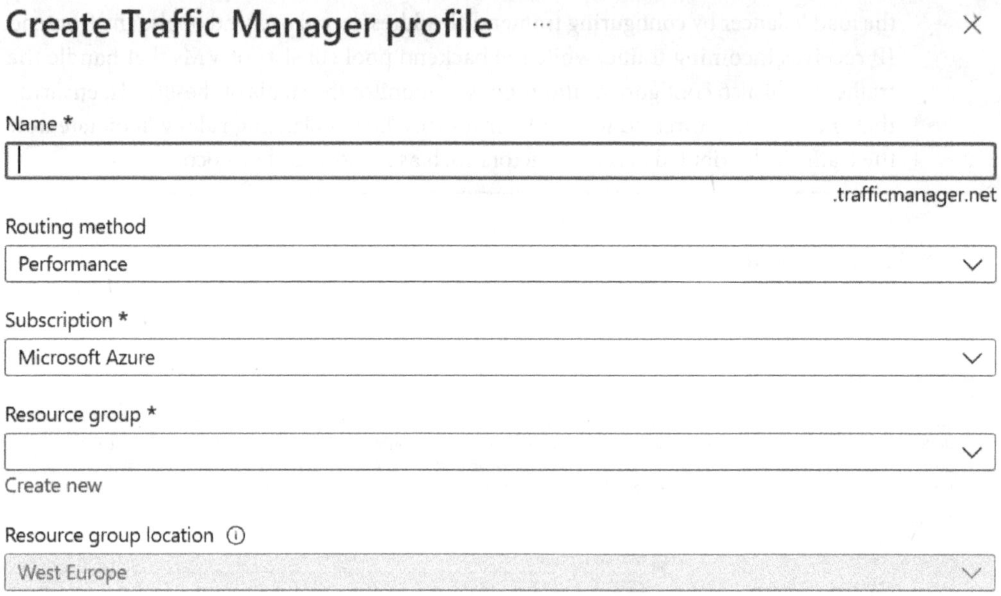

Create Traffic Manager profile ⋯   ✕

Name *

[   ]

.trafficmanager.net

Routing method

[Performance   ⌄]

Subscription *

[Microsoft Azure   ⌄]

Resource group *

[⌄]

Create new

Resource group location ⓘ

[West Europe   ⌄]

Figure 4.16 – Azure Traffic Manager profile creation page

Continuous monitoring and optimization are integral to maintaining optimal network performance. Azure Monitor provides real-time insights into network performance by collecting and analyzing metrics, logs, and diagnostic data. This allows you to proactively manage network resources, identifying and resolving issues before they impact performance. Network Watcher complements Azure Monitor by offering tools for troubleshooting network flows, such as packet capture and connection monitoring, which are essential for diagnosing and optimizing network performance.

Applying best practices in network design

This ensures that the network architecture is secure, scalable, and cost-efficient. Scalability is embedded into the design by leveraging the hub-and-spoke model, which supports easy expansion as new workloads or departments are added to the cloud environment. This model allows for adding new spokes or expanding existing ones without disrupting the overall architecture.

Security best practices are rigorously applied throughout the network. This includes using NSGs, Azure Firewall, encryption, and identity management to protect resources at multiple levels. Regular security audits and compliance checks are conducted to ensure the network remains aligned with industry standards and organizational policies. The network design also emphasizes cost efficiency by optimizing resource usage, minimizing redundancy, and reducing operational costs. This involves selecting the most appropriate Azure services and configurations that balance performance, security, and cost considerations.

Comprehensive documentation of the network design is maintained to support ongoing management and troubleshooting. This documentation includes details on IP address management, security policies, connectivity configurations, and VNet peering setups. Keeping this documentation up to date is crucial for ensuring that the network continues to meet the organization's needs as it evolves.

By following these steps and applying best practices, CloudNet Solutions can successfully transition to a hybrid cloud environment that is secure, scalable, and efficient. This network design not only meets the current needs of the organization but is also flexible enough to adapt to future challenges and opportunities. As the project progresses, continuous monitoring, optimization, and adherence to best practices will ensure that the network infrastructure supports the company's long-term business objectives.

Summary

As we conclude this chapter, you've now gained a comprehensive understanding of how to design and implement a robust Azure network topology. We began by laying the foundation with a well-structured VNet topology, then moved on to implementing essential security measures to protect your resources. We established secure hybrid connectivity to integrate your on-premises infrastructure with Azure and optimized network performance to ensure smooth operations. Finally, we discussed best practices to ensure that your network design is scalable, secure, and cost-efficient.

With these skills and knowledge, you are well equipped to tackle the challenges of creating and managing a complex Azure network environment. In the next chapter, we'll build on this foundation by exploring how to deploy and manage web applications in Azure. You'll learn how to leverage Azure's powerful app services to create scalable, high-performance web apps, further extending your capabilities in cloud infrastructure management. Let's move forward and continue building your Azure expertise.

Get This Book's PDF Version and Exclusive Extras

UNLOCK NOW

Scan the QR code (or go to packtpub.com/unlock). Search for this book by name, confirm the edition, and then follow the steps on the page.

Note: Keep your invoice handly. Purchase made directly from packt don't require one.

5

Implementing a Serverless Solution

What is the first thing that comes to mind when talking about the word *serverless*? Or even a serverless solution? First, let's start with serverless. As cloud computing continues to evolve, serverless technology has emerged as a transformative model that enables developers to build and deploy applications without the burden of managing underlying server infrastructure. Serverless computing abstracts away the complexities of server management, allowing developers to focus solely on writing code and solving business problems. In this chapter, we will explore the concept of serverless technology, understand what constitutes a serverless solution, and learn how to leverage Azure's serverless offerings to implement scalable, event-driven applications.

Specifically, the chapter will cover the following topics:

- Core concepts and benefits of serverless computing
- Creating and deploying serverless functions using Azure Functions
- Implementing event-driven architectures with serverless components
- Exploring integration options for serverless solutions, such as connecting to databases and APIs
- Setting up monitoring and logging for serverless applications to ensure reliability and performance
- Applying best practices for security and scalability in serverless applications

What are serverless technology and serverless solutions?

Serverless technology is a cloud-computing execution model where the cloud provider dynamically manages the allocation and provisioning of servers. Despite its name, serverless computing does not mean there are no servers involved; rather, it signifies that developers do not need to worry about server maintenance, scaling, or infrastructure management. Instead, they can deploy their code in the form of functions, which are executed in response to specific events. This model allows for automatic scaling, high availability, and built-in fault tolerance.

With serverless computing, you pay only for the execution time of your code rather than for pre-allocated server capacity. This pay-as-you-go model makes serverless technology an efficient and cost-effective solution for running applications, especially those with variable or unpredictable traffic patterns.

A **serverless solution** refers to an application architecture that relies on serverless services to perform backend functions, execute code, and handle application logic. These solutions typically use event-driven architectures, where the execution of code is triggered by specific events, such as HTTP requests, database changes, or messages in a queue.

In a serverless solution, various components, such as microservices, functions, and managed services, work together seamlessly to deliver the desired functionality. These components can include serverless functions (e.g., Azure Functions), managed databases (e.g., Azure Cosmos DB), and messaging services (e.g., Azure Service Bus). By integrating these services, developers can build highly scalable and resilient applications without worrying about server provisioning, scaling, or maintenance.

Serverless solutions are ideal for a wide range of use cases, including real-time data processing, web and mobile backends, automation, and integration workflows. They allow organizations to rapidly develop and deploy applications, reducing time to market and lowering operational costs. Next, we will discover the core concepts and benefits of serverless computing solutions.

Understanding the core concepts and benefits of serverless computing

Serverless computing represents a significant shift in how applications are built and deployed in the cloud. By abstracting the infrastructure layer, serverless computing allows developers to focus purely on writing code and implementing business logic without having to manage or maintain the underlying servers. This model has transformed how applications are developed, offering numerous benefits that make it an attractive option for modern cloud-based architectures. In *Figure 5.1*, an example of serverless architecture is illustrated.

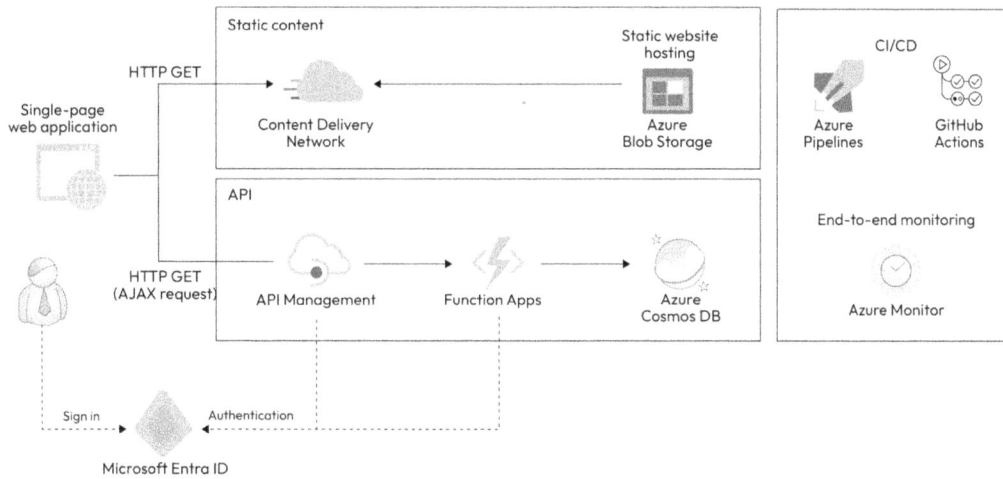

Figure 5.1 – Example of serverless architecture

This architecture is built upon key principles that define the serverless model, which we will explore in the following section.

What is serverless computing?

At its core, **serverless computing** is a cloud execution model where the cloud provider automatically provisions, scales, and manages the infrastructure required to run code in response to specific events. Despite the term *serverless*, physical servers are still involved (as mentioned earlier), but their management is entirely handled by the cloud provider, such as Microsoft Azure, AWS, or Google Cloud. Developers write functions—small, discrete pieces of code—that are triggered by events, such as HTTP requests, changes in a database, or messages in a queue.

Serverless computing typically involves two main types of services:

- **Function as a service** (**FaaS**): This is the core of serverless computing, where developers deploy individual functions that are executed in response to events. Azure Functions is an example of a FaaS offering, allowing you to run event-driven code without explicitly managing the hosting environment.

- **Backend as a service** (**BaaS**): This refers to managed services that provide backend capabilities, such as databases (e.g., Azure Cosmos DB), authentication (e.g., Entra ID B2C), and messaging (e.g., Azure Service Bus), which can be seamlessly integrated into serverless applications. (Here, we call them BaaS to categorize those services into one group.)

Key concepts and features in serverless computing

Some key concepts in serverless computing are as follows:

- **Event-driven execution**: Serverless computing is inherently event-driven. Functions are executed in response to events, which can include HTTP requests, changes in data, or scheduled triggers. This makes serverless ideal for scenarios that require real-time processing, such as IoT data processing, automated workflows, or chatbots.

- **Microservices architecture**: Serverless encourages the use of microservices architecture, where applications are composed of small, loosely coupled functions that perform specific tasks. Each function is independent and can be updated, scaled, or deployed separately, enhancing modularity and flexibility.

- **Automatic scaling**: One of the most compelling features of serverless computing is automatic scaling. The cloud provider automatically scales the number of function instances based on the incoming event rate. For example, if a function is triggered by an HTTP request, the cloud provider can create multiple instances of that function to handle a spike in traffic, ensuring high availability and responsiveness.

- **Pay-as-you-go pricing**: Serverless computing follows a consumption-based pricing model. You pay only for the time your code is running and the resources it consumes, rather than paying for pre-allocated infrastructure. This makes serverless a cost-effective solution, particularly for applications with variable or unpredictable workloads.

- **Stateless functions**: Serverless functions are generally stateless, meaning they do not maintain a persistent state between invocations. Any required state management must be handled through external storage solutions, such as databases or distributed caches. This stateless nature makes functions lightweight and easily scalable.

- **No infrastructure management**: In a serverless model, developers are not concerned with infrastructure management tasks such as server provisioning, maintenance, patching, or scaling. The cloud provider takes care of these aspects, allowing developers to focus on writing code and implementing functionality.

Benefits of serverless computing

Serverless computing offers several benefits, including the following:

- **Cost efficiency**: One of the most significant advantages of serverless computing is cost efficiency. Since you only pay for the compute resources consumed during function execution, there are no costs associated with idle server capacity. This is particularly advantageous for applications with sporadic usage patterns or for start-ups that need to minimize operational costs while scaling.

- **Scalability and high availability**: Serverless platforms automatically scale the number of instances based on demand, ensuring that your application can handle sudden spikes in traffic without manual intervention. This elasticity provides high availability and resilience, as serverless functions can quickly adapt to changing workloads.

- **Faster time to market**: Serverless accelerates the development process by eliminating the need to set up and manage infrastructure. Developers can deploy and iterate on their applications quickly, which reduces the time to market for new features and services. The simplicity of deploying individual functions also allows for rapid experimentation and Agile development practices.

- **Reduced operational overhead**: By outsourcing infrastructure management to the cloud provider, organizations can reduce operational overhead and focus more on application development and innovation. This not only streamlines operations but also reduces the risk of errors related to server configuration, patching, and maintenance.

- **Focus on business logic**: Serverless computing allows developers to concentrate on writing business logic rather than managing servers. This shift in focus can lead to more efficient development cycles and better alignment with business objectives. Developers can implement functionality faster and with fewer distractions related to infrastructure concerns.

- **Global reach**: Serverless platforms provided by major cloud providers, such as Azure Functions, are globally distributed. This means that functions can be deployed closer to end users, reducing latency and improving the overall user experience. This global reach is particularly beneficial for applications serving a distributed user base or for IoT solutions that collect data from various geographic locations.

- **Built-in security and compliance**: Cloud providers handle many aspects of security for serverless applications, including data encryption, patch management, and compliance certifications. This built-in security framework helps ensure that serverless solutions meet industry standards and regulatory requirements.

Understanding the core concepts and benefits of serverless computing is fundamental for leveraging this technology effectively. Serverless computing simplifies development, enhances scalability, and optimizes cost efficiency, making it a powerful choice for modern cloud-based applications. By focusing on writing code and solving business problems rather than managing servers, developers can create innovative solutions that respond dynamically to user demands and business needs.

In the next sections of this chapter, we will explore how to create and deploy serverless functions using Azure Functions, implement event-driven architectures, and integrate serverless components into comprehensive solutions. These practical applications will demonstrate the power of serverless technology and how it can transform the way we build and operate applications in the cloud.

Creating and deploying serverless functions using Azure Functions

Now that we have a solid understanding of the core concepts and benefits of serverless computing, the next step is to delve into the practical aspects of creating and deploying serverless functions using Azure Functions. Azure Functions is Microsoft's event-driven, serverless compute service that enables you to run small pieces of code (functions) without the need for infrastructure management. This section will cover the steps to set up Azure Functions, write your first function, deploy it, and manage it effectively. *Figure 5.2* shows the steps from *Code* to *Events + Data*, which leads to *Azure Functions*.

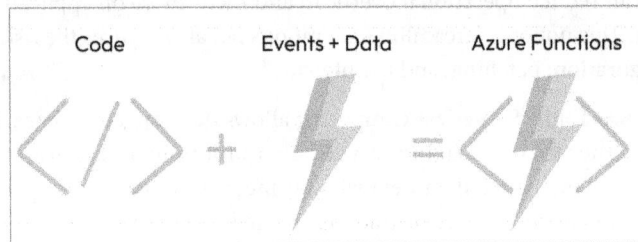

Figure 5.2 – Azure Functions

What is Azure Functions?

Azure Functions is a FaaS platform that provides a way to execute code in response to various events, such as HTTP requests, changes in data, scheduled timers, or messages from other Azure services. It is designed to support a range of use cases, from automating workflows to processing data streams and running backend services for web and mobile applications.

Functions in Azure are designed to be lightweight and modular, typically performing a single task or responding to a specific event. They are stateless by default, meaning that any state required between invocations must be managed externally, such as in a database or a distributed cache. Azure functions can be written in multiple programming languages, including C#, JavaScript, Python, Java, and PowerShell, providing flexibility for developers. *Figure 5.3* shows an architectural example in which you can see a step-by-step guide to how Azure Functions works.

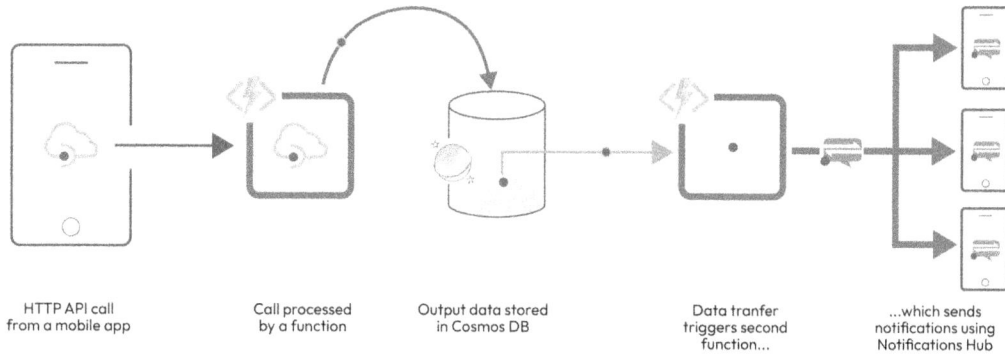

Figure 5.3 – Azure Functions architectural example

Advantages of Azure Functions

Functionality in an **Azure Functions-based architecture** refers to the specific tasks and operations that individual functions perform within the broader application context. Each function represents a single, focused unit of work that contributes to the overall functionality of the application. These functions work together to form a complete system, where each part is responsible for a specific aspect of the workflow.

Azure Functions offers many benefits, including the following:

- **Modularity and reusability**: One of the key benefits of using Azure Functions in application architecture is the modularity it provides. Each function can be developed, tested, and deployed independently, allowing for greater agility in development. This modular approach also makes functions reusable across different parts of the application or even in different applications. For instance, `SendConfirmationEmailFunction` can be reused in both order processing and customer support scenarios.

- **Scalability and resilience**: Functions are inherently scalable. Azure automatically manages the execution environment, scaling the number of function instances based on demand. If there is a sudden spike in order submissions, Azure can scale out `SubmitOrderFunction` to handle multiple requests simultaneously. This auto-scaling ensures that the application remains responsive and available even during peak loads.

- **Decoupling and flexibility**: Using Azure Functions enables a loosely coupled architecture where each function interacts through well-defined events and messaging systems (e.g., Azure Queue or Event Grid). This decoupling allows functions to be developed and deployed independently, making the application more flexible and easier to maintain. It also allows different teams to work on different functions simultaneously without conflicts.

- **Cost-effectiveness**: Azure Functions operates on a pay-as-you-go model. This means that you are only billed for the time your functions are actually executing rather than for idle server time. This cost model makes Azure Functions an economical choice for applications with varying workloads, where certain functions might only run a few times a day or during specific business hours.

- **Integration with Azure services**: Azure Functions seamlessly integrate with other Azure services, such as Azure Cosmos DB for data storage, Azure Logic Apps for workflow automation, and Azure AI Services for AI capabilities. This integration capability allows developers to build rich, data-driven applications that leverage the full power of the Azure ecosystem.

- **Monitoring and diagnostics**: Azure Functions come with built-in monitoring capabilities via Azure Monitor and Application Insights. These tools provide real-time insights into function performance, enabling proactive identification of issues and optimization of function execution. Developers can set up custom metrics, track execution times and error rates, and even create alerts to notify the team of critical events.

- **Custom domain**: The Azure Functions custom domain feature allows you to assign a personalized domain name to your function app instead of using the default Azure-provided URL. This enhances branding and improves user trust by providing a consistent and recognizable web address. The setup involves configuring a custom domain in the Azure portal and updating DNS settings to point to Azure's servers, often secured with SSL/TLS for encrypted connections.

- **Backup**: The Backup feature in Azure Functions provides automated, scheduled backups of your app's content, configurations, and any connected storage. This ensures that in the event of accidental data loss, corruption, or deployment issues, you can quickly restore your function app to a previous state. Backups can be stored in Azure Storage accounts, and users can configure the frequency and retention period to align with business continuity and disaster recovery needs.

When building modern, cloud-native applications, leveraging serverless technologies such as Azure Functions can provide a flexible and scalable architecture. In the next section, we'll explore how to design an application architecture using Azure Functions, focusing on how different functions can interact to form a cohesive and efficient system. This architecture not only simplifies deployment and scaling but also allows developers to focus on the business logic, with minimal concerns about infrastructure.

Application architecture overview

An application architecture designed with Azure Functions typically follows a microservices pattern, where the overall application is broken down into smaller, independent units of functionality. Each function is event-driven and responsible for a specific task and can operate independently of the others.

A common architecture pattern for building applications with Azure Functions involves several key components:

- **Event sources**: These are the triggers that initiate function execution. Events can come from various sources such as HTTP requests (for APIs), messages from Azure Queue Storage, changes in Azure Cosmos DB, or events routed through Azure Event Grid.

- **Azure Functions (event handlers)**: These are the core processing units of the architecture. Each function handles specific tasks, such as processing a user registration, handling a payment transaction, or updating a database record.

- **Data storage**: Functions often need to read from or write to data storage. This can include Azure Blob Storage for storing files, Azure Cosmos DB for NoSQL data, Azure SQL Database for relational data, or Azure Table storage for simple key-value data.

- **Integration services**: Azure Functions can integrate with other Azure services such as Azure Logic Apps for workflow automation, Azure Service Bus for reliable messaging, and Azure API Management for API gateway functionalities.

- **Monitoring and diagnostics**: To ensure the application is running smoothly, Azure Monitor and Application Insights are used to track performance, detect errors, and provide detailed logging and telemetry.

- **Security and authentication**: Azure Functions can integrate with Entra ID for identity and access management. This ensures that only authenticated users or applications can invoke specific functions.

Now that you know what an Azure function is and how it can help you leverage your applications, let's set up an Azure function in the portal for our project.

Setting up Azure Functions

Before you can create and deploy your first function, you need to set up the necessary environment and resources in Azure. This involves creating a function app, which serves as a container for your functions and provides a runtime environment for execution.

To create a function app, follow these steps:

1. Log in to the Azure portal at `https://portal.azure.com/`.

2. Navigate to **Create a resource** | **Web** | **Function App**.

3. Configure the basic settings for your function app:

   - **Hosting Option**: Choose the hosting option on the first page to determine your app scale, resources available per instance, and pricing. *Figure 5.4* shows how to choose from current hosting plans.

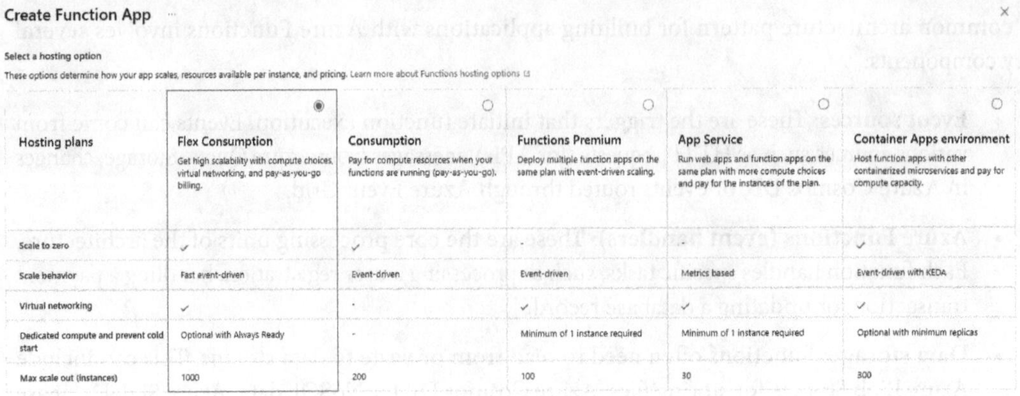

Create Function App

Select a hosting option

These options determine how your app scales, resources available per instance, and pricing. Learn more about Functions hosting options

Hosting plans	Flex Consumption Get high scalability with compute choices, virtual networking, and pay-as-you-go billing.	Consumption Pay for compute resources when your functions are running (pay-as-you-go).	Functions Premium Deploy multiple function apps on the same plan with event-driven scaling.	App Service Run web apps and function apps on the same plan with more compute choices and pay for the instances of the plan.	Container Apps environment Host function apps with other containerized microservices and pay for compute capacity.
Scale to zero	✓	✓	-	-	✓
Scale behavior	Fast event-driven	Event-driven	Event-driven	Metrics based	Event-driven with KEDA
Virtual networking	✓	-	✓	✓	✓
Dedicated compute and prevent cold start	Optional with Always Ready	-	Minimum of 1 instance required	Minimum of 1 instance required	Optional with minimum replicas
Max scale out (instances)	1000	200	100	30	300

Figure 5.4 – Azure function app hosting options

- **Subscription**: Choose the Azure subscription where you want to create the function app.
- **Resource Group**: Create a new resource group or select an existing one, such as `Serverless-Resources`.
- **Function App Name**: Enter a unique name for your function app, such as `MyFirstFunctionApp`.
- **Region**: Select the Azure region closest to your users or business needs for optimal performance.
- **Runtime Stack**: Choose the programming language you want to use, such as .NET Core, Node.js, or Python.
- **Version**: Select the latest version supported for your runtime stack.
- **Operating System**: Choose between **Windows** or **Linux**, depending on your requirements and language support.

4. Once all settings are configured, click **Review + create** and then **Create** to provision the function app. This may take a few minutes.

Next, follow these steps to create your first function:

1. After the function app is created, navigate to it from the Azure portal by selecting the **Go to resource** button.

2. On the function app's page, select **Create function**, as shown in *Figure 5.5*.

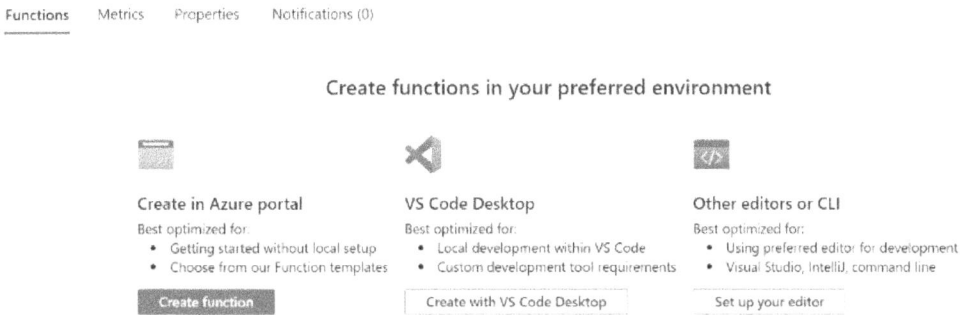

Functions   Metrics   Properties   Notifications (0)

Create functions in your preferred environment

Create in Azure portal   VS Code Desktop   Other editors or CLI
Best optimized for: Best optimized for: Best optimized for:
• Getting started without local setup   • Local development within VS Code   • Using preferred editor for development
• Choose from our Function templates   • Custom development tool requirements   • Visual Studio, IntelliJ, command line

Create function   Create with VS Code Desktop   Set up your editor

Figure 5.5 – Creating a function in a function app

3. Select a template for your function. For example, choose the HTTP trigger template, which creates a function that runs in response to an HTTP request.

4. Configure the function's settings:

   - **Function App Type**: Create new function app

   - **Function Name**: Enter a name for your function, such as `HelloWorldFunction`

   - **Authorization Level**: Choose **Function** to require a key for access, or **Anonymous** or **Admin** for different levels of access

5. Click **Create** to generate the function. Azure will set up the necessary environment and display a code editor where you can write the function code.

   In the following example, the function reads a query string parameter named name and returns a greeting. If no name is provided, it returns a bad request message:

```
// Example HTTP-triggered function in C#
public static class HelloWorldFunction
{
    [FunctionName("HelloWorldFunction")]
    public static async Task<IActionResult> Run(
        [HttpTrigger(AuthorizationLevel.Function, "get", "post",
Route = null)] HttpRequest req,
        ILogger log)
    {
        log.LogInformation("C# HTTP trigger function processed a
request.");
        string name = req.Query["name"];
        return name != null
            ? (ActionResult)new OkObjectResult($"Hello, {name}")
```

```
                : new BadRequestObjectResult("Please pass a name on
the query string.");
      }
    }
}
```

Now, let's see how to test your function:

1. Once the code is written, test your function using the Azure portal. Click on **Test/Run** in the function editor.

2. Enter a value for the name parameter (e.g., name=Azure) and click **Run**. The function will execute, and the output will be displayed below the code editor, showing either a greeting or, if no name was provided, an error message.

There are different deployment methods available for users. Deployment in Azure Functions can be done directly from the Azure portal for simple use cases, but in real-world scenarios, you often use a version control system such as GitHub or Azure DevOps for **continuous integration and continuous deployment (CI/CD)**.

To deploy from a repository, follow these steps:

1. Navigate to your function app's settings, select **Deployment Center**, and choose your source.

2. Authorize and configure the repository, branch, and build settings.

Azure will set up an automated deployment process that triggers whenever new code is pushed to the specified branch.

Managing and scaling Azure Functions

Azure Functions provides built-in tools for managing and scaling your serverless functions automatically. The Consumption plan automatically scales the number of function instances based on the rate of incoming events, ensuring that your application can handle traffic spikes and high workloads.

Here are the key features that enhance the management and scalability of your serverless architecture:

- **Auto-scaling**: With the Consumption plan, Azure Functions can automatically scale out to meet demand by adding more instances as needed. This scaling is seamless and managed entirely by Azure, meaning you do not need to configure or provision additional servers.

- **Premium and dedicated plans**: For scenarios that require additional scaling, always-on capabilities, or isolated environments, you can use Premium or Dedicated (App Service) plans. These plans provide more control over scaling, VNet integration, and advanced performance options.

- **Monitoring and logging**: Azure Functions integrates with Azure Monitor and Application Insights, providing comprehensive monitoring and logging capabilities. You can track metrics such as function execution times, error rates, and resource consumption. Setting up alerts based on these metrics allows you to be proactive in managing performance and identifying potential issues.

- **Security**: Secure access to Azure Functions using API keys, Entra ID authentication, or managed identities. These security measures help ensure that only authorized users and applications can execute your functions.

Creating and deploying serverless functions using Azure Functions provides a powerful way to build scalable, event-driven applications without the burden of infrastructure management. By following the steps outlined previously, you can set up a function app, write your first function, test and deploy it, and manage its performance and security. This approach allows developers to focus on building functionality and delivering business value, making Azure Functions an essential tool in the serverless computing toolkit.

In the next section, we will explore how to implement event-driven architectures using Azure Functions and other serverless components, further expanding our ability to create responsive and scalable applications in the cloud. This will include integrating with Azure's messaging services, databases, and other tools to build comprehensive serverless solutions.

Implementing event-driven architectures with serverless components

Now that we have covered the creation and deployment of Azure Functions, the next step is to explore how these functions can be used as part of a broader event-driven architecture. Event-driven architectures are a natural fit for serverless computing because they allow applications to react to events in real time, providing a scalable and efficient way to process and respond to various triggers. This section will detail how to implement event-driven architectures using Azure Functions and other serverless components.

What is an event-driven architecture?

An **event-driven architecture** (**EDA**) is a software architecture pattern that revolves around the production, detection, and reaction to events. In this model, the system components interact with each other through events rather than through direct calls. An event is a change in state or an update, such as a new user sign-up, an item added to a shopping cart, or a file uploaded to cloud storage. These events trigger specific actions or workflows defined in the system. The following figure shows an example of an EDA.

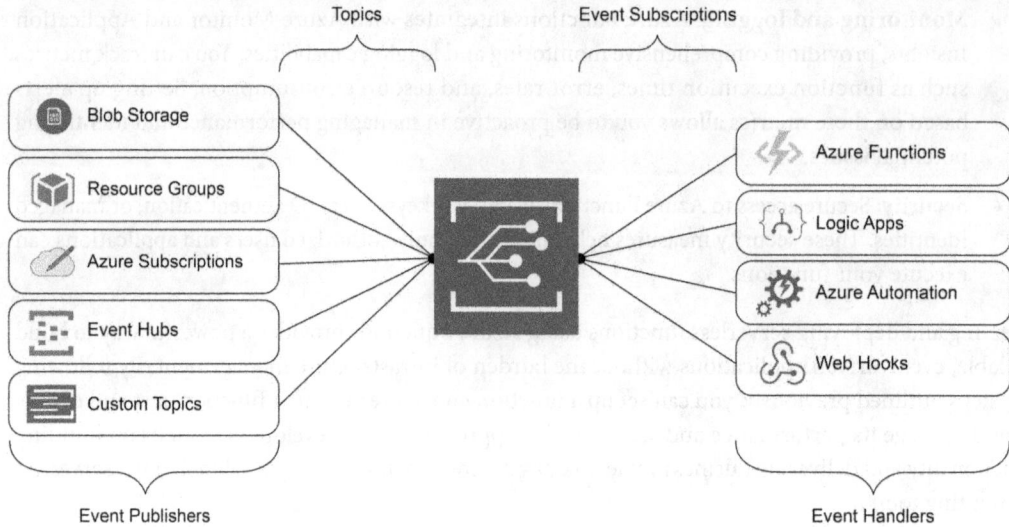

Figure 5.6 – EDA example

In an EDA, there are typically three main components:

- **Event producers**: These are the sources that generate events. Examples include HTTP requests, changes in a database, file uploads, or messages from IoT devices.

- **Event consumers**: These are the services or functions that react to the events. Azure functions often serve as event consumers, executing code in response to the events.

- **Event routers**: These manage the flow of events from producers to consumers, ensuring that the events are delivered and processed correctly. Azure Event Grid, Azure Service Bus, and Azure Logic Apps are common event routers in Azure.

The decoupling of event producers and consumers enables scalability, flexibility, and improved system responsiveness. Each component can be updated or scaled independently, leading to more maintainable and adaptable systems.

Types of Azure triggers

Azure Functions can act as the backbone of an EDA, handling various types of events and performing tasks based on those events. Azure provides built-in triggers that make it easy to set up and respond to events, integrating seamlessly with other Azure services. The details of these triggers are as follows:

- **HTTP trigger**: This is one of the most common triggers used with Azure Functions. It allows a function to respond to HTTP requests, making it suitable for building APIs, webhooks, or microservices that need to handle web requests directly. When an HTTP request is made to the function's endpoint, Azure Functions executes the associated code.

Example use case: A user submits a form on a website, which sends an HTTP request to an Azure function. The function processes the form data and stores it in a database or sends a confirmation email.

- **Timer trigger**: Timer triggers are used to execute functions on a predefined schedule, similar to cron jobs in Unix/Linux systems. This is useful for periodic tasks such as data cleanup, report generation, or regular system health checks.

Example use case: A function runs every night at midnight to aggregate daily sales data from different sources and store it in a reporting database.

- **Azure Blob Storage trigger**: This trigger executes a function whenever a new file is uploaded to or modified in an Azure Blob Storage container. This is useful for scenarios involving file processing, such as image resizing, video encoding, or data transformation.

Example use case: An e-commerce site uploads product images to Azure Blob Storage. An Azure function automatically resizes these images for various device formats when they are uploaded.

- **Azure Queue Storage trigger**: Queue Storage triggers allow a function to process messages from Azure Queue Storage. This is often used for decoupling tasks and ensuring that messages are processed asynchronously.

Example use case: Orders placed on an online store are added to a queue. An Azure function reads messages from the queue and processes each order sequentially, ensuring that the order is logged, inventory is updated, and a confirmation email is sent to the customer.

- **Azure Event Grid trigger**: Event Grid is a fully managed event routing service that enables event-driven programming across various Azure services. Functions subscribed to Event Grid can handle events from multiple sources, such as resource creation, database updates, or custom applications.

Example use case: A function is triggered whenever a new user is added to Entra ID. The function can then create a user profile, send a welcome email, or assign default permissions.

- **Azure Service Bus trigger**: Service Bus triggers allow Azure Functions to process messages from Azure Service Bus queues or topics. Service Bus is a robust messaging platform suitable for high-scale and high-reliability messaging scenarios.

Example use case: A function subscribes to a topic that distributes customer support tickets across multiple teams. When a new ticket is published, the function assigns it to the appropriate support team based on the ticket's content.

Designing an event-driven workflow

To build a robust EDA using Azure Functions, you need to design workflows that define how events are handled. Here's how you can implement a basic workflow:

1. **Define the events**: Identify the key events that your application needs to respond to. These could include HTTP requests, file uploads, database changes, or system notifications.

2. **Choose the triggers**: Based on the events, select the appropriate Azure Functions triggers. For example, if your application needs to process uploaded files, use the Blob Storage trigger. If you need to handle user requests, use the HTTP trigger.

3. **Develop the functions**: Write the Azure functions that perform the desired tasks when an event occurs. Ensure that each function is small, focused, and performs a specific action. This modular approach makes it easier to update, test, and maintain the functions.

4. **Set up event routing**: Use services such as Azure Event Grid, Azure Service Bus, or Azure Logic Apps to route events from producers to consumers. Configure the routing rules to ensure that events are delivered to the correct functions based on predefined conditions.

5. **Monitor and log events**: Implement monitoring and logging using Azure Monitor and Application Insights. These tools provide visibility into function execution, performance metrics, and error handling, helping you troubleshoot issues and optimize performance.

Example scenario – implementing an EDA for order processing

Consider an online retail company that needs to process customer orders efficiently. The company has decided to use an EDA with Azure Functions to handle different tasks related to order processing, listed as follows:

1. **Order submission**: Customers place orders through the website, which sends an HTTP request to an Azure function (`ProcessOrderFunction`). This function validates the order details and writes a message to an Azure queue (`order-queue`).

2. **Order processing**: A second Azure function (`HandleOrderFunction`) is triggered by new messages in the order queue. This function reads the message, processes the order (e.g., checks inventory and calculates shipping), and writes the order details to a database.

3. **Notification and shipping**: When the order is processed, an event is published to Azure Event Grid. This event triggers multiple functions:

    - `SendConfirmationEmailFunction`: This sends a confirmation email to the customer
    - `UpdateInventoryFunction`: This updates the inventory database to reflect the sold items
    - `PrepareShipmentFunction`: This initiates the shipment process by sending details to the shipping department

4. **Monitoring and alerting**: Azure Monitor tracks the performance of all functions. Alerts are configured to notify the operations team if any function fails or if processing times exceed acceptable thresholds.

In the next section, we will explore integration options for serverless solutions, such as connecting Azure Functions to databases, APIs, and other services. This will provide a complete picture of how to create end-to-end serverless applications that meet diverse business needs.

Exploring integration options for serverless solutions

In the realm of serverless computing, integration is a key factor that enhances the capability of serverless functions. Azure Functions, as a part of an application's architecture, often needs to interact with various data sources, external APIs, and other cloud services to perform comprehensive operations. This section will explore different integration options for Azure Functions, detailing how these functions can connect to databases, APIs, and other Azure services to build complete serverless solutions.

Integration is essential in serverless architecture because serverless functions typically handle specific, granular tasks. To build full-featured applications, these functions need to collaborate with other services to retrieve data, process information, trigger workflows, or interact with third-party systems. By integrating with databases, APIs, and other cloud services, Azure Functions can handle complex scenarios such as data processing, authentication, notification, and communication across various platforms.

Azure provides multiple ways to integrate functions with other services, offering pre-built connectors, SDKs, bindings, and triggers that facilitate seamless integration.

Integrating with databases

The following are some ways of integrating Azure Functions with databases:

- **Azure Cosmos DB integration**: Azure Cosmos DB is a multi-model database service with global distribution capabilities. It is widely used with Azure Functions due to its scalability, low latency, and ability to handle JSON documents natively.

  Here are some key features and benefits of integrating Azure Cosmos DB with Azure Functions:

  - **Binding**: Azure Functions can directly bind to Cosmos DB, allowing it to read from and write to the database with minimal configuration. By using the Cosmos DB input binding, a function can automatically retrieve data from a specified database and collection based on a query. Similarly, the output binding allows a function to save data to Cosmos DB.

- **Trigger**: Azure Functions can be triggered by changes in Cosmos DB. For example, when a new document is added to a collection, a function can be triggered to perform additional processing, such as sending a notification or updating a cache.

In the following example, `ProcessOrderFunction` is triggered whenever a new document is added to the `Orders` collection in `EcommerceDB`:

```
[FunctionName("ProcessOrderFunction")]
public static void Run(
    [CosmosDBTrigger(
        databaseName: "EcommerceDB",
        collectionName: "Orders",
        ConnectionStringSetting = "CosmosDBConnectionString",
        LeaseCollectionName = "leases")] IReadOnlyList<Document>
documents,
    ILogger log)
{

    foreach (var doc in documents)
    {
        log.LogInformation($"New order received: {doc}");
        // Perform order processing logic here
    }
}
```

- **Azure SQL Database integration**: Azure Functions can connect to Azure SQL Database to perform CRUD operations. This is typically done using the SQL bindings, ADO.NET, Entity Framework, or any other standard database access libraries supported by the function's runtime environment.

Here are some key features and benefits:

- **Binding example**: You can use SQL binding to connect to Azure SQL Database and perform operations such as reading data from tables or inserting records.

- **Direct access**: Functions can also directly execute SQL commands using ADO.NET. This method provides more control over SQL execution but requires managing connections and handling exceptions manually.

In the following example, the `GetCustomerData` function queries the `Customers` table in Azure SQL Database using an HTTP trigger:

```
[FunctionName("GetCustomerData")]
public static async Task<IActionResult> Run(
    [HttpTrigger(AuthorizationLevel.Function, "get", Route =
"customer/{id}")] HttpRequest req,
    int id, ILogger log)
```

```
{
    string connectionString = Environment.
GetEnvironmentVariable("SqlConnectionString");
    using (SqlConnection conn = new
SqlConnection(connectionString))
    {
        conn.Open();
        var query = "SELECT * FROM Customers WHERE CustomerID =
@id";
        using (SqlCommand cmd = new SqlCommand(query, conn))
        {
            cmd.Parameters.AddWithValue("@id", id);
            var reader = await cmd.ExecuteReaderAsync();
            // Process the result and return response
        }
    }
}
```

These examples illustrate how Azure Functions can be used to integrate with databases, enabling seamless data processing and retrieval. Next, we explore how serverless solutions can interact with external APIs.

Integrating with external APIs

The methods to integrate serverless solutions with external APIs are as follows:

- **Calling external APIs**: Azure Functions can make HTTP requests to external APIs to consume data or interact with third-party services. This capability is useful for scenarios such as fetching data from a weather service, sending SMS messages via a third-party provider, or integrating with payment gateways.

  An example is the HTTP client. Use the `HttpClient` class to send HTTP requests from within an Azure function. This approach allows functions to call RESTful APIs, handle responses, and manage exceptions.

  In the following example, the `FetchWeatherData` function calls a weather API to get current weather conditions for a specified city:

```
[FunctionName("FetchWeatherData")]
public static async Task<IActionResult> Run(
    [HttpTrigger(AuthorizationLevel.Function, "get", Route =
"weather/{city}")] HttpRequest req,
    string city, ILogger log)
{
    string apiKey = Environment.
GetEnvironmentVariable("WeatherApiKey");
```

```
    string apiUrl = $"https://api.weather.com/v3/weather/
conditions?city={city}&apikey={apiKey}";
    using (HttpClient client = new HttpClient())
    {
        var response = await client.GetAsync(apiUrl);
        string responseBody = await response.Content.
ReadAsStringAsync();
        // Process the weather data and return the result
    }
}
```

- **Using managed identity for secure API calls**: Azure Functions can use a managed identity to securely access resources, eliminating the need to manage credentials explicitly. This approach is particularly useful when functions need to authenticate with Azure services or external APIs that support Entra AD authentication.

Integrating with other Azure services

The following are some options for integrating serverless solutions with other Azure services:

- **Azure Service Bus integration**: Azure Service Bus is a messaging service that facilitates reliable communication between different components of a cloud application. Azure Functions can use Service Bus triggers to respond to messages in queues or topics.

  A function configured with a Service Bus trigger will automatically execute when a new message is available in a specified queue or topic.

  In the following example, the ProcessQueueMessage function is triggered when a new message is added to the order queue:

```
[FunctionName("ProcessQueueMessage")]
public static void Run(
    [ServiceBusTrigger("order-queue", Connection =
"ServiceBusConnectionString")] string message,
    ILogger log)
{
    log.LogInformation($"Processing order message: {message}");
    // Add business logic to process the message
}
```

- **Azure Logic Apps integration**: Logic Apps provides a way to design workflows that automate business processes and integrate with various services. Azure Functions can be called from Logic Apps, enabling more complex workflows and orchestration scenarios.

A logic app can call an Azure function using the HTTP connector, passing data to the function and handling the response to continue the workflow.

Example use case: A Logic Apps workflow detects a new file in Azure Blob Storage, calls an Azure function to process the file contents, and then sends a notification email with the results.

Monitoring and managing integration

Azure Monitor and **Application Insights** play a critical role in managing integrated serverless solutions. These tools allow you to track metrics, set up alerts, and analyze telemetry data to ensure that all integrated components are functioning correctly.

Here are some key features and benefits:

- **Custom metrics**: Define custom metrics to monitor specific aspects of function execution, such as the number of messages processed or the number of successful API calls.

- **Distributed tracing**: Use distributed tracing to track the flow of a request through multiple functions and services. This helps in diagnosing issues and optimizing performance in complex workflows.

- **Error handling and retry policies**: Implement error handling and retry policies within functions to gracefully handle failures and ensure reliability. For example, if an API call fails due to a network issue, the function can retry the call after a short delay.

In the next section, we will explore how to set up monitoring and logging for serverless applications to ensure reliability and performance. This will include configuring Azure Monitor and Application Insights and setting up alerts to proactively manage serverless solutions.

Setting up monitoring and logging for serverless applications to ensure reliability and performance

Effective monitoring and logging are critical components of managing serverless applications, especially when using Azure Functions. Since serverless applications automatically scale and respond to various events, it's important to have a robust monitoring strategy to track performance, detect issues, and ensure smooth operation. This section will cover the essential tools and practices for monitoring Azure Functions, ensuring it performs reliably and meets business requirements.

Importance of monitoring and logging

Monitoring and logging in serverless applications provide visibility into the function's execution, performance metrics, and errors. By tracking these elements, you can quickly identify and resolve issues, optimize performance, and ensure that the application meets the expected service levels. Key benefits include the following:

- **Proactive issue detection**: Monitoring allows you to detect anomalies and failures in real time, enabling quick resolution before they impact users

- **Performance optimization**: Analyzing metrics such as execution time, memory usage, and request rates helps optimize function performance and resource usage

- **Security compliance**: Logging access attempts and function execution details can help ensure compliance with security standards and detect unauthorized access

Azure tools for monitoring and logging

Azure provides the following built-in tools to monitor and log Azure Functions effectively:

- **Azure Monitor**: Azure Monitor is a robust platform for gathering, analyzing, and responding to telemetry data from cloud resources. For Azure Functions, it provides metrics on execution count, success and failure rates, average response time, and memory usage.

  To set up monitoring, in the Azure portal, navigate to your function app and select **Metrics** under the **Monitoring** section. Here, you can view built-in metrics and create custom dashboards to monitor specific aspects of your functions.

  You can set up alerts based on metric thresholds. For example, if the error rate exceeds a certain percentage, Azure Monitor can send an alert via email or SMS, prompting immediate investigation.

- **Application Insights**: Application Insights is a flexible **application performance management (APM)** service designed for developers and DevOps teams. It provides detailed monitoring and diagnostics data for Azure Functions, including dependency tracking, custom telemetry, and distributed tracing.

  To enable Application Insights, navigate to your function app in the Azure portal and click on **Application Insights** under the **Settings** menu. Enable it and link to an existing Application Insights resource or create a new one.

  Application Insights provides powerful search capabilities to filter logs, view traces, and analyze telemetry. You can use the Application Insights portal to create custom queries, track performance trends, and view real-time data.

  Application Insights supports *distributed tracing*, allowing you to trace the flow of requests across multiple functions and services. This is particularly useful in complex, multi-function workflows, where it's essential to understand how data flows between components.

- **Log Analytics**: Azure Log Analytics allows you to collect and query logs from Azure Functions. It integrates with Azure Monitor to provide a unified view of your logs and metrics.

  Log Analytics supports querying logs using **Kusto Query Language** (**KQL**), which helps you analyze logs for troubleshooting, performance optimization, and insights.

  You can create custom dashboards in the Azure portal that display metrics and logs from multiple function apps, providing a comprehensive overview of your serverless environment.

Best practices for monitoring and logging

The following are some best practices to keep in mind for monitoring and logging:

- **Define key metrics**: Identify and track **key performance indicators** (**KPIs**) relevant to your application, such as request count, execution time, failure rate, and memory usage. Monitoring these metrics helps ensure that your functions are running efficiently.

- **Implement custom telemetry**: Use Application Insights to log custom events and traces, providing more context about function execution and business logic. This is useful for monitoring specific actions within your function, such as user interactions or API calls.

- **Set up alerts and automated responses**: Configure alerts for critical metrics to detect issues early. Use automated responses, such as scaling operations or sending notifications, to handle incidents proactively.

- **Regularly review logs**: Establish a routine to review logs and analyze trends. This helps identify performance bottlenecks, security incidents, and opportunities for optimization.

- **Optimize function performance**: Use insights from monitoring to optimize function performance. This may include adjusting code, optimizing data access patterns, or configuring scaling settings to handle varying loads efficiently.

- **Ensure security and compliance**: Log access attempts and function execution details to meet security and compliance requirements. Review security logs regularly to detect unauthorized access attempts.

Setting up effective monitoring and logging is crucial for maintaining the reliability and performance of serverless applications. By leveraging Azure Monitor, Application Insights, and Log Analytics, you can gain visibility into function execution, track performance metrics, detect issues, and optimize your serverless environment.

In the next section, we will discuss best practices for security and scalability in serverless applications. These best practices will help you design and implement secure, scalable serverless solutions that are resilient and cost-effective.

Best practices for security and scalability in serverless applications

In the serverless model, while the cloud provider manages infrastructure, it is still crucial to implement certain best practices to ensure the security and scalability of your applications. Azure Functions offers built-in features and settings to help secure and efficiently scale serverless solutions. In this section, we'll summarize the key strategies and best practices to achieve a secure and scalable serverless architecture.

Some of the best practices in the realm of *security* are as follows:

- **Use managed identities**: Azure Functions can use managed identities to securely access Azure resources such as Key Vault, SQL Database, or Storage accounts without managing credentials. This eliminates the need to hardcode secrets or connection strings in your functions, reducing the risk of data exposure.

- **Secure access with API keys and authentication**: Protect your functions with API keys, OAuth tokens, or Entra ID authentication. This ensures that only authorized users and applications can invoke sensitive functions. For public-facing APIs, consider using Azure API Management to enforce security policies and manage access.

- **Encrypt sensitive data**: Always use HTTPS for communication to protect data in transit. Store sensitive information such as API keys, connection strings, and certificates securely in Azure Key Vault. Functions can access these secrets at runtime without exposing them in the code.

- **Implement role-based access control (RBAC)**: Use Azure RBAC to restrict access to Function Apps and resources. Assign the minimum necessary permissions to users and applications to follow the principle of least privilege.

- **Monitor and audit function activity**: Use Azure Monitor and Application Insights to track access attempts, function execution details, and potential security incidents. Set up alerts for suspicious activities, such as repeated failed authentication attempts or unexpected high usage.

- **Regularly update and patch**: Although Azure manages infrastructure updates, ensure that any dependencies, libraries, or frameworks used within your functions are up to date. Regularly review and update code to protect against vulnerabilities.

- **Private endpoints**: From a network security perspective, it's recommended to have private endpoints configured for better network security and to make sure the traffic stays private in the backend.

Some of the best practices in the realm of *scalability* are as follows:

- **Leverage automatic scaling**: Azure Functions on the Consumption plan automatically scales based on the number of incoming events. Configure function timeouts and limits to handle long-running operations effectively and ensure that your functions are designed to run efficiently.

- **Use stateless functions**: Keep functions stateless to ensure scalability and reliability. Any required state should be managed externally using Azure services such as Cosmos DB, Redis Cache, or Azure Blob Storage. This allows functions to scale independently without relying on a shared state.

- **Optimize function performance**: Optimize the code within your functions to minimize execution time and resource consumption. This includes reducing dependencies, avoiding unnecessary computations, and using efficient data processing techniques. Shorter execution times lead to faster response rates and lower costs.

- **Implement asynchronous processing**: Use asynchronous programming models and messaging services such as Azure Service Bus, Event Grid, or Queue Storage to handle tasks that can be processed asynchronously. This reduces the load on functions and improves overall system performance.

- **Monitor and adjust scaling policies**: Regularly monitor function performance and adjust scaling settings as needed. Use Azure Monitor to track metrics such as execution count, average response time, and memory usage to understand how functions behave under different loads.

- **Test for scalability**: Perform load testing to ensure that your functions can handle expected traffic volumes. Identify bottlenecks and optimize the architecture to support growth, ensuring that the application remains responsive and reliable during peak loads.

By implementing these security and scalability best practices, you can design serverless applications that are both secure and efficient. Leveraging Azure's built-in features, such as managed identities, automatic scaling, and monitoring tools, helps maintain a robust and resilient serverless environment. These practices are essential for protecting sensitive data, ensuring high availability, and optimizing resource usage, ultimately leading to a better user experience and more efficient operations.

Summary

In this chapter, we explored the power of serverless computing with Azure Functions, learning how to create, deploy, and manage scalable, event-driven applications without the need to handle infrastructure. We covered various triggers, integrations with Azure services such as Cosmos DB and Service Bus, and connecting to external APIs. Key topics included setting up monitoring and logging using Azure Monitor and Application Insights and implementing best practices for security and scalability.

In the next chapter, we will dive into building and managing scalable data solutions, focusing on using Azure's data services to handle large-scale storage, processing, and analytics. We'll cover tools such as Azure SQL Database, Cosmos DB, and Data Lake, and discuss optimizing performance, ensuring security, and managing data effectively.

Get This Book's PDF Version and Exclusive Extras

UNLOCK NOW

Scan the QR code (or go to packtpub.com/unlock). Search for this book by name, confirm the edition, and then follow the steps on the page.

Note: Keep your invoice handly. Purchase made directly from packt don't require one.

6

Principles and Practices of Scalable Data Management

So far, we've learned about Entra ID, networking, serverless, and storage in Azure; however, as data becomes a vital asset for modern organizations, building and managing scalable data solutions is essential to ensure that data-driven applications perform efficiently and can handle growth in both volume and complexity. Azure offers a wide range of services tailored for scalable data storage, processing, and analytics, making it a powerful platform for building data solutions that meet both current and future business needs.

In this chapter, we will dive into the strategies and best practices for designing scalable data solutions on Azure. You'll learn how to leverage Azure's data services such as Azure SQL Database, Azure Cosmos DB, and Azure Data Lake, along with best practices for performance optimization, data security, and cost management. We'll also explore how to integrate and manage these data solutions across large-scale applications to ensure reliability and performance at every stage.

By the end of this chapter, you'll be able to confidently design and implement data solutions that can grow with your organization's needs while maintaining robust performance and security.

Here's what we are going to cover in this chapter:

- Understand the key components of scalable data solutions on Azure

- Design and implement scalable databases using Azure SQL Database and Cosmos DB

- Learn how to build scalable data lakes and warehouses with Azure Data Lake

- Integrate data processing and analytics services to support real-time and batch workloads

- Apply best practices for performance optimization and cost management in data solutions

- Ensure security and compliance for large-scale data solutions

Let's get started in the beautiful world of data with Microsoft Azure.

Why build scalable data solutions on Azure?

Building scalable data solutions on Azure offers numerous advantages, from handling growing volumes of data to ensuring performance and reliability across a wide variety of workloads. Azure provides a comprehensive set of tools and services designed to store, manage, process, and analyze large-scale data efficiently. Let's dive deeper into why Azure is the ideal platform for scalable data solutions and explore some practical examples:

- **Scalability on demand**: One of the most significant benefits of Azure is its ability to scale resources dynamically based on demand. Whether you're dealing with a sudden spike in web traffic, growing amounts of IoT sensor data, or an expanding customer base, Azure can handle the increasing workloads without compromising performance.

  For example, an e-commerce business running on Azure SQL Database can automatically scale up during high-traffic periods, such as Black Friday sales. This ensures that the website remains responsive and transactions can be processed quickly, even under heavy load. Similarly, a company using Azure Cosmos DB for global customer data management can benefit from Cosmos DB's auto-scaling capabilities, ensuring fast access to data for users around the world.

- **Seamless integration with big data and analytics tools**: Azure offers seamless integration with big data processing and analytics tools, enabling businesses to derive insights from their data in real-time or batch mode. Azure Data Lake and Azure Synapse Analytics allow organizations to store and process vast amounts of structured and unstructured data, making it easier to perform data analysis, machine learning, and business intelligence tasks at scale.

  For example, a financial services company can use Azure Data Lake to store large datasets related to customer transactions and market trends. By integrating this data with Azure Synapse Analytics, they can run complex queries and analytics to detect fraud patterns, optimize investment strategies, or forecast market trends.

- **Cost-effective storage and management**: Azure provides a variety of storage options that allow businesses to store data cost-effectively based on how frequently the data is accessed. Azure Storage offers hot, cool, and archive tiers, ensuring that you only pay for what you need. Hot tiers are ideal for frequently accessed data, while cool and archive tiers are used for infrequently accessed data, significantly lowering costs.

  For example, a healthcare provider might use the Azure archive storage tier to store old medical records that must be retained for legal reasons but are infrequently accessed. Newer records that are accessed more frequently can be stored in the hot or cool tiers, reducing overall storage costs.

- **Global reach and reliability**: Azure's global network of data centers allows organizations to deploy data solutions close to their users, improving performance and reducing latency. Azure's global presence is especially beneficial for businesses with users or customers spread across different geographical regions. With services such as Azure Cosmos DB and Azure **Content Delivery Network** (**CDN**), businesses can ensure fast access to data no matter where their customers are located.

For example, a global news organization can use Azure Cosmos DB to store and distribute real-time news updates to users worldwide. By replicating the data across multiple regions, they can ensure that users receive the latest updates with minimal latency, regardless of where they are located.

- **Enhanced security and compliance**: Azure offers built-in security features that ensure your data is protected at all times. Data encryption (both at rest and in transit), **role-based access control (RBAC)**, advanced threat protection, and integration with Entra ID ensure that your data solutions meet strict security and compliance requirements.

   For example, a healthcare organization must adhere to regulations such as HIPAA that require strict data security and privacy measures. Azure provides encryption and compliance management tools that help ensure that the healthcare provider's patient data is stored securely and meets regulatory requirements.

- **Flexibility to handle multiple data models**: Azure offers multiple services that cater to different data models, allowing businesses to choose the right database for the right workload. For instance, Azure SQL Database is designed for structured relational data, while Azure Cosmos DB can handle unstructured or semi-structured data across multiple models such as document, graph, key-value, and column family. This flexibility ensures that businesses can manage different types of data using the most appropriate services, improving efficiency and performance.

   For example, a logistics company may use Azure SQL Database to manage structured shipping data while using Azure Cosmos DB to handle unstructured GPS tracking data from delivery vehicles.

Building scalable data solutions on Azure offers significant benefits, from managing increasing data volumes to ensuring optimal performance and reliability for diverse workloads. In this section, we have explored how Azure's robust suite of tools and services facilitates efficient data storage, management, processing, and analysis at scale.

Designing scalable databases using Azure SQL Database and Cosmos DB

When it comes to building a scalable database solution, choosing the right platform for your data model and access patterns is crucial. Azure provides two key services—**Azure SQL Database** for structured, relational data and **Azure Cosmos DB** for globally distributed, NoSQL data models. Each service is designed to handle different types of workloads, and both offer powerful scalability options to ensure that your database can grow as your application and data needs to expand.

Features of Azure SQL Database

Azure SQL Database is a fully managed, relational **database as a service (DBaaS)** built on Microsoft SQL Server technologies. It offers features like automated backups, scaling, high availability, and integrated security. Azure SQL Database is ideal for applications that need structured, relational data storage, such as financial systems, e-commerce platforms, CRM systems, and **enterprise resource planning (ERP)** applications.

The following are some key features of Azure SQL Database:

- **Automatic scaling and elastic pools**: Azure SQL Database provides the flexibility to scale up or down based on your workload. You can increase the computing resources for your database as your application demands grow. If you manage multiple databases with varying workloads, **elastic pools** allow you to share resources across those databases, helping you manage costs effectively while ensuring that each database gets the resources it needs.

    An e-commerce platform can benefit from elastic pools during seasonal sales peaks. When traffic spikes during Black Friday, the platform can use elastic pools to allocate more resources to handle the higher transaction volume without affecting other databases in the system.

- **High availability and disaster recovery**: Azure SQL Database comes with built-in **high availability (HA)** features such as geo-replication and automated backups. It offers the option to replicate data across different geographic regions, ensuring that your data is protected in the event of a disaster or outage.

    A financial services company can ensure that their transactional data is replicated across regions, providing uninterrupted services to their users, even during regional outages.

- **Intelligent performance features**: Azure SQL Database includes features such as **automatic index tuning** and **Query Performance Insight**, which help optimize the performance of your queries without manual intervention. This ensures that as your database grows, your application performance remains optimized.

- **Security and compliance**: Azure SQL Database provides advanced data security features, including **encryption at rest and in transit**, **Always Encrypted**, and **row-level security**. These features help protect sensitive data and ensure compliance with industry regulations such as GDPR, HIPAA, and PCI DSS.

Here is a link to the full features if you'd like to know more – `https://learn.microsoft.com/en-us/azure/azure-sql/database/features-comparison?view=azuresql`.

A healthcare application storing patient information can use Always Encrypted to protect sensitive medical records, ensuring that only authorized applications can access the data.

Setting up Azure SQL Database

Here's how Azure SQL Database can be set up:

1. First, we'll create a SQL database. To do so, in the Azure portal, navigate to **Create a resource | Databases | SQL Database**.
2. Configure the **Subscription**, **Resource group**, **Database name**, and **Server** settings.
3. Select the appropriate pricing tier (**Basic**, **Standard**, or **Premium**) based on your performance and storage needs.

    Figure 6.1 shows the **Create SQL Database** screen.

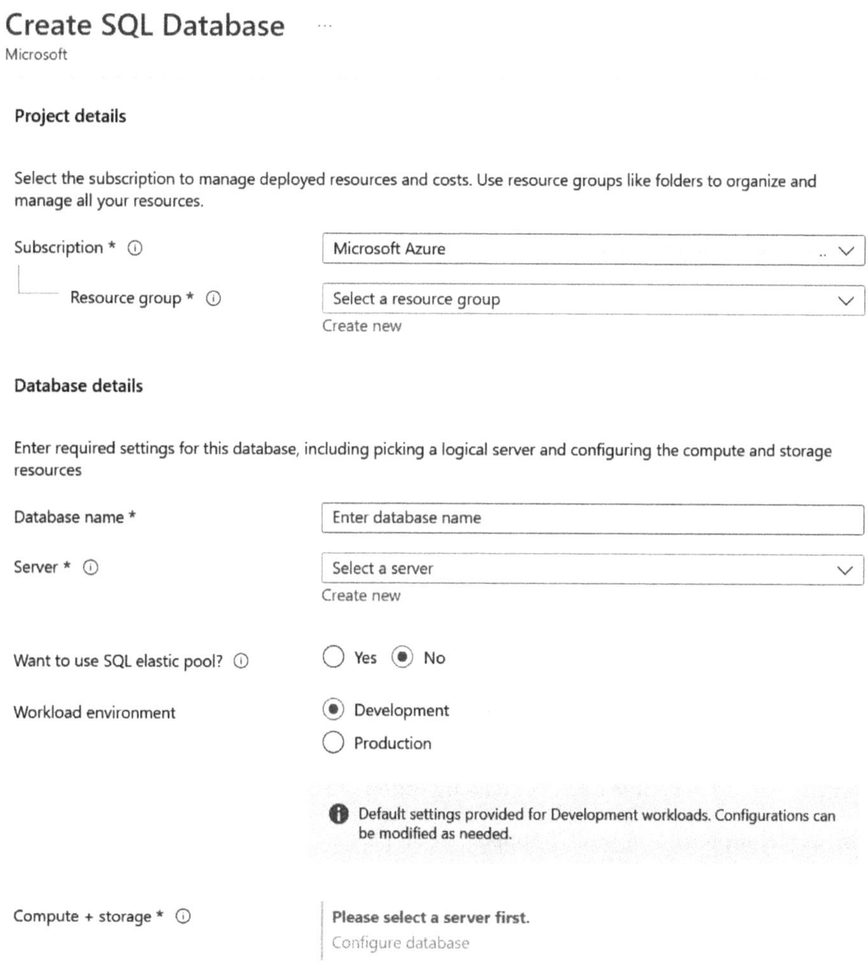

Figure 6.1 – Create SQL Database

4. Next, enable **Auto-Scaling** to ensure that the database can automatically scale up or down based on workload.

    Use elastic pools if managing multiple databases with varying usage patterns, to optimize resource allocation.

5. We'll now set up HA. To do this, enable **Geo-Replication** to replicate your data across multiple regions for disaster recovery.

6. Set up automated backups to ensure data recovery in the event of an outage or accidental deletion.

7. Lastly, we will apply security measures. To do this, enable **transparent data encryption** (TDE) to protect data at rest.

8. Use Entra ID for user authentication and RBAC for managing access to the database.

Features of Azure Cosmos DB

Azure Cosmos DB is a fully managed, globally distributed NoSQL database service that provides low-latency access to data, automatic scaling, and support for multiple data models, including document, key-value, graph, and column family. Cosmos DB is designed for applications that require HA, global distribution, and the ability to handle large volumes of unstructured or semi-structured data.

The following are some key features of Azure Cosmos DB:

- **Global distribution**: Cosmos DB allows you to replicate your data across multiple regions worldwide with a few clicks. This ensures low-latency data access for users around the globe, as well as HA in the case of a regional outage.

  A social media platform can use Cosmos DB to store user-generated content, such as posts and comments, ensuring that users can access and interact with the platform quickly, regardless of their location.

- **Automatic scaling**: Cosmos DB offers **automatic and manual scaling** options based on **request units** (**RUs**), a performance currency that represents the throughput of operations. As your application's workload increases, Cosmos DB automatically adjusts to ensure optimal performance without manual intervention.

  A real-time IoT platform monitoring thousands of sensors can benefit from Cosmos DB's automatic scaling to handle bursts of data ingestion during peak times.

- **Multi-model support**: Cosmos DB supports multiple data models, including document (JSON), key-value, graph, and column family, making it versatile for a wide range of applications. This flexibility allows developers to choose the model that best fits their data and query requirements.

  A gaming application can use the **document model** to store player profiles and the **graph model** to manage relationships between players for social interactions within the game.

- **Low-latency and HA**: Cosmos DB provides 99.999% availability for multi-region deployments and low-latency access to data (less than 10 ms read/write latency), ensuring fast data access even under heavy loads.

  An e-commerce platform with a global customer base can use Cosmos DB to ensure customers experience minimal delays during transactions, whether they are in the US, Europe, or Asia.

- **Security and compliance**: Cosmos DB provides advanced security features such as encryption at rest, Entra ID integration, firewall rules, and VNet service endpoints to ensure that your data is protected and compliant with security standards.

Setting up Azure Cosmos DB

The steps to set up Azure Cosmos DB are as follows:

1. In the Azure portal, we will first create a Cosmos DB account. Go to **Create a resource | Databases | Azure Cosmos DB**.

2. Select the API that matches your data model, as shown in the following figure:

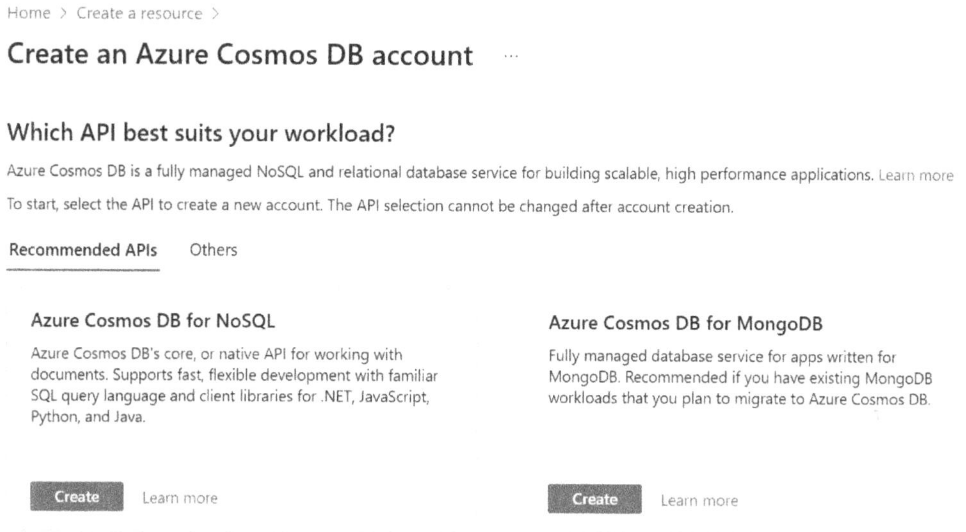

Home > Create a resource >

Create an Azure Cosmos DB account   ...

Which API best suits your workload?

Azure Cosmos DB is a fully managed NoSQL and relational database service for building scalable, high performance applications. Learn more

To start, select the API to create a new account. The API selection cannot be changed after account creation.

Recommended APIs   Others

Azure Cosmos DB for NoSQL

Azure Cosmos DB's core, or native API for working with documents. Supports fast, flexible development with familiar SQL query language and client libraries for .NET, JavaScript, Python, and Java.

Azure Cosmos DB for MongoDB

Fully managed database service for apps written for MongoDB. Recommended if you have existing MongoDB workloads that you plan to migrate to Azure Cosmos DB.

Create   Learn more   Create   Learn more

Figure 6.2 – Create an Azure Cosmos DB account

3. Configure the global distribution by selecting the regions where your data should be replicated.

4. Next, let's configure **Throughput (Request Units)**. To do so, set the initial RUs based on your expected workload.

5. Enable **Autoscale** to allow Cosmos DB to adjust RUs dynamically as demand fluctuates.

6. Use the Cosmos DB global distribution feature to replicate your data to multiple regions for low-latency access.

7. Configure multi-master replication if your application requires data to be written in multiple regions simultaneously.

8. Lastly, to carry out security configuration, enable *data encryption at rest* and ensure secure data transmission by enabling TLS encryption.

9. Set up RBAC and manage access via Entra ID.

Consider a global e-commerce platform that handles millions of transactions daily across multiple regions. The platform needs a reliable, scalable database solution that can handle a variety of workloads, from transactional data to product catalog information and user interactions.

Azure Cosmos DB is the ideal solution for this scenario. With its global distribution, Cosmos DB replicates data across multiple regions, ensuring that users anywhere in the world experience low latency when browsing products or completing transactions. It supports multi-model data, meaning it can easily store different types of information, such as product catalogs, customer profiles, and user activities—all in their native formats. This flexibility is perfect for managing diverse e-commerce data efficiently.

Cosmos DB's elastic scalability means that the database can automatically scale up during periods of high demand, such as during holiday sales, without manual intervention. It also provides high availability with a 99.999% uptime SLA, ensuring that the platform remains accessible even if there are regional failures. This reliability is essential to handle millions of daily transactions smoothly. Additionally, Cosmos DB's low latency reads and writes make it perfect for processing real-time transactions, such as checking out and payment, which is crucial for enhancing customer experience.

Now that we know about Azure Cosmos DB and how it can help us achieve the solution we are looking for, let us discover relational data with Azure SQL Database and unstructured data with Cosmos DB and their differences:

- **Relational data with Azure SQL Database**:

  - The platform uses Azure SQL Database to store structured, transactional data such as customer orders, payment details, and inventory management. By using elastic pools, the company ensures that databases handling different markets (e.g., North America, Europe, and Asia) share resources efficiently, scaling dynamically as demand shifts between regions.

  - To ensure HA, the platform configures geo-replication, ensuring data is replicated to multiple regions for disaster recovery.

- **Unstructured data with Cosmos DB**:

    - For handling unstructured data such as product recommendations, user-generated reviews, and browsing history, the platform uses Azure Cosmos DB. With global distribution, Cosmos DB ensures low-latency access to product information and user data across continents.

    - During high-traffic sales events, Cosmos DB's auto-scaling ensures the system can handle spikes in data requests without impacting performance.

By using both Azure SQL Database for structured relational data and Cosmos DB for unstructured, globally distributed data, this e-commerce platform creates a scalable, high-performance solution that meets the diverse needs of their global business.

This hybrid approach enables businesses to efficiently store, manage, and scale data solutions based on their unique needs, ensuring performance, availability, and security on a global scale.

In the next section, we will learn how to build scalable data lake and warehouse solutions.

Building scalable data lakes and warehouses with Azure Data Lake

As businesses grow, so do their data needs. The ability to manage and analyze large volumes of structured and unstructured data is crucial to driving insights, optimizing operations, and making data-driven decisions. **Azure Data Lake** is designed specifically for these challenges, offering a scalable, high-throughput, and cost-effective storage solution that can accommodate vast amounts of data, whether structured, semi-structured, or unstructured. Paired with powerful analytics and integration tools, Azure Data Lake allows businesses to store, process, and analyze data efficiently on top of Azure Storage accounts.

What is Azure Data Lake?

Azure Data Lake is a fully managed, highly scalable data storage solution designed for big data workloads. It allows organizations to store vast amounts of unstructured data in its raw format, making it ideal for use cases such as data analytics, machine learning, IoT data storage, and real-time reporting. Azure Data Lake supports the storage of virtually any type of data—such as logs, images, videos, or documents—allowing businesses to collect and retain data from various sources. To learn more about Azure Data Lake, you can go to `https://learn.microsoft.com/en-us/azure/storage/blobs/data-lake-storage-introduction`.

The underlying storage in Azure Data Lake is based on Azure Blob Storage, providing enterprise-grade durability, redundancy, and scalability. Azure Data Lake can handle both *batch* and *real-time processing*, making it versatile for multiple use cases, including data analytics and building data pipelines for transformation and reporting.

Here are some key features of Azure Data Lake:

- **Scalability and elasticity**: Azure Data Lake offers virtually unlimited storage, scaling automatically to accommodate the growth of data without the need for manual intervention. As your data grows, the system automatically scales to handle the increased load, ensuring that performance remains consistent.

  For example, a social media company collecting user activity data in the form of logs and event data can use Azure Data Lake to store terabytes or even petabytes of information while ensuring that the data is easily accessible for analysis.

- **Hierarchical namespace for efficient data management**: One of the key features of Azure Data Lake is its **hierarchical namespace**, which allows you to organize data into a structured, directory-based system similar to a filesystem. This feature enhances data management by supporting features such as directory-level security and access control, enabling you to manage data more efficiently.

  For example, a financial institution can organize data related to transactions, customer information, and risk analysis into separate directories, applying security and access controls at different levels to protect sensitive information while maintaining logical data organization.

- **Support for data lakes and warehouses**: Azure Data Lake is often paired with **Azure Synapse Analytics** (formerly SQL Data Warehouse) to build a complete data ecosystem. While Azure Data Lake stores the raw data, Synapse Analytics can be used to query, process, and transform that data into structured formats ready for reporting and analysis. This combination of services allows businesses to build end-to-end data pipelines that support real-time and batch analytics.

  For example, a retail company using Azure Data Lake to store transaction logs, customer reviews, and inventory data can leverage Synapse Analytics to query and analyze the data in real time, providing insights into customer behavior and sales trends.

- **Cost-effective storage**: Azure Data Lake offers cost-efficient storage through *tiered pricing*, allowing organizations to optimize storage costs based on data access patterns. Frequently accessed data can be stored in hot storage, while rarely accessed data can be moved to cool or archive storage tiers to reduce costs.

  For example, a media company that stores video footage for archival purposes can move older content to cooler storage tiers, minimizing storage costs while ensuring that the data is still accessible when needed.

- **Built-in security and compliance**: Azure Data Lake offers enterprise-grade security features such as encryption at rest and in transit, RBAC, and integration with Entra ID for identity and access management. These features ensure that data is protected and only accessible to authorized users.

For example, a healthcare organization that stores patient records and medical images in Azure Data Lake can implement strict RBAC policies and encryption to ensure that sensitive data is protected, meeting HIPAA and GDPR compliance standards.

Building scalable data pipelines with Azure Data Lake

Azure Data Lake is commonly used as the foundation for **data lakes** and **data warehouses**, allowing businesses to create scalable data pipelines that support various types of processing—whether it's real-time streaming data from IoT devices or batch processing for large-scale analytics.

For more information about data lakes and data warehouses and the differences between both, you can refer to the following links at Microsoft Learn:

- `https://learn.microsoft.com/en-us/azure/architecture/data-guide/scenarios/data-lake`

- `https://learn.microsoft.com/en-us/azure/architecture/example-scenario/data/data-warehouse`

Here are the steps to set up Azure Data Lake and build a data pipeline:

1. The first step is to create a Data Lake storage account. To do so, in the Azure portal, navigate to **Create a resource | Storage account**.

2. Continue the creation of a storage account as mentioned in previous chapters and make sure to check the box for **Enable hierarchical namespace** in the **Advanced** tab, as shown in the following figure:

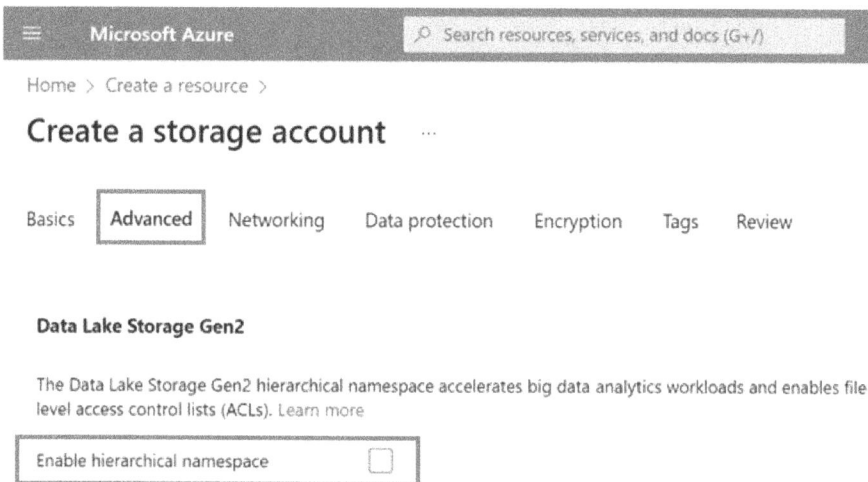

Figure 6.3 – Enable hierarchical namespace

3. Navigate to **Data Lake Gen2 upgrade** under **Settings** in the storage account you just created.

4. Review and validate the storage account.

5. Click **Start upgrade** and Data Lake Gen2 will be ready afterward.

Figure 6.4 shows how to upgrade your storage account to Azure Data Lake.

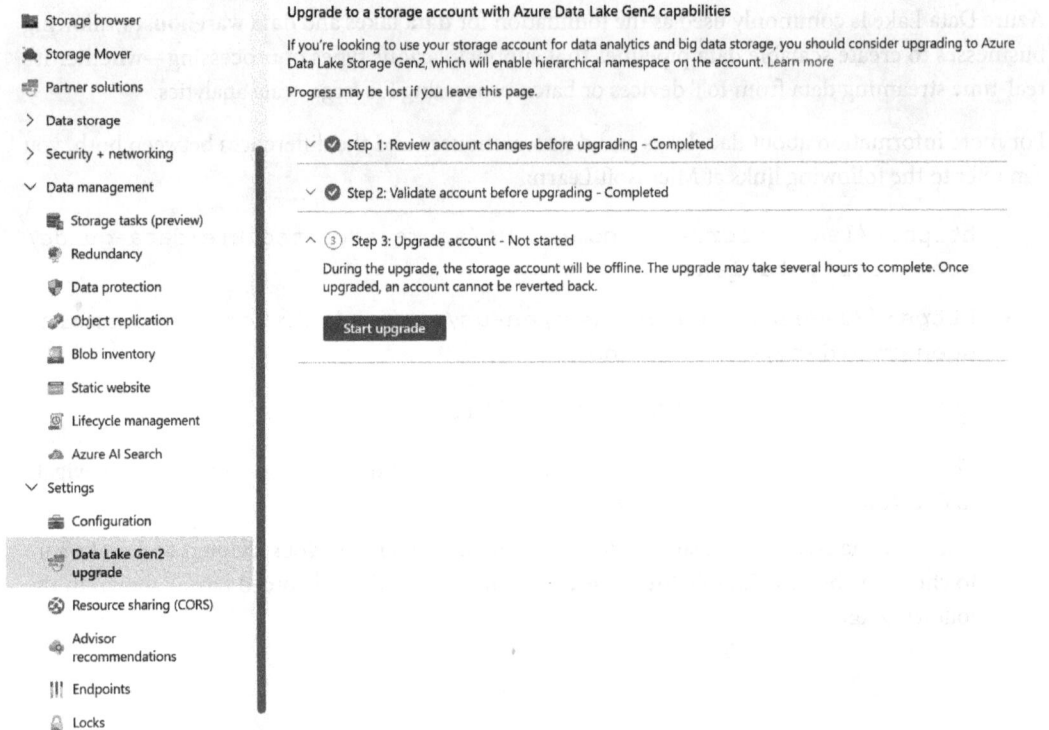

Figure 6.4 – Upgrading to Azure Data Lake

6. Next, to organize your data with a hierarchical namespace, create directories for different types of data, such as **raw data**, **processed data**, and **curated data**. This structure helps streamline the data processing pipeline and ensures efficient access control at each stage.

7. Apply access controls and security policies to different directories based on the sensitivity of the data.

8. We will now ingest data from multiple sources to use **Azure Data Factory** or **Azure Databricks**, including relational databases, IoT devices, and on-premises systems.

9. Automate the ingestion process to continuously collect and store data in Azure Data Lake in real-time or scheduled batches.

10. Now, we will process and analyze data with Azure Synapse Analytics. To do so, use Azure Synapse Analytics to run queries, process large datasets, and transform raw data into structured formats for reporting and analytics.

11. Leverage Apache Spark or SQL within Synapse Analytics to process data at scale, making it ready for consumption by business intelligence tools such as Power BI or third-party analytics platforms.

12. Next, implement data lifecycle management by setting up **lifecycle management policies**. This will automatically move data to lower-cost storage tiers as it becomes less frequently accessed. For example, after 90 days, move older logs to the cool tier, and after a year, transfer them to the archive tier. This ensures that you're optimizing costs without sacrificing access to long-term data.

13. Lastly, use Azure Monitor and Azure Cost Management to track storage utilization, access patterns, and data retrieval times.

Configure alerts for performance issues or cost spikes, ensuring that your data solution remains scalable and cost-effective.

A sample scenario for building a scalable data lake for a smart city

Let's consider an example where a smart city is using Azure Data Lake to manage and analyze massive amounts of data generated by IoT devices deployed throughout the city. These devices include sensors for monitoring traffic, air quality, and energy consumption across various districts.

The following bullet points will explain different solutions and methods on how to achieve the example scenario.

- **Data ingestion and storage**: The city's IoT devices generate large amounts of data in real time, including air quality metrics, traffic patterns, and electricity usage. Using Azure Data Factory, this data is ingested and stored in Azure Data Lake in raw format, allowing for flexible analysis and historical data archiving. The data is stored in directories by data type (e.g., "traffic," "air quality," and "energy consumption") using a hierarchical namespace to keep it organized.

- **Real-time and batch processing**: For real-time analysis of traffic data, Azure Synapse Analytics is used to query the incoming data streams and generate insights about traffic congestion in different areas of the city. This allows city planners to make adjustments in real time, such as optimizing traffic signal timings to reduce congestion. Batch processing is used to analyze long-term trends in air quality and energy consumption, helping the city improve sustainability practices.

- **Cost optimization**: The city manages a vast amount of data, much of which is accessed infrequently. As such, Azure Data Lake's lifecycle management automatically moves older data, such as historical energy usage records, to cooler storage tiers, significantly reducing storage costs. Data that is more than a year old is transferred to the archive tier, where it remains secure but accessible when needed for regulatory or historical analysis.

- **Data security and compliance**: The data stored includes sensitive information about the city's infrastructure, requiring strong security measures. Using RBAC and integration with Entra ID, the city ensures that only authorized personnel can access specific data directories. Encryption at rest and in transit guarantees that the data remains secure, complying with regulatory requirements like GDPR and national data protection laws.

In this scenario, the smart city is able to build a scalable, cost-effective data pipeline using Azure Data Lake and Azure Synapse Analytics, enabling real-time insights and long-term strategic planning.

Building a scalable data lake with Azure Data Lake and integrating it with data processing tools such as Azure Synapse Analytics provides businesses with a powerful foundation for managing large-scale data operations. Whether you're handling IoT data, customer transactions, or unstructured data from various sources, Azure Data Lake offers the flexibility, scalability, and cost-effectiveness needed to support growing data needs.

In the next section, we are going to discover data processing and analytics services for real-time and batch workloads.

Integrating data processing and analytics services to support real-time and batch workloads

One of the major challenges in modern data architecture is effectively processing and analyzing large volumes of data in both real-time and batch modes. Real-time workloads allow businesses to react immediately to events, while batch processing is essential for handling large datasets over specific intervals for detailed analysis. Azure provides a comprehensive suite of services that allow organizations to integrate real-time and batch data processing seamlessly, ensuring scalability, reliability, and performance for various workloads.

Why integrate real-time and batch data processing?

Organizations often deal with diverse data sources that require different processing methods. For instance, real-time data from IoT sensors, social media streams, or financial transactions needs to be processed immediately to trigger alerts or generate insights in real time. On the other hand, batch processing is essential for large-scale reporting, trend analysis, or data consolidation, where data can be processed at set intervals to uncover broader insights.

By integrating real-time and batch processing, businesses can build robust data pipelines that handle both time-sensitive and large-scale analytical needs, improving decision-making, operational efficiency, and responsiveness to dynamic events.

Key Azure services

Azure offers several services to handle both real-time and batch data processing, which can be seamlessly integrated to build a comprehensive data solution. Some of the key services include Azure Stream Analytics, Azure Databricks, Azure Synapse Analytics, and Azure Data Factory. Let's learn more about these:

- **Azure Stream Analytics**: This is a fully managed service that processes real-time data streams from various sources, such as IoT devices, event hubs, social media feeds, or log files. It allows businesses to gain insights from real-time data streams and take immediate action based on those insights.

  Here are some key features of Azure Stream Analytics:

  - **Low-latency processing**: It processes millions of events in real time with minimal latency, ensuring that insights can be acted on instantly

  - **SQL-like query language**: It offers a familiar SQL-based language for writing real-time queries, making it easier for data engineers to create complex data transformations and analytics

  - **Integration with Event Hubs and IoT Hub**: It seamlessly integrates with Azure Event Hubs, IoT Hub, and Blob Storage, providing a unified platform for ingesting and analyzing real-time data

  For example, a financial trading platform can use Azure Stream Analytics to analyze real-time stock market data, detect sudden price changes, and automatically execute trades based on predefined strategies.

- **Azure Databricks**: This is an Apache Spark-based analytics platform optimized for big data and machine learning workloads. It supports both real-time streaming and batch processing, making it highly versatile for building end-to-end data pipelines.

  Here are some key features of Azure Databricks:

  - **Unified data processing**: It supports real-time and batch workloads within the same platform, enabling businesses to process large datasets, build machine learning models, and run data transformations at scale

  - **Apache Spark integration**: Built on Apache Spark, Databricks provides distributed data processing capabilities for large-scale data operations

  - **Real-time streaming**: It supports real-time data ingestion and streaming analytics using Spark Streaming, allowing businesses to process live data and analyze it as it arrives

  For example, an e-commerce company can use Azure Databricks to handle both real-time customer browsing data (for immediate recommendations) and batch processing for nightly sales reporting, enabling them to optimize their sales strategies in real time while maintaining detailed daily performance analytics.

- **Azure Synapse Analytics**: This is a limitless analytics service that combines big data and data warehousing. It enables organizations to query large volumes of data on demand, whether structured or unstructured, and perform real-time or batch analytics.

Here are some key features of Azure Synapse Analytics:

- **Integrated data workflows**: It supports both real-time and batch processing, making it an ideal platform for combining live data analysis with scheduled data processing.

- **Serverless and dedicated pools**: It offers serverless and dedicated SQL pools for querying data, allowing organizations to run analytics across vast datasets without complex infrastructure management.

- **Unified experience**: It provides a unified experience for managing data pipelines, running queries, and performing data transformations from one platform.

For example, a logistics company can use Azure Synapse Analytics to monitor real-time fleet data to optimize delivery routes while using batch processing to analyze fuel consumption and vehicle performance trends over time.

- **Azure Data Factory** (**ADF**): This is a cloud-based data integration service that enables the creation, scheduling, and orchestration of data pipelines. ADF is crucial for **extract, transform, and load** (ETL) processes, enabling businesses to move data between various sources, transform it as needed, and load it into the destination.

Some key features of ADF are as follows:

- **Batch and incremental data processing**: It orchestrates both batch and incremental data processing pipelines, ensuring that data is moved and transformed efficiently

- **Real-time data movement**: ADF supports real-time data movement through integration with services such as Event Hubs and Stream Analytics, allowing businesses to process and react to real-time data streams

- **Scalable data pipelines**: ADF allows you to build scalable data pipelines that can handle large datasets or real-time streams, transforming data as it moves between sources

For example, a healthcare provider can use ADF to collect and process real-time patient data (such as vital signs from IoT-enabled devices) while also orchestrating batch pipelines for consolidating medical records and generating daily reports for healthcare professionals.

Building a unified data processing pipeline

To fully support real-time and batch workloads, integrating these Azure services is essential. The following is a step-by-step approach to building a unified data processing pipeline that handles both real-time and batch data streams:

1. **Ingest real-time data**:

    I.   Set up Azure Event Hubs to collect real-time data from sources such as IoT sensors, application logs, or social media streams.

    II.   Use Azure Stream Analytics to process the real-time data stream and generate immediate insights. For example, in a smart building scenario, temperature sensors might send real-time data that is analyzed for anomalies.

2. **Process data in real time**:

    I.   Stream the data from Azure Stream Analytics into Azure Databricks or Azure Synapse Analytics for further real-time analytics or to trigger actions based on live data.

    II.   In the case of our smart building example, the data could be analyzed to automatically adjust air conditioning systems if a temperature threshold is exceeded.

3. **Orchestrate batch data pipelines**: Use ADF to orchestrate batch data ingestion and transformation tasks. Schedule nightly or hourly jobs to extract data from sources such as on-premises databases, external APIs, or cloud services, and load it into Azure Data Lake or Azure SQL Database.

    For example, after processing the day's real-time sensor data, you might schedule a batch pipeline that aggregates sensor readings from the entire day for long-term storage and trend analysis.

4. **Batch processing for analytics and reporting**:

    I.   Run Azure Synapse Analytics or Azure Databricks batch processing jobs to generate reports or dashboards based on the transformed data. This can include aggregating daily data, calculating KPIs, or generating forecasts.

    II.   Continuing with the smart building scenario, the building management team can run batch reports analyzing energy consumption and HVAC system efficiency across all locations.

5. **Integrate with BI tools for data visualization**: Once the data is processed, integrate it with Power BI or other business intelligence tools to visualize real-time and batch insights. This allows decision-makers to view dashboards and reports that combine real-time alerts with long-term performance analysis.

A scenario for smart retail store analytics

Consider a *smart retail store* that aims to improve customer experience by integrating real-time and batch analytics. The store collects data from various sources, including customer movement tracking (real-time), **Point of Scale (POS)** transactions (real-time), and inventory data (batch).

The following bullet points will explain how you can achieve the mentioned scenario for smart retail store analytics:

- **Real-time data ingestion and processing**:

  - Azure Event Hubs is set up to ingest real-time data from IoT sensors that track customer movement in the store.

  - Azure Stream Analytics processes this data in real time, analyzing foot traffic patterns and customer behavior. For example, if a section of the store is overcrowded, the system triggers a staff alert to manage the flow.

- **Batch data orchestration and processing**:

  - At the end of each day, ADF orchestrates the batch ingestion of sales and inventory data from the POS systems. This data is cleaned, transformed, and loaded into Azure Data Lake for storage.

  - Azure Synapse Analytics runs nightly queries that consolidate sales data, customer purchases, and inventory levels to generate daily sales performance reports.

- **Real-time and batch insights**:

  - Store managers can access real-time dashboards displaying current foot traffic, allowing them to make decisions about staffing and customer assistance.

  - In parallel, detailed sales and inventory reports are generated from the batch-processed data, helping the management team plan for inventory restocking, marketing strategies, and long-term operational efficiency.

  In this scenario, the smart retail store leverages both real-time and batch processing to optimize day-to-day operations while ensuring long-term strategic planning.

In the next section, we will be discovering more about best practices for performance optimization and cost management in your data solutions.

Best practices for performance optimization and cost management in data solutions

As data solutions scale, it's essential to ensure that the infrastructure performs efficiently while controlling costs. Without proper management, the costs of running large-scale data platforms can escalate quickly, and performance can degrade as the system grows. Azure provides several built-in tools and strategies to optimize both the performance and the cost-efficiency of data solutions. Applying best practices helps businesses strike a balance between powerful, responsive data operations and cost control, ensuring that solutions are sustainable over the long term.

Let's dive into the best practices for performance optimization and cost management when building data solutions on Azure.

Best practices for performance optimization

The following are some best practices to keep in mind in order to achieve performance optimization:

- **Choose the right service tier**: Azure offers various service tiers for its data services such as Azure SQL Database, Cosmos DB, and Azure Data Lake. Selecting the appropriate tier based on your workload is crucial for optimizing performance and minimizing unnecessary resource consumption. Each tier provides different levels of compute, storage, and throughput capacity, which are directly related to both performance and cost.

  If you are managing a high-transaction environment such as an e-commerce platform, choosing a *Premium* tier for Azure SQL Database with high throughput and low latency might be necessary to handle spikes in user activity. On the other hand, for a staging environment used for testing, a lower-tier plan would suffice.

- **Use data partitioning and sharding**: For services such as Cosmos DB and Azure SQL Database, partitioning and sharding are key techniques to improve performance by distributing data across multiple storage locations. Data partitioning divides the dataset into smaller segments that can be managed and accessed independently, reducing the load on any single part of the system and improving query efficiency.

  In Cosmos DB, choosing the right partition key is critical. If you're managing a retail application, using something such as *Order ID* as a partition key ensures that large-scale queries (such as fetching all orders for a customer) are distributed evenly, preventing bottlenecks during peak times.

- **Implement caching strategies**: Caching frequently accessed data can significantly boost performance by reducing the need to repeatedly query the underlying database or data lake. Azure provides caching solutions such as **Azure Cache for Redis** that store frequently used data in memory, speeding up response times and reducing query load on the primary data store.

A web application that displays product details could use Azure Cache for Redis to cache popular products or categories, ensuring that users receive instant responses without repeatedly querying the main database.

- **Optimize queries and indexes**: Efficient querying and indexing are fundamental to ensuring that databases perform optimally as they scale. For relational databases such as Azure SQL Database, indexing can drastically reduce query times by organizing data in a way that allows the database to retrieve information more quickly. Similarly, in Cosmos DB, setting up appropriate indexes can enhance query performance.

  In Azure SQL Database, regularly review the performance of queries and set up indexes for frequently queried columns. Use the **SQL Query Performance Insight** tool to identify slow-running queries and adjust indexing or optimize the query structure.

- **Leverage auto-scaling**: Azure provides auto-scaling options for services such as Cosmos DB, Azure SQL Database, and Azure Data Lake, allowing these systems to automatically scale resources based on demand. This ensures optimal performance during high-load periods while preventing overprovisioning during low-use times.

  A media streaming service can benefit from auto-scaling in Cosmos DB to accommodate sudden increases in traffic during major live events. By scaling out resources dynamically, the system can maintain low latency while avoiding performance degradation.

Best practices for cost management

The following are some best practices to keep in mind for managing costs:

- **Optimize storage with lifecycle management**: For data services such as Azure Blob Storage and Azure Data Lake, it's essential to use tiered storage to manage costs. Azure offers hot, cool, and archive tiers, where frequently accessed data is stored in the hot tier, and less frequently accessed data can be moved to cooler, cheaper storage tiers. Lifecycle management policies can be set up to automate the process of moving data between these tiers as its usage changes over time.

  A healthcare organization storing patient records might use hot storage for recent records that are accessed regularly, but after a year, they can automatically move older records to a cool or archive tier to save on storage costs.

- **Use Reserved Instances for long-term workloads**: For services such as Azure SQL Database and Azure Synapse Analytics, Reserved Instances offer significant cost savings for long-term, predictable workloads. By committing to a specific service capacity for one or three years, businesses can reduce costs compared to pay-as-you-go pricing.

  A retail company running a data warehouse on Azure Synapse Analytics can use reserved capacity pricing if they have predictable daily processing needs, saving up to 72% compared to on-demand pricing.

- **Monitor resource usage and optimize**: Azure provides tools such as **Azure Cost Management and Billing** to help businesses monitor and optimize resource usage. With this tool, you can track usage patterns, set budgets, and receive alerts when spending exceeds predefined thresholds. This helps ensure that resources are used efficiently, and costs are kept in check.

  A logistics company might set up cost alerts for its ADF pipelines. If a particular data pipeline starts consuming more resources than expected, they'll receive an alert and can investigate the issue to prevent runaway costs.

- **Right-size resources for your workloads**: Overprovisioning resources can lead to unnecessary costs. Regularly review your resource allocations to ensure they match the actual needs of your workloads. **Right-sizing** resources means reducing underutilized services while ensuring that your applications have sufficient capacity to handle peak loads without waste.

  A financial services company using Azure SQL Database might review performance metrics to discover that its current provisioned capacity exceeds demand. By reducing the service tier or enabling auto-scaling, they can avoid paying for unused resources.

- **Leverage serverless for event-driven workloads**: Serverless architectures such as **Azure Functions** and Cosmos DB's serverless mode allow you to pay only for the exact resources consumed by your application. This can be highly cost-efficient for applications with unpredictable or intermittent workloads, as you don't have to provision and pay for idle resources.

  A news website might use Azure Functions to process incoming user-generated content during major news events. Rather than maintaining a full-time server for intermittent traffic spikes, they only pay for compute resources when articles are submitted, allowing for cost-efficient scaling.

Combining performance optimization with cost management

The key to successful data solutions is balancing performance with cost. Azure provides a rich set of tools and services that allow businesses to optimize their data workloads without overspending. By following best practices such as selecting the right service tiers, implementing auto-scaling, and using lifecycle management policies for storage, organizations can ensure that their data platforms are both efficient and cost-effective.

Azure's monitoring tools also play a crucial role in this balancing act, helping you track both performance and spending in real time. With Azure Monitor, Azure Cost Management, and built-in telemetry from data services such as Azure SQL Database and Cosmos DB, businesses can continuously fine-tune their solutions to maintain optimal performance while minimizing costs.

Consider a global retailer that uses Azure SQL Database for transaction data and Azure Data Lake for customer insights and inventory tracking. The retailer has seen significant growth in both data volume and transaction volume, leading to a need for better performance and cost management.

The following list will discuss the options and how they help you with the mentioned scenario:

- **Performance optimization**:

  - The retailer implements partitioning in Azure SQL Database, allowing them to handle millions of transactions per day without a performance hit.

  - They set up Azure Cache for Redis to cache frequently accessed product details, reducing query times and improving the shopping experience for customers.

- **Cost management**:

  - To manage their growing data storage, they apply lifecycle management policies to their Azure Data Lake. Data that is no longer actively used is automatically moved to the archive tier, reducing storage costs by 40%.

  - The retailer also uses Azure Cost Management to monitor their daily cloud spend and receives alerts if usage exceeds predefined limits, allowing the team to address inefficiencies in real time.

By following these best practices, the retailer ensures that its data platform is optimized for performance while maintaining cost efficiency, enabling it to scale globally without excessive overhead.

In the next section, we will be covering security and compliance for large-scale data solutions with examples and best practices of real-world scenarios.

Ensuring security and compliance for large-scale data solutions

As businesses increasingly rely on cloud-based data solutions, ensuring the security and compliance of sensitive data becomes paramount. Data breaches, unauthorized access, and non-compliance with industry regulations can have severe consequences, including financial loss and reputational damage. When dealing with large-scale data solutions, the challenge becomes even more significant as the volume of data grows, and the number of potential access points increases.

Azure provides a wide range of built-in security features and compliance tools designed to safeguard data, maintain privacy, and ensure that businesses meet regulatory requirements across industries. From encryption and identity management to advanced threat protection and compliance monitoring, Azure enables organizations to design data architectures that are secure, compliant, and resilient.

Let's explore the key best practices and Azure tools available to ensure security and compliance for large-scale data solutions.

Best practices for ensuring security and compliance

The following are some best practices to keep in mind in order to ensure security and compliance:

- **Encrypt data at rest and in transit**: Encryption is one of the fundamental ways to protect data from unauthorized access, ensuring that even if data is intercepted or accessed by an unauthorized party, it remains unreadable. Azure provides encryption at both rest and in transit, ensuring that data is protected throughout its lifecycle. Let's learn more about these:

  - **Encryption at rest**: Azure automatically encrypts all data stored in services such as Azure SQL Database, Cosmos DB, Azure Data Lake, and Blob Storage. This includes using TDE for databases, ensuring that the stored data is always encrypted.

  - **Encryption in transit**: Data in transit (moving between data centers, users, or applications) is encrypted using **Transport Layer Security** (**TLS**) to prevent unauthorized access during transmission.

  For example, a healthcare provider storing sensitive patient data in Azure Data Lake can ensure the data is encrypted using AES-256 encryption while at rest. Additionally, data transfers between their on-premises systems and Azure are encrypted using TLS.

- **Implement RBAC**: RBAC ensures that only authorized users have access to specific data and resources within your Azure environment. By applying the principle of *least privilege*, you can ensure that users only have access to the data they need for their roles, reducing the risk of accidental or malicious access.

  In Azure, Entra ID integrates seamlessly with RBAC, allowing you to manage users and their roles across multiple Azure services. Each service can have granular access controls, allowing you to assign different levels of permissions (such as read, write, or administrative access) to users or groups.

  For example, a financial institution managing a large-scale data warehouse can restrict access to sensitive financial data by creating specific RBAC roles for data analysts, administrators, and external auditors. Data analysts may have *read-only* access to the data, while administrators have full control to manage the database, and auditors have temporary access to compliance reviews.

- **Use Azure Key Vault for secret management**: Managing sensitive information such as encryption keys, API keys, passwords, and certificates securely is crucial for large-scale data solutions. **Azure Key Vault** provides a secure environment for storing and managing secrets, ensuring that sensitive information is protected and accessible only by authorized applications or users.

  Azure Key Vault integrates with other Azure services, allowing you to automatically rotate keys, manage access controls, and track the usage of secrets to ensure compliance.

  For example, a logistics company using Cosmos DB to store real-time tracking data can store its database connection strings and encryption keys in Azure Key Vault. This ensures that only the authorized application has access to the database keys, reducing the risk of data breaches.

- **Enable Advanced Threat Protection**: Azure offers **Advanced Threat Protection (ATP)**, a set of intelligent security features that monitor and protect against potential security threats across Azure services, such as Azure SQL Database, Cosmos DB, and Azure Storage. ATP continuously analyzes your environment for suspicious activities and alerts you when potential vulnerabilities or breaches are detected. Let's learn more about these:

  - **SQL Database threat detection**: It monitors SQL Database for unusual activities such as SQL injections or abnormal login patterns

  - **Cosmos DB threat detection**: It analyzes traffic patterns and access logs for anomalies that might indicate potential breaches

  These alerts are automatically sent to the appropriate security teams, enabling a rapid response to emerging threats.

  For example, a retail company processing customer orders in Azure SQL Database receives an alert from ATP about an unusual spike in failed login attempts. The security team investigates and identifies an attempted brute-force attack, allowing them to respond quickly and prevent unauthorized access.

- **Ensure compliance with Azure Policy and Blueprints**: For businesses operating in highly regulated industries such as finance, healthcare, or government, meeting compliance requirements is critical. Azure provides compliance management tools such as **Azure Policy** and **Azure Blueprints** that help you enforce compliance across your data solutions. Let's learn more about these:

  - **Azure Policy** allows you to create, assign, and manage policies that enforce specific compliance rules, such as requiring encryption on all storage accounts, restricting access to specific IP ranges, or mandating that only approved resources are deployed within the environment.

  For example, a global e-commerce platform can use Azure Policy to enforce strict data residency policies, ensuring that customer data from the EU is only stored in European data centers.

  - **Azure Blueprints** enables automated deployment of secure, compliant environments. It allows you to package policies, role assignments, and templates into reusable blueprints.

  The same e-commerce platform can use Azure Blueprints to ensure that infrastructure is deployed in accordance with GDPR and PCI DSS requirements.

- **Regularly audit and monitor access logs**: Continuous monitoring and auditing are essential to maintain security and compliance. Azure provides robust logging and monitoring tools such as Azure Monitor, **Azure Security Center**, and **Azure Sentinel** to track access patterns, detect unusual activities, and maintain a detailed audit trail of user interactions with data. Let's learn more about these:

  - **Azure Monitor**: This captures real-time telemetry data across all your Azure services, providing insights into resource usage, access patterns, and potential performance or security issues.

- **Azure Security Center**: This offers a unified security management solution that helps you track the security health of your data environments and identify vulnerabilities.

- **Azure Sentinel**: This is a cloud-native **security information and event management (SIEM)** service that aggregates security data from multiple sources, including Azure services, on-premises systems, and third-party security solutions, to provide real-time threat detection and incident response.

For example, a healthcare organization can use Azure Monitor to keep an eye on who accesses sensitive patient data in Azure Data Lake. The logs are reviewed regularly to ensure that only authorized personnel are accessing the information, and Azure Security Center alerts the IT team to any unusual or unauthorized access attempts.

Ensuring security and compliance for a global financial institution

Consider a *global financial institution* that handles sensitive customer data, including financial transactions, account details, and personal information. This institution is subject to stringent regulatory requirements such as PCI DSS and GDPR and must ensure that its data solutions are secure, compliant, and capable of scaling across multiple regions.

Let's discover what options and solutions we have for the mentioned scenario:

- **Data encryption and access control**:

  - The institution uses Azure SQL Database and Cosmos DB to store sensitive financial data. They enable TDE to ensure all stored data is encrypted. All communications between their on-premises systems and Azure are encrypted using TLS.

  - RBAC is implemented via Entra ID, ensuring that only authorized users—such as database administrators and financial analysts—can access specific datasets. Temporary access is granted to auditors through RBAC, ensuring secure access for compliance reviews.

- **Secret management and key rotation**:

  - The institution stores all encryption keys and API keys in Azure Key Vault. By using Key Vault, they automate key rotation and manage access controls, ensuring that sensitive information remains secure and inaccessible to unauthorized users.

- **Threat detection and monitoring**:

  - ATP is enabled for all databases, providing real-time monitoring for potential threats such as SQL injections or unusual login attempts. The institution receives alerts if suspicious activity is detected, allowing them to respond quickly to any threats.

  - Additionally, Azure Sentinel is used to aggregate security logs from multiple data centers across the globe, providing a unified view of the organization's security posture and enabling proactive incident response.

- **Compliance with regulatory standards:**

  - To comply with GDPR and PCI DSS, the institution uses Azure Blueprints to automate the deployment of compliant infrastructure in each region where it operates. Azure Policy enforces the encryption of all data at rest and ensures that customer data is only stored in approved regions.

  - Regular compliance audits are conducted using Azure's built-in auditing tools, ensuring that the organization continuously meets regulatory requirements.

Summary

In this chapter, we explored the essential aspects of building and managing scalable data solutions using Azure. We began by discussing the importance of creating scalable databases with services such as Azure SQL Database and Cosmos DB, focusing on how these platforms help manage large data volumes efficiently while ensuring high availability and performance. We then moved on to Azure Data Lake, learning how to build scalable data lakes and warehouses for storing massive amounts of structured and unstructured data, using tools such as Azure Synapse Analytics to integrate real-time and batch workloads. In the next chapter, we will cover CI/CI flows with pipelines.

7

Building a Continuous Integration and Continuous Delivery Pipeline

In today's fast-paced software development environment, the ability to deliver high-quality applications efficiently and reliably is crucial for business success. **Continuous integration** (**CI**) and **continuous delivery** (**CD**) are core practices that help software development teams streamline their workflow, maintain code quality, and release features more frequently. By automating the integration and delivery processes, CI/CD pipelines allow teams to focus more on innovation and less on repetitive manual tasks. This ensures that software reaches production faster, with fewer errors and greater consistency.

In this chapter, we will explore how to build and manage a CI/CD pipeline, leveraging Azure DevOps and GitHub Actions. We will walk through the essential components of setting up a CI/CD pipeline, from integrating code repositories, running automated tests, and configuring build environments to deploying services in a consistent, repeatable manner. Azure provides powerful tools for setting up these pipelines, including **Azure DevOps Pipelines**, **GitHub Actions**, and **Azure Repos**, making the process accessible for development teams of any size.

The focus of this chapter is to help you understand the benefits of implementing CI/CD practices, learn how to build a pipeline for your Azure projects, and explore best practices for automating deployments to various environments. By the end of this chapter, you will be equipped with the skills to create a fully functioning CI/CD pipeline that integrates with Azure services, helping your team deliver robust, reliable software with agility and speed.

In this chapter, we will be covering the following learning objectives:

- Understand the core concepts and benefits of CI/CD
- Learn how to build and configure a CI/CD pipeline using Azure DevOps or GitHub Actions
- Explore integrating automated testing into your CI/CD process to ensure code quality
- Configure build and release stages to automate the deployment of applications to Azure services

The importance of CI/CD pipelines

Before diving into the learning objectives, first, let's explore the question *Why build a CI/CD pipeline?* This will help us better understand the overall idea of CI/CD.

The implementation of CI/CD pipelines has revolutionized the software development process. Traditionally, manual integration and deployment processes were time-consuming and prone to human error, leading to delays, inconsistency, and quality issues. CI/CD addresses these problems by creating a fully automated workflow that handles code integration, testing, and deployment seamlessly.

CI emphasizes merging all developer working copies to a shared repository multiple times a day, automatically testing and building the code with each change. This ensures that errors are detected early before they compound into larger problems.

CD extends CI by automating the deployment process, allowing teams to release software at any time with the click of a button. This fosters a culture of incremental releases, where small, well-tested changes can be deployed frequently to production, improving overall software stability and user satisfaction.

By building a CI/CD pipeline on Azure, developers can leverage powerful automation tools and integrate closely with Azure's cloud infrastructure, streamlining the entire process of coding, testing, and deploying applications. This approach ensures that your applications are delivered with quality, speed, and consistency—vital elements for staying competitive in the market.

Understanding the core concepts and benefits of CI/CD

The first learning objective of this chapter is to understand the core concepts and benefits of CI and CD. These practices are central to modern DevOps culture, and understanding them thoroughly is essential for building effective, automated pipelines that allow teams to deliver quality software rapidly and efficiently.

CI

CI is a software development practice where developers frequently merge their code changes into a central repository. After every commit, automated builds and tests run to verify the integration. CI encourages developers to commit changes often, typically multiple times a day, ensuring that small, incremental changes are validated as they are made.

The key features of CI are as follows:

- **Automated builds**: Every time new code is committed to the repository, the CI server automatically triggers a build to ensure that the code compiles correctly.

- **Automated testing**: Unit tests, integration tests, and even UI tests are run as part of the CI process, ensuring that new changes don't introduce errors. This helps in maintaining code quality and catching issues early in the development cycle.

- **Feedback mechanism**: When the build or tests fail, the development team is immediately notified so they can fix the issue quickly. This prevents issues from snowballing and keeps the codebase in a deployable state at all times.

Moving on from the features, let's see a few benefits of CI, which are as follows:

- **Early detection of errors**: CI helps detect integration issues early, as the code is built and tested every time a change is committed. This means that bugs are caught at the point of introduction, making them much easier and cheaper to fix.

- **Reduced integration problems**: Since all changes are merged frequently, integration becomes less painful, as smaller changes are easier to merge and verify compared to large changes accumulated over longer periods.

- **Improved team collaboration**: CI encourages a culture of collaboration and code-sharing among developers. As everyone works with the same shared repository, it prevents divergence and ensures that developers are always working with the latest version of the code.

- **Enhanced security and compliance**: Automated security checks and compliance validation ensure that the code adheres to industry standards and regulations.

Here's a basic visual representation of the CI workflow:

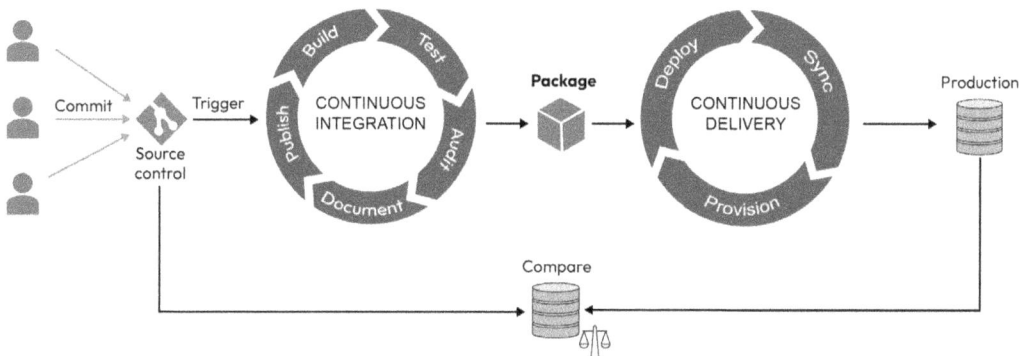

Figure 7.1 – CI workflow

The preceding figure illustrates a CI workflow:

1. Developers make changes to their code and push these to a central repository (e.g., Azure Repos or GitHub).

2. The CI system is triggered, automatically pulling the latest changes and running build scripts.

3. Automated tests are executed to ensure code integrity.

4. If any step fails, the responsible developer is notified.

CD

CD builds upon CI by automating the deployment process, making it possible to release new changes to production with minimal manual intervention. Once changes are committed and successfully built and tested in CI, they move into the delivery phase, where they are automatically prepared for release to various environments—staging, testing, or even production.

CD focuses on automating as much of the software release process as possible so that software can be deployed at any time with the confidence that it has already passed the necessary checks.

Here are the key features of CD:

- **Automated deployments**: After passing through CI, code is automatically deployed to environments such as staging or testing for further checks.

- **Pipeline visualization**: Most CD tools, such as Azure DevOps and GitHub Actions, provide a visual representation of the entire delivery pipeline, from build to deployment, making it easier for teams to monitor each stage.

- **Configuration management**: CD relies on infrastructure-as-code and consistent configuration management to deploy identical environments. Tools such as **Terraform** or Azure's **ARM templates** help automate the provisioning of infrastructure.

The benefits of CD are highlighted as follows:

- **Shorter release cycles**: With CD, teams can deploy software frequently—often multiple times a day—which means features and updates reach users faster

- **Reduced human error**: Automation significantly reduces the risk of manual errors during deployment, making the release process more reliable and consistent

- **Increased product stability**: Frequent releases with smaller increments reduce the risks associated with large-scale deployments, leading to more stable and predictable software delivery

Here's a visual overview of how CD works:

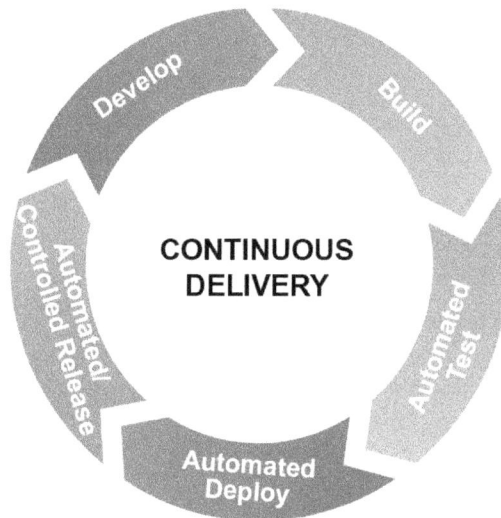

Figure 7.2 – CD workflow

Let's understand the workflow:

1. After the code passes CI, the successful build is automatically moved to the delivery phase.
2. The system deploys the build to environments such as staging or quality assurance.
3. Manual approval might be required before deploying to production.

Figure 7.1 also illustrates how CD looks alongside CI to demonstrate the ecosystem of CI/CD.

Now that we have covered CI/CD core concepts, features, and benefits, let's continue with the next section.

CD and continuous deployment: the next step

It is worth noting that **continuous deployment** is a step beyond CD. In continuous deployment, every change that passes the CI/CD pipeline tests is automatically deployed to production, removing the need for manual approval. While it shares a similar philosophy, continuous deployment requires even higher levels of automation and confidence in the testing process.

Tools and services for implementing CI/CD

Let's look at a few tools and services for implementing CI/CD:

- **Azure DevOps**: Azure DevOps provides a comprehensive set of tools for CI/CD, including **Azure Pipelines**, which allows you to automate the building, testing, and deployment processes. Azure Pipelines integrates with source control systems such as **GitHub**, **Bitbucket**, and **Azure Repos**.

- **GitHub Actions**: GitHub Actions offers a flexible, built-in CI/CD solution for projects hosted on GitHub. It allows developers to create workflows that automatically build, test, and deploy code whenever changes are pushed to the repository.

- **Jenkins, Travis CI, and CircleCI**: These are popular CI/CD tools that provide similar functionality. They integrate with various cloud services, including Azure, allowing developers to build their own customized CI/CD workflows.

Example scenario

Imagine a software development team working on an online retail platform. The team uses Azure DevOps to set up a CI/CD pipeline:

- **CI**: Every time a developer adds a new feature—such as updating the product catalog–the new code is pushed to Azure Repos. The CI pipeline runs unit tests and integration tests, and builds the software to ensure it's ready for deployment.

- **CD**: After a successful build, the CD pipeline automatically deploys the changes to a **staging environment** where **quality assurance** (**QA**) engineers test the new feature in an environment that closely resembles production.

- **Automated approval**: Once the QA tests are completed and approved, the code is automatically deployed to **production**, making the new feature available to customers quickly and with minimal risk.

By leveraging CI/CD, this team minimizes manual intervention, ensures high-quality releases, and delivers new features faster to customers—resulting in a better user experience and more efficient development process.

CI/CD are foundational practices in modern software development that significantly enhance the ability to deliver high-quality software frequently and reliably. CI/CD pipelines automate key processes—such as building, testing, and deploying software—enabling teams to focus more on writing code and innovating, rather than managing integrations and releases manually. With Azure DevOps and GitHub Actions, you can build these automated workflows to deliver software faster, improve quality, and stay competitive in the ever-changing technology landscape.

In the next section, we will dive into the practical aspects of building and configuring a CI/CD pipeline using Azure DevOps or GitHub Actions and explore the steps needed to integrate this pipeline into your Azure projects.

Building and configuring a CI/CD pipeline using Azure DevOps or GitHub Actions

The second learning objective in this chapter is to understand how to build and configure a CI/CD pipeline using Azure DevOps or GitHub Actions. This involves setting up source code management, creating automated CI workflows for building and testing, and configuring CD pipelines for deploying the application. These pipelines help ensure that code quality is maintained, deployments are consistent, and new features are delivered to customers as quickly and reliably as possible.

In this section, we will take a hands-on approach to creating a complete CI/CD pipeline, starting from **source code management** all the way through to automated testing and deployment into Azure. We'll explore both tools—Azure DevOps and GitHub Actions—to understand their roles in automating the development process and how they can be used to manage the entire application lifecycle efficiently.

CI/CD pipeline overview

The following diagram shows the complete flow of a CI/CD pipeline from building and testing code to deploying it in Azure.

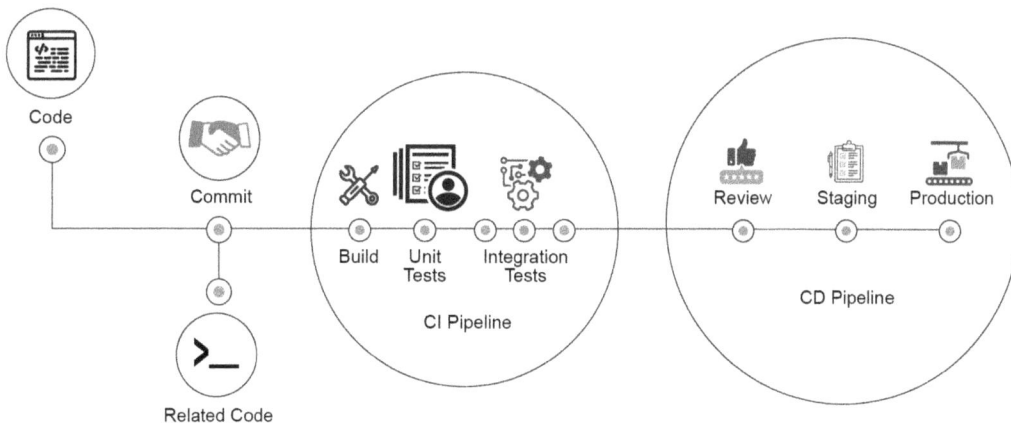

Figure 7.3 – CI/CD pipeline flow

Here are the stages:

1. **Build stage**: The code is built and packaged.
2. **Test stage**: Unit tests, integration tests, and end-to-end tests are executed.
3. **Release stage**: The application is deployed to staging and production environments with manual approval gates if needed.

With this understanding of the CI/CD pipeline structure, you are now ready to configure and implement it step by step. In the next section, we will walk through the process of setting up source code management as the foundation of your CI/CD pipeline.

Step 1 – setting up source code management

Before we begin with CI/CD, it's crucial to have a **version control system** that manages the source code and tracks changes. Both Azure DevOps and GitHub provide source code management options:

- **Azure Repos**: This is a service within Azure DevOps that provides Git repositories to host your code and manage version control

- **GitHub repositories**: GitHub, integrated with GitHub Actions, is a popular platform for managing open source and private code bases, enabling easy collaboration and integration

For example, we will use GitHub to host the source code for our application, which will then be integrated with either GitHub Actions or Azure DevOps for CI/CD. The following diagram illustrates how version control is integrated with CI/CD processes:

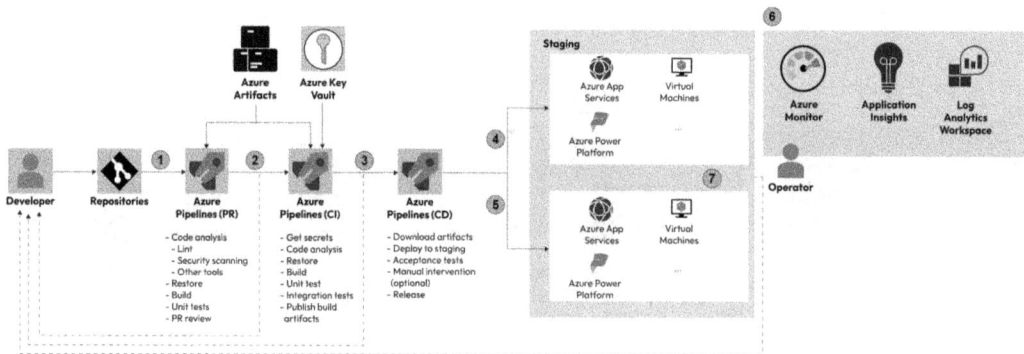

Figure 7.4 – Version control integration diagram

In the preceding figure, you can see what the process of a CI/CD pipeline looks like from above:

1. Developers push code to GitHub.
2. GitHub triggers either GitHub Actions or Azure DevOps to initiate the CI/CD pipeline.

Step 2 – creating a CI pipeline

The next step is to create a CI pipeline that automatically builds and tests the code every time changes are pushed to the repository. This ensures that code quality is maintained and errors are caught early in the development process.

Configuring a CI pipeline in Azure DevOps

Azure Pipelines is a cloud-hosted CI/CD pipeline solution for building and testing your code automatically for CI/CD. Follow these steps:

1. **Create a new pipeline**: In Azure DevOps, navigate to the **Pipelines** section and click **Create Pipeline**. Select your GitHub repository or Azure Repos repository as the source.

2. **Define the build process**: Azure DevOps uses a YAML file (`azure-pipelines.yml`) to define the build process. This YAML file specifies all steps involved in building, testing, and packaging the application.

   Here is the example YAML configuration:

   ```
   trigger:
     branches:
       include:
         - main
   pool:
     vmImage  'ubuntu-latest'
   steps:
   - task  UseDotNet@2
     inputs:
       packageType  'sdk'
       version  '6.x'
   - script  dotnet build
     displayName  'Build Project'
   - script  dotnet test
     displayName  'Run Unit Tests'
   ```

   This configuration will trigger a build whenever there are changes to the `main` branch. The pipeline uses an Ubuntu virtual machine to install .NET SDK, build the project, and run unit tests.

Configuring a CI pipeline with GitHub Actions

GitHub Actions allows you to create workflows to build, test, and deploy your code directly from your GitHub repository.

To create a workflow file GitHub Actions uses a YAML file (`.github/workflows/ci.yml`) to define CI workflows. The YAML file is stored in the `.github/workflows/` directory of your repository.

Here's an example workflow file configuration:

```
name  Azure Projects CI/CD
on:
  push:
    branches:
      - main
  pull_request:
    branches:
      - main
jobs:
  build:
    runs-on  ubuntu-latest
    steps:
    - name  Checkout code
      uses  actions/checkout@v2
    - name  Set up .NET
      uses  actions/setup-dotnet@v1
      with:
        dotnet-version  6.0
    - name  Build Project
      run  dotnet build
    - name  Run Tests
      run  dotnet test
```

This GitHub Actions workflow is triggered when there is a push or pull request on the main branch. It checks out the code, installs the .NET SDK, and then builds and tests the project automatically.

The following diagram illustrates how a CI workflow runs on GitHub Actions:

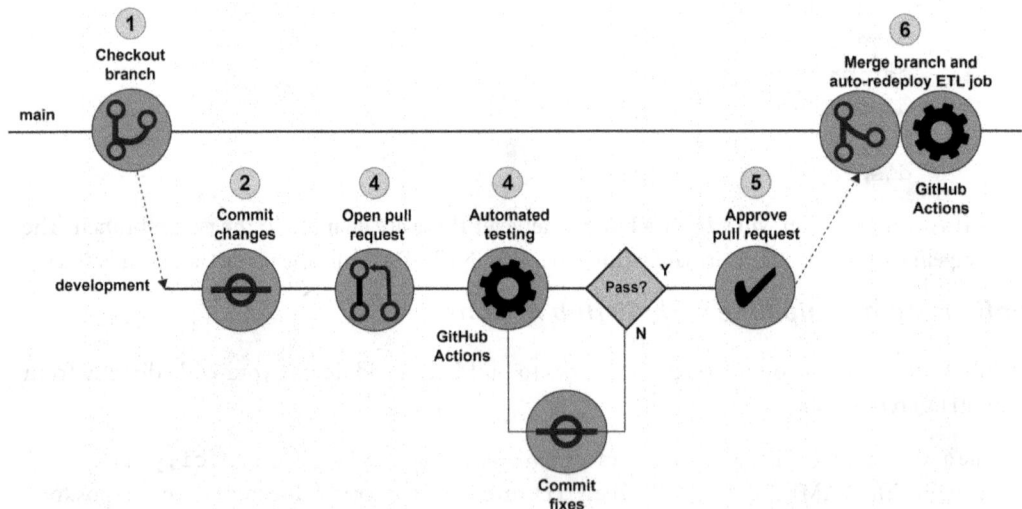

Figure 7.5 – CI workflow on GitHub Actions

Let's understand the workflow:

1.   The code is pushed to the GitHub repository.

2.   GitHub Actions automatically triggers a CI job.

3.   The job runs build and test scripts to ensure code quality.

Step 3 – setting up CD

Once the CI pipeline successfully builds and tests the code, we need to automate the process of delivering this code to different environments, such as staging or production.

Configuring a CD pipeline in Azure DevOps

To set up a CD pipeline in Azure DevOps follow these steps:

1.   **Release pipeline setup**: Navigate to the **Releases** section in Azure DevOps and create a new release pipeline. Link it to the output of the CI pipeline.

2.   **Define environments**: Define multiple environments such as staging, QA, and production. Each environment can have different deployment conditions—staging might require automated deployment, while production might need manual approval.

3.   **Configure deployment tasks**: Add tasks to the release pipeline that will deploy the build artifacts to the desired environment. For example, you can deploy to **Azure App Service**.

Let's look at an example deployment task:

I.   Use the Azure App Service **Deploy** task to publish your web application to Azure.

II.   Set up deployment slots (staging and production) to make sure your changes are thoroughly tested before going live.

Configuring a CD pipeline with GitHub Actions

For GitHub Actions, you can create a new workflow to automate deployment after a successful build.

Let's look at an example GitHub Actions CD workflow:

```
name   Azure Projects
on:
  push:
    branches:
      - main
jobs:
  deploy:
    runs-on   ubuntu-latest
```

```
steps:
- name  Checkout code
  uses  actions/checkout@v2
- name  Set up .NET
  uses  actions/setup-dotnet@v1
  with:
    dotnet-version  6.0
- name  Deploy to Azure Web App
  uses  azure/webapps-deploy@v2
  with:
    app-name  'my-azure-app'
    publish-profile  ${{ secrets.AZURE_PUBLISH_PROFILE }}
    package  '.'
```

In this example, GitHub Actions is configured to deploy the application to Azure App Service after successful changes are pushed to the main branch. The AZURE_PUBLISH_PROFILE secret is used to authenticate and securely deploy to Azure.

The following diagram illustrates the CD workflow:

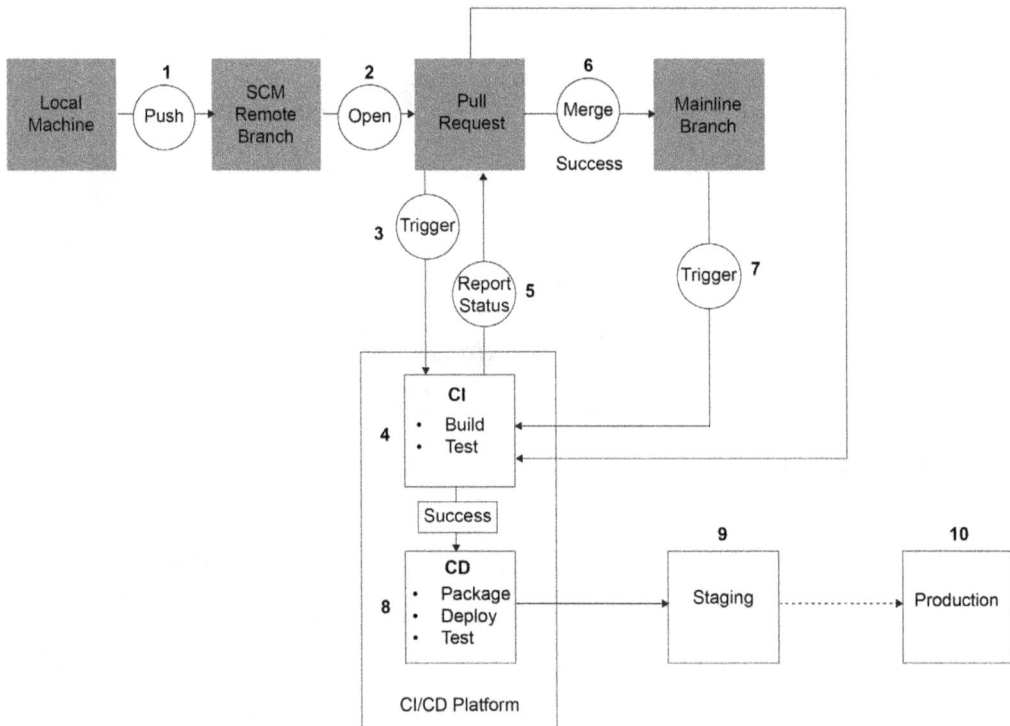

Figure 7.6 – CD workflow diagram

Let's understand the workflow:

1. The code is tested and built successfully.

2. The CD pipeline is triggered, deploying the application to a staging or production environment.

Step 4 – managing environment variables and secrets

It's important to manage configuration settings, environment variables, and sensitive information such as **API keys** or **database connection strings** securely within your pipeline.

To ensure a robust and secure pipeline, leveraging built-in tools and services to manage sensitive information is essential, such as through these methods:

- **Azure Key Vault integration**: Azure DevOps and GitHub Actions can integrate with Azure Key Vault to manage sensitive information securely. Secrets can be retrieved dynamically during the pipeline execution, ensuring that sensitive information is never hard-coded into configuration files.

- **GitHub Secrets**: GitHub Actions uses GitHub Secrets to store sensitive information securely. Secrets are encrypted and can be accessed during the workflow execution.

Step 5 – automating approval and manual intervention

While automation is a core benefit of CI/CD pipelines, there are times when manual intervention is required, such as approvals before deploying to production. Azure DevOps allows you to add **manual approval gates** before releasing to critical environments. Similarly, GitHub Actions can be configured to require a **manual review** step before proceeding with deployment to sensitive environments.

By understanding the basics of CI/CD pipeline creation, you can now move on to integrating additional components such as **automated testing** to further enhance the robustness of your application delivery process.

In the next section, we will discuss integrating automated testing into your CI/CD pipeline to ensure code quality and reduce risks when deploying software updates.

Integrating automated testing into your CI/CD pipeline to ensure code quality

The third learning objective of this chapter is to understand how to integrate automated testing into your CI/CD pipeline to ensure that your code is robust, reliable, and ready for deployment. Automated testing is an essential aspect of the CI/CD process, as it allows teams to identify and rectify issues early in the development cycle, improving overall software quality and reducing risks associated with code changes.

Automated testing is a cornerstone of building reliable and robust CI/CD pipelines. By integrating unit tests, integration tests, and end-to-end tests into your CI/CD workflow, you ensure that the software you deliver is thoroughly tested at every stage, catching issues early and reducing risks. Tools such as Azure DevOps and GitHub Actions provide excellent support for configuring automated tests, reporting results, and notifying teams of issues in real time.

In this section, we will discuss the different types of testing that can be automated, how to implement them within Azure DevOps and GitHub Actions, and how automated testing fits into the overall CI/CD process.

Types of automated tests

When developing robust software, implementing a comprehensive testing strategy is essential to ensure quality and reliability. Here are some key tests that play a crucial role in the software development lifecycle:

- **Unit tests**: Unit testing involves testing individual units or components of the software to validate that each part performs as expected. These tests are typically fast to execute and provide immediate feedback to developers. They are the foundation of automated testing and are usually integrated into the CI process.

  For instance, in a web application, unit tests might be written to verify the functionality of individual methods that perform calculations, manipulate strings, or handle business logic.

- **Integration tests**: Integration testing validates how different modules or services work together. This ensures that various components in an application interact correctly. Integration tests are generally slower to execute compared to unit tests because they involve setting up and managing the interaction between multiple services.

  For example, in an e-commerce platform, integration tests might check how the payment gateway interacts with the order processing system to ensure orders are correctly processed and confirmed.

- **End-to-end (E2E) tests**: E2E tests simulate the end user experience by testing the entire application workflow from start to finish. These tests are essential for validating user journeys, such as adding an item to a cart, checking out, and receiving a confirmation email.

  For example, in a banking application, an E2E test could involve simulating a user logging in, transferring funds, and logging out, verifying that each step works seamlessly.

- **Performance tests**: Performance testing ensures that the application can handle anticipated load levels without significant degradation in performance. This type of testing often requires a dedicated environment to simulate real-world user activity.

  For example, performance tests for a media streaming service might simulate thousands of users streaming video simultaneously to ensure the system can maintain quality under load.

Integrating tests into your pipeline

Integrating tests into your pipeline is a critical step. By automating the testing process, you can catch errors early and streamline your development workflow. There are two popular platforms for implementing unit testing within your CI/CD pipelines: Azure DevOps and GitHub Actions.

Using Azure DevOps

In Azure DevOps, unit tests are usually integrated into the **build pipeline** as part of the CI process. Here is how you can set up unit testing.

Here's the test step we will be following – Azure DevOps pipelines are configured using a YAML file (`azure-pipelines.yml`). In the pipeline configuration, you can add a script to run unit tests immediately after the `build` step.

Here is an example configuration:

```
trigger:
  branches:
    include:
      - main
pool:
  vmImage 'ubuntu-latest'
steps:
- task UseDotNet@2
  inputs:
    packageType 'sdk'
    version '6.x'
- script dotnet build
  displayName 'Build Project'
- script dotnet test
  displayName 'Run Unit Tests'
```

In this configuration, unit tests are run as soon as the code is built. Any failure will stop the pipeline and prevent the changes from moving forward until they are resolved.

Using GitHub Actions

For GitHub Actions, you can define a similar workflow to build the application and run unit tests. You can create a YAML file (`.github/workflows/ci.yml`) to define the workflow.

Here is an example workflow configuration:

```
name Project Pipeline
on:
  push:
```

```
      branches:
        - main
jobs:
  build:
    runs-on ubuntu-latest
    steps:
    - name Checkout code
      uses actions/checkout@v2
    - name Set up .NET
      uses actions/setup-dotnet@v1
      with:
        dotnet-version 6.0
    - name Build Project
      run dotnet build
    - name Run Unit Tests
      run dotnet test
```

In this GitHub Actions workflow, the `dotnet test` command is used to run all unit tests. If any tests fail, the workflow fails, ensuring that errors are caught early.

Adding integration and E2E tests

For integration tests and E2E tests, additional tools and frameworks may be required. These tests often need a more comprehensive environment setup since they involve more than one part of the system.

In Azure DevOps, integration tests can be effectively managed with features such as the following:

- **Environment setup**: Before running integration tests, Azure DevOps allows you to configure pre-deployment steps to provision necessary resources (e.g., test databases)

- **Service connections**: You may need to set up service connections to external services that are part of the integration, such as databases or APIs

To configure integration tests in your pipeline, consider the following steps:

1. Add a step in the pipeline to spin up test instances of dependent services.

2. Use scripts to run integration tests that validate the interaction between components.

E2E testing with Selenium or Cypress in GitHub Actions

E2E tests using tools such as Selenium or Cypress can be integrated into GitHub Actions by adding a dedicated job that provisions a browser environment to run the tests.

Here is an example E2E test configuration:

```
jobs:
  e2e:
    runs-on ubuntu-latest
    steps:
    - name Checkout code
      uses actions/checkout@v2
    - name Set up Node.js
      uses actions/setup-node@v2
      with:
        node-version 14
    - name Install Cypress
      run npm install cypress
    - name Run E2E Tests
      run npx cypress run
```

This job sets up Node.js, installs Cypress, and runs E2E tests that simulate how a user interacts with the application.

Implementing testing stages in the CI/CD pipeline

In both Azure DevOps and GitHub Actions, you can organize your pipeline into multiple stages—such as *build*, *test*, and *deploy*—each dedicated to a specific aspect of the process:

- The **build stage** compiles the code

- The **test stage** runs all tests—unit, integration, and E2E

- The **deploy stage** deploys the application to a target environment if all tests pass successfully

This structure ensures that only tested, high-quality code reaches production, reducing the risk of introducing bugs and regressions.

Configuring testing reports and notifications

Both Azure DevOps and GitHub Actions allow you to configure test reports and send notifications if a test fails. Reporting tools such as **JUnit** or **xUnit** can be used to generate detailed testing reports that provide insights into failures, helping developers diagnose and resolve issues quickly.

To leverage these capabilities effectively, consider the following options:

- **Azure DevOps test reports**: Azure DevOps can generate rich reports for each test run, including logs, pass/fail statistics, and failure details. These reports are available in the pipeline summary.

- **GitHub Actions with third-party tools**: You can integrate GitHub Actions with third-party reporting services such as **Codecov** or **Coveralls** to visualize test coverage and results, providing better insights into code quality.

Real-world example of automated testing for a food delivery application

Consider a food delivery application that needs to be highly reliable, with features such as food ordering, payment processing, and order tracking. Automated testing is implemented at various levels:

- **Unit tests**: These verify the functionality of core business logic, such as calculating delivery charges based on distance or applying promotions.

- **Integration tests**: Integration tests validate interactions between the payment gateway and the order processing system. This ensures that when a payment is completed, the order status is updated correctly.

- **E2E tests**: E2E tests simulate a customer journey where a user browses the menu, selects items, places an order, and completes payment. These tests validate the full workflow to ensure there are no breaking points.

By integrating all these tests into a CI/CD pipeline using Azure DevOps, the development team ensures that the application is rigorously tested before deployment, reducing risks and ensuring that new updates are reliable and consistent.

In the next section, we will cover how to configure build and release stages to automate the deployment of applications to Azure services, ensuring that the entire process—from coding to delivery—is automated, consistent, and reliable.

Configuring build and release stages to automate application deployment to Azure services

The final learning objective of this chapter is to configure build and release stages to automate the deployment of applications to Azure services. Configuring build and release stages in your CI/CD pipeline automates the process of preparing and deploying applications to Azure services, making the delivery process faster, more consistent, and less prone to errors. In this section, you will learn how to set up build and release pipelines using Azure DevOps and GitHub Actions, how to deploy applications to services such as Azure App Service and **Azure Kubernetes Service** (**AKS**), and how to use different deployment strategies to minimize downtime.

In this section, we will walk through how to automate the deployment process after building, testing, and ensuring the code quality. Deploying software to cloud environments like Azure can be complex and repetitive, which is why automating these processes is essential for maintaining consistency, reducing errors, and enabling faster, more frequent releases.

We'll focus on understanding the components of the build and release stages, how to configure them using Azure DevOps and GitHub Actions, and best practices for automating application deployment to services such as Azure App Service, AKS, and Azure Functions.

Build stage – preparing code for deployment

The build stage is responsible for taking the source code and turning it into a deployable package. This stage typically involves compiling the code, running any necessary scripts, packaging the artifacts, and ensuring that they are ready for the deployment environment.

Configuring the build stage with Azure DevOps

In the following steps, we will be creating stages with Azure DevOps:

1. **Setting up a build pipeline**:

    I.   Configure the build pipeline in Azure DevOps to pull the latest code from your repository.

    II.   Add steps to execute the necessary `build` scripts and generate artifacts.

    III. Ensure the artifacts, such as binaries, Docker images, or other build outputs, are stored for deployment.

2. **Defining the YAML file**:

    I.   Create or update an `azure-pipelines.yml` file to define the steps of your build process.

    II.   Specify each stage, including `build` scripts, artifact generation, and storage configurations.

    III. Validate the YAML file to ensure it adheres to Azure DevOps syntax and requirements.

    Here is an example build configuration:

```
trigger:
  branches:
    include:
      - main
pool:
  vmImage  'ubuntu-latest'
steps:
- task  UseDotNet@2
  inputs:
    packageType  'sdk'
    version  '6.x'
- script  dotnet publish -c Release -o $(Build.
ArtifactStagingDirectory)
  displayName  'Publish Artifacts'
- task  PublishBuildArtifacts@1
```

```
    inputs:
      pathToPublish  '$(Build.ArtifactStagingDirectory)'
      artifactName  'drop'
```

In this YAML file, the `dotnet publish` command creates a release build of the application, which is then stored as an artifact using the `PublishBuildArtifacts` task.

Configuring the build stage with GitHub Actions

Similar to the steps and examples in the previous subsection, GitHub Actions can be configured to create a build pipeline that compiles and packages the application.

Here is a workflow configuration for building artifacts:

```
name  Azure Projects
on:
  push:
    branches:
      - main
jobs:
  build:
    runs-on  ubuntu-latest
    steps:
    - name  Checkout code
      uses  actions/checkout@v2
    - name  Set up .NET
      uses  actions/setup-dotnet@v1
      with:
        dotnet-version  6.0
    - name  Publish Artifacts
      run  dotnet publish -c Release -o ./publish
```

In this workflow, after building the project, the `dotnet publish` command packages the application, making it ready for deployment.

Release stage – automating application deployment

The release stage takes the artifacts generated during the build stage and deploys them to the desired environment, such as staging, testing, or production. Automating this process reduces manual intervention and ensures consistency.

Configuring the release stage in Azure DevOps

Azure DevOps release pipelines automate the process of deploying applications across different environments. Release pipelines are visually configured to include various stages, such as staging and production, each with its own set of tasks.

Here are the steps to set up a release pipeline:

1. **Create a release pipeline**: Go to **Releases** in Azure DevOps and create a new release pipeline. Link it to the artifacts generated by the build pipeline.

2. **Define deployment stages**: Set up different stages for environments, such as staging and production. Each stage can include tasks such as deploying the web app to Azure App Service or AKS.

3. **Add a deployment task for Azure App Service**: Use the Azure App Service **Deploy** feature to create a deployment task. Configure it to deploy from the `drop` folder where the build artifacts were published.

   Here is an example deployment configuration:

   ```
   - task  AzureWebApp@1
     inputs:
       azureSubscription  'Your-Azure-Subscription'
       appName  'my-azure-web-app'
       package  '$(System.DefaultWorkingDirectory)/drop/**/*.zip'
   ```

   This task will take the package and deploy it to Azure App Service, making it accessible to users.

Configuring the release stage with GitHub Actions

In GitHub Actions, the release stage is configured using a similar workflow that deploys the published artifacts to the desired Azure environment.

Here is an example of the GitHub Actions deployment workflow to show how it can be configured:

```
name  Deploy to Azure Projects
on:
  push:
    branches:
      - main
jobs:
  deploy:
    runs-on  ubuntu-latest
    steps:
    - name  Checkout code
      uses  actions/checkout@v2
    - name  Set up .NET
      uses  actions/setup-dotnet@v1
      with:
        dotnet-version  6.0
    - name  Deploy to Azure Web App
      uses  azure/webapps-deploy@v2
      with:
        app-name  'my-azure-web-app'
        publish-profile  ${{ secrets.AZURE_PUBLISH_PROFILE }}
        package  './publish'
```

In this workflow, the `azure/webapps-deploy` action deploys the application to Azure App Service using a `publish profile` secret stored securely in GitHub Secrets.

Deploying to AKS

If your application is containerized, AKS is a popular choice for deploying and managing containers at scale. Here's how deployment can be automated:

1. **Containerize the application**: Use Docker to containerize your application. Publish the Docker image to a container registry, such as **Azure Container Registry (ACR)**.

2. **Deploy to AKS**: Configure Azure DevOps or GitHub Actions to deploy the Docker image from ACR to AKS. Use a Kubernetes manifest file to define the deployment specifications.

    Here is an example configuration for GitHub Actions:

    ```
    - name  Set up Docker Buildx
      uses  docker/setup-buildx-action@v1
    - name  Log in to Azure Container Registry
      uses  azure/docker-login@v1
      with:
        login-server  mycontainerregistry.azurecr.io
        username  ${{ secrets.AZURE_CLIENT_ID }}
        password  ${{ secrets.AZURE_CLIENT_SECRET }}
    - name  Build and Push Docker Image
      run  |
        docker build -t mycontainerregistry.azurecr.io/my-app:latest

        docker push mycontainerregistry.azurecr.io/my-app:latest
    - name  Deploy to AKS
      uses  azure/k8s-deploy@v1
      with:
        kubeconfig  ${{ secrets.KUBECONFIG }}
        manifests  |
          ./k8s/deployment.yaml
    ```

This workflow builds the Docker image, pushes it to ACR, and then deploys it to AKS using a Kubernetes manifest file.

Implementing deployment strategies

When deploying applications, it's important to consider different deployment strategies to ensure minimal downtime and risk:

- **Blue-green deployment**: This involves maintaining two identical environments—*blue* and *green*. The blue environment is active, while the new version is deployed to the green environment. After verification, traffic is switched to the green environment, minimizing downtime.

- **Canary deployment**: This involves releasing new features to a small subset of users before rolling them out to everyone. This allows teams to verify that the new version works correctly with minimal risk.

- **Rolling updates**: With rolling updates, the application is gradually updated across the deployment. This ensures that parts of the application remain active and available while others are updated.

- **Feature flags**: Feature flags allow you to enable or disable specific features at runtime without redeploying the application. This enables safer experimentation, gradual rollouts, and instant rollbacks if needed, enhancing control over feature releases.

- **A/B testing**: A/B testing involves directing users to different versions of a feature to compare their performance. By analyzing user behavior and feedback, teams can make data-driven decisions to optimize user experience and application functionality.

In this section, we delved into the automation of deployment processes in cloud environments such as Azure. By exploring the build and release stages, you learned how to streamline deployments using tools such as Azure DevOps and GitHub Actions. This approach ensures consistency, minimizes errors, and accelerates delivery.

Configuring approval gates

For environments such as production, it's common to implement manual approval gates; consider the following options:

- Azure DevOps allows you to add **pre-deployment approvals** in the release pipeline. This ensures that a designated person reviews the deployment before it proceeds.

- In GitHub Actions, similar control can be implemented by requiring approvals for pull requests that trigger deployments.

Monitoring and rollbacks

To ensure that deployments are successful and to respond quickly if issues arise, you can implement these strategies:

- **Monitoring with Azure Monitor and Application Insights**: Use **Azure Monitor** and **Application Insights** to track the performance of your application post-deployment. This helps in identifying issues that may have arisen due to the deployment.

- **Automatic rollbacks**: If a deployment fails or results in unexpected issues, configuring an automatic rollback ensures that the previous stable version is reinstated, minimizing disruption to users.

By implementing monitoring and rollback strategies, you can quickly detect and resolve issues, ensuring stable and reliable deployments. These practices help maintain application health and minimize downtime, reinforcing the effectiveness of your CI/CD pipeline.

Summary

In this chapter, we explored the foundational concepts and advantages of CI/CD, emphasizing how they streamline software development through faster, more reliable releases. We learned how to build and configure a CI/CD pipeline using tools such as Azure DevOps and GitHub Actions, enabling automated workflows that enhance productivity. Additionally, we integrated automated testing within the CI/CD process to maintain high code quality and prevent issues before deployment. Finally, we configured build and release stages to automate the deployment of applications to Azure services, ensuring consistent and efficient delivery of software updates.

In the next chapter, we will explore how to design and build a containerized solution on Azure, focusing on how to package applications as containers and manage them effectively using AKS.

Join the CloudPro Newsletter with 44000+ Subscribers

Want to know what's happening in cloud computing, DevOps, IT administration, networking, and more? Scan the QR code to subscribe to **CloudPro**, our weekly newsletter for 44,000+ tech professionals who want to stay informed and ahead of the curve.

`https://packt.link/cloudpro`

8

Designing and Building a Containerized Solution on Azure

In today's cloud-driven era, **containerization** has emerged as a powerful approach for developing and deploying applications in a more efficient, scalable, and portable manner. **Containers**, with their lightweight and self-contained architecture, allow developers to package applications and their dependencies together, ensuring that the application runs consistently across different environments, whether it's a developer's laptop, on-premises servers, or in the cloud.

Azure Kubernetes Service (**AKS**) is Azure's managed Kubernetes offering, allowing you to deploy, manage, and scale containerized applications using the popular Kubernetes orchestrator. This chapter is dedicated to understanding how to design and build containerized solutions on Azure, focusing on the best practices of containerization, the use of AKS, and how to leverage the benefits of containers for modern, scalable applications.

Building containerized solutions offers several advantages over traditional **virtual machine** (**VM**)-based deployments. Containers provide isolation and portability, enabling developers to create consistent runtime environments across multiple platforms. Containerized solutions help optimize resource usage, enhance scalability, and reduce overhead by packaging application code along with its dependencies, allowing for seamless migration and scaling.

AKS simplifies the orchestration of containerized applications. It automates tasks such as scaling, health monitoring, and load balancing, making it an ideal choice for managing containerized applications at scale.

We will delve into container architecture, the process of creating and managing containers, and how to automate deployments using Azure DevOps or GitHub Actions. By the end of this chapter, you'll have a strong understanding of how to build containerized applications and orchestrate them with Kubernetes, ensuring they can scale, recover from failures, and handle diverse workloads efficiently.

In this chapter, we will be covering the following learning objectives:

- Understand the basics of containers and their significance in modern application development
- Build and run Docker containers for application development and deployment
- Set up and manage a Kubernetes cluster using AKS
- Deploy, scale, and update containerized applications on AKS

Now, let's get started with the first learning objective.

Understand the basics of containers and their significance in modern application development

The first learning objective of this chapter is to understand the fundamentals of containers and containerization. This is crucial for anyone looking to build modern applications in the cloud, especially using platforms such as AKS. Containers allow developers to package applications and their dependencies into portable, isolated units that run consistently across various environments, making it easier to develop, test, and deploy software at scale.

In this section, we will dive deep into what containers are, how they differ from traditional VMs, and why containerization has become the cornerstone of modern cloud-native application development. We will also explore best practices for creating, managing, and deploying containerized applications.

What are containers?

Containers are lightweight, stand-alone, and executable software packages that include everything needed to run an application—such as the code, runtime, libraries, environment variables, and system tools. Unlike VMs, which encapsulate the entire OS, containers share the host OS kernel but isolate the application environment. This allows containers to be significantly more efficient and portable.

Containers ensure that applications run consistently across different environments, whether on a developer's local machine, a test server, or in a production cloud environment. This consistency makes them particularly useful for **DevOps** and **microservices** architectures, where applications are broken down into smaller, independently deployable services.

How containers differ from VMs

Although both containers and VMs provide isolation, they do so in fundamentally different ways. Understanding the differences in the following table helps clarify why containers are more lightweight and flexible than VMs.

Feature	Virtual Machines	Containers
Isolation	Full isolation with a separate OS for each VM	Process-level isolation with a shared OS kernel
Resource usage	Requires resources for full OS and applications	Shares host OS, resulting in lower overhead
Startup time	Slow (minutes)	Fast (seconds or milliseconds)
Portability	Difficult to move between different environments	Highly portable across different environments
Overhead	Heavyweight, requires dedicated resources per VM	Lightweight, minimal overhead

Table 8.1 – Containers versus VMs

Figure 8.1 depicts a container architecture diagram:

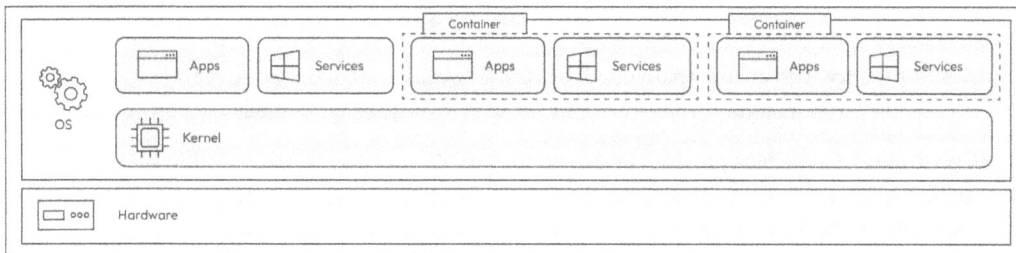

Figure 8.1 – Container architecture diagram

Figure 8.2 depicts a VM architecture diagram:

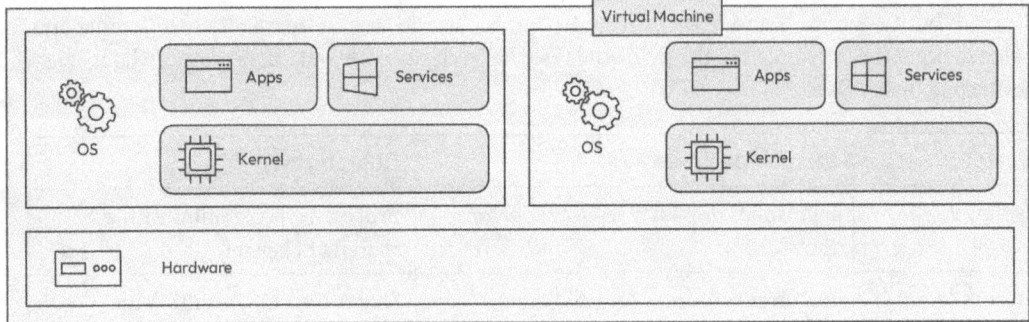

Figure 8.2 – VM architecture diagram

As seen in the preceding diagram, containers run on top of the host OS and share the OS kernel, whereas VMs require their own separate OS, leading to higher overhead and slower startup times.

Benefits of using containers

Containers have become essential in modern application development for several reasons:

- **Portability**: Containers package the application along with its dependencies and configuration, making it easy to move the containerized application between different environments (development, testing, staging, and production). This portability eliminates the *it works on my machine* problem, ensuring that the application behaves the same across all environments.

  A best practice is to ensure that your **Dockerfile** includes all necessary dependencies for the application to run smoothly in any environment. Keep the base image minimal to improve efficiency.

- **Consistency**: Containers provide consistency by bundling all dependencies within the container, including libraries, environment settings, and system dependencies. This makes containers particularly effective for DevOps pipelines, where consistency across development, testing, and production environments is key.

  A best practice is to maintain version control for your Dockerfiles and configuration settings. Always test containers in a staging environment before deploying them to production.

- **Isolation**: Each container operates in isolation, meaning that the software running inside the container does not affect other containers running on the same host. This ensures that different applications and services can run on the same host without conflicts.

  A best practice is to use containers to break down large, monolithic applications into **microservices**. This provides better isolation and allows for independent scaling and deployment.

- **Efficiency**: Containers share the host OS kernel, which means they require fewer resources than VMs. This makes them lightweight and much faster to start. Containers also allow multiple instances of an application to run on a single server, making them ideal for **cloud-native applications** that need to scale quickly.

  A best practice is to regularly monitor container resource usage using tools such as Azure Monitor or Prometheus to optimize resource consumption. Scale containers dynamically using Kubernetes to handle varying workloads efficiently.

- **DevOps and CI/CD**: Containers play a vital role in **continuous integration** (CI) and **continuous delivery** (CD) pipelines. With containers, you can automate the testing and deployment of your applications in a consistent environment. Docker, in particular, integrates seamlessly with CI/CD tools such as **Azure DevOps** and **GitHub Actions**.

  A best practice is to use CI/CD pipelines to automate the build, test, and deployment of containerized applications. Set up automated tests for container builds to catch issues early in the development cycle.

How containers work

At a high level, containers are created using **Docker**, a platform that automates the process of creating, running, and managing containers. Containers are built from **images**, which are read-only templates that include the application code, dependencies, and runtime:

- **Docker images**: A Docker image is a blueprint for creating containers. It contains everything needed to run the application, including system libraries, dependencies, and the application code itself. Images are built using a Dockerfile, which defines the instructions for creating the image.

- **Docker containers**: Once an image is created, it can be used to launch a Docker container. A container is a running instance of an image, complete with its own isolated environment. Containers can be started, stopped, and scaled as needed.

- **Dockerfile**: The Dockerfile is the script that tells Docker how to build the image. It includes instructions such as which base image to use, which dependencies to install, and which commands to run when the container starts.

  Here is an example Dockerfile:

```
# Use a base image
FROM node:14
# Set the working directory inside the container
WORKDIR /app
# Copy package.json and install dependencies
COPY package.json .
RUN npm install
# Copy the rest of the application code
```

```
COPY . .
# Expose the application on port 3000
EXPOSE 3000
# Start the application
CMD ["npm", "start"]
```

In this example, a simple Node.js application is being containerized. The Dockerfile defines the base image (node:14), installs the necessary dependencies (npm install), and specifies how to start the application (npm start).

Best practices for containerization

To get the most out of containers, it's essential to follow best practices when building and managing them:

- **Keep images lightweight**: Use minimal base images to reduce the size of your container and improve startup time. This also reduces the attack surface for security vulnerabilities.

  Use images such as **Alpine Linux** or minimal versions of popular distributions to keep containers lean.

- **Use multi-stage builds**: Docker supports **multi-stage builds**, which allow you to create smaller, more efficient images by separating the build process into multiple stages. The final image only includes the necessary binaries and dependencies, while the build artifacts are discarded:

```
FROM node:14 as builder
WORKDIR /app
COPY . .
RUN npm install && npm run build
FROM node:14-alpine
WORKDIR /app
COPY --from=builder /app/build /app
CMD ["npm", "start"]
```

  This example creates a multi-stage build where the first stage compiles the application, and the second stage creates a minimal image with only the necessary build artifacts.

- **Leverage Docker volumes for persistence**: Containers are ephemeral by nature, meaning that any data stored within the container is lost when the container stops or is removed. Use **Docker volumes** to store persistent data outside of the container, ensuring that important data is not lost between restarts.

- **Security best practices**: Some of these are as follows:

  - Run containers with **non-root users** to minimize security risks

- Regularly scan your Docker images for known vulnerabilities using tools such as **Docker Scan** or **Aqua Security**
- Use signed and trusted images from verified sources to reduce the risk of using compromised base images

- **Use Kubernetes for orchestration**: While Docker helps with building and managing individual containers, **Kubernetes** is necessary for managing containers at scale. Kubernetes provides features such as **automatic scaling**, **self-healing**, and **load balancing**, making it ideal for large-scale, containerized applications.

Hypothetical use case – microservices in a retail application

Consider a retail application with multiple services, such as a **product catalog**, **order management**, **payment processing**, and **user authentication**. Each service is containerized and runs in its own isolated environment, allowing independent development and scaling:

- **Product catalog**: The catalog service is written in Node.js and containerized using Docker. The image includes the necessary dependencies (such as Express.js) and is deployed to a Kubernetes cluster.

- **Order management**: The order management service is written in Python and runs in its own container, interacting with the **PostgreSQL** database. Each microservice is isolated but can communicate with other services through **API gateways**.

- **Scaling**: The payment processing service needs to handle high volumes of transactions during sales periods. With Kubernetes, additional instances of the payment service container can be automatically deployed to handle the increased load.

By using containers, the development team can work independently on different services, deploy them frequently, and scale them as needed without affecting other parts of the application.

Understanding the fundamentals of containers and containerization is a critical first step in building modern, scalable, and portable applications. Containers provide an isolated and consistent environment for applications, enabling seamless movement across development, testing, and production environments. By following best practices such as using minimal images, multi-stage builds, and leveraging Kubernetes for orchestration, you can ensure that your containerized applications are efficient, scalable, and secure.

In the next section, we will explore how to build and deploy containers using Docker, where you'll get hands-on experience in creating Docker containers and running them locally and in the cloud.

Build and run Docker containers for application development and deployment

The second learning objective of this chapter is to build and run Docker containers for application development and deployment. Docker containers play a pivotal role in modern application development by providing isolated environments that package an application and its dependencies, ensuring consistency across different environments. In this section, we will cover the process of building Docker containers, running them locally, and deploying them to production environments, such as Azure.

We will break down the steps to create Docker images using Dockerfiles, understand how to run and manage containers, and explore best practices for container development and deployment.

Why Docker containers?

Docker simplifies the process of packaging applications into containers, which can be deployed on any system that runs Docker. Whether you're working in development, testing, or production, Docker ensures that the application runs the same way everywhere.

By using Docker, developers can do the following:

- Package an application and its dependencies together, creating a consistent and portable environment
- Enable faster development by containerizing each part of an application (e.g., services or databases) and running them independently
- Easily scale and manage applications in production environments such as AKS

Building Docker containers – a high-level overview

The process of building a Docker container involves defining the necessary steps in a Dockerfile. A Dockerfile is a script that tells Docker how to assemble a container image. It contains instructions such as specifying the base image, installing dependencies, copying application code, and defining the command to run when the container starts:

1. **Choosing a base image:** Start by selecting a base image that aligns with your application's technology stack. For example, if you're developing a Node.js application, you might use node:14 as your base image. It's important to choose lightweight images to reduce the overall size and speed up deployment.

   A best practice is to use lightweight images such as Alpine Linux to minimize container size, which improves performance and security.

2. **Adding dependencies**: The next step is to install any necessary dependencies. In a Node.js application, this could be running npm install to install the required packages for your app.

   A best practice is to always pin the versions of dependencies in your Dockerfile to avoid unexpected issues when updating packages.

3. **Copying application code**: The application source code is then copied into the container. This allows the container to run the code as if it were on any other machine.

   A best practice is to structure your Dockerfile so that dependency installation happens before copying the full source code. This enables Docker to cache earlier layers, speeding up future builds when the application code changes.

4. **Setting environment variables and ports**: Finally, you'll expose any necessary ports and define environment variables that your app needs to run.

   A best practice is to externalize sensitive data such as passwords or API keys through environment variables or secret management tools (e.g., Azure Key Vault), instead of hardcoding them into your Dockerfile.

Running Docker containers

Once you have built a Docker image, the next step is to run it as a container. Running a Docker container is as simple as executing a command that launches the container with the desired configuration:

- **Mapping ports**: When running a container, you'll often need to expose it to the outside world by mapping container ports to the host machine's ports. For instance, mapping port 3000 on your container to port 3000 on your local machine allows you to access the application in the browser.

  A best practice is to use standard port mappings across development, testing, and production environments to avoid unnecessary configuration changes.

- **Managing containers**: Docker provides powerful tools for managing running containers, such as starting, stopping, and viewing logs from containers.

  A best practice is to use Docker Compose to manage multi-container applications, where different parts of your application (such as a web app, database, and cache) run as separate containers.

Best practices for Dockerfile and container management

When building and running Docker containers, there are several best practices to ensure efficient, secure, and maintainable containerized applications, such as the following:

- **Keep your Dockerfile clean and lean**:
  - Use minimal base images such as Alpine Linux
  - Organize Dockerfile commands logically to minimize rebuild times
  - Remove unnecessary files and dependencies during the build process to reduce image size

- **Leverage multi-stage builds**: Multi-stage builds allow you to separate the build environment from the final production environment, ensuring that only necessary binaries and dependencies are included in the final image. This practice results in smaller, more efficient containers.

  For example, in a multi-stage build, you can use one stage to compile the source code and another to build the runtime environment, only including what's needed in the final image.

- **Optimize image layers**: Each instruction in the Dockerfile creates a layer in the resulting image. It's a best practice to minimize the number of layers by grouping related commands together, as this can significantly reduce image size and build times.

  For example, instead of having separate commands for copying files and installing dependencies, group them to make the build process more efficient.

- **Use volumes for persistent data**: Containers are designed to be ephemeral. If you need to store persistent data (such as database files or logs), use Docker volumes to store the data outside the container's filesystem. This ensures data persistence even if the container is stopped or deleted.

  A best practice is to use **Docker volumes** or **Azure Files** for data persistence, ensuring that critical data is not lost when containers are stopped.

- **Security considerations**:

  - Run containers with non-root users to limit the potential attack surface

  - Regularly scan your Docker images for vulnerabilities using tools such as Aqua Security or Docker Scan

  - Sign and verify images using **Docker Content Trust** to ensure that only trusted images are deployed to production environments

Pushing Docker images to a registry

Once your Docker image is built, you need to push it to a container registry for easy deployment. A container registry is a centralized store for Docker images that can be accessed from anywhere:

- **Docker Hub**: The default public registry for Docker images. It's easy to use and ideal for open source projects.

- **Azure Container Registry (ACR)**: ACR is a private registry provided by Azure that integrates seamlessly with other Azure services, such as AKS and Azure DevOps. This is ideal for managing containerized applications in production environments.

  A best practice can be to use ACR for private images and integrate it with your CI/CD pipelines to streamline the build and deployment process.

- **Tagging images**: Tagging images with version numbers or environment-specific tags (e.g., `:latest`, `:staging`, or `:prod`) is important for version control and environment isolation.

  A best practice can be to tag Docker images with specific versions or semantic versioning to avoid confusion and ensure you are deploying the correct version of your app.

Deploying Docker containers to Azure

After pushing your Docker image to a registry, the next step is deploying the container to a cloud environment such as **AKS** or **Azure App Service**.

- **AKS**: AKS is a fully managed Kubernetes service that automates the deployment, scaling, and operations of containerized applications. AKS is ideal for applications that need to scale dynamically and require advanced orchestration features like rolling updates and self-healing.

  A best practice can be to use **Helm charts** to deploy complex applications to AKS. Helm charts are Kubernetes packages that help manage application deployment and versioning in a Kubernetes environment.

- **Azure App Service**: Azure App Service also supports containerized applications. It is easier to set up and manage than AKS for smaller applications or simple use cases that don't require advanced orchestration.

  A best practice can be that for smaller applications or web services, **Azure App Service for Containers** is a simpler alternative to AKS, providing built-in scaling and security features.

Hypothetical containerizing of a microservice architecture

Consider a microservices-based application where each service—such as user authentication, order management, and payment processing—is containerized and deployed independently. By using Docker, each microservice can be developed, tested, and deployed in isolation, with its dependencies packaged into a container. This provides scalability, as each service can be deployed and scaled based on individual resource demands.

Imagine a scenario where an e-commerce company runs several services, such as the following:

- **Authentication service**: Runs in a container with all necessary dependencies (e.g., user validation libraries). It's deployed independently to AKS.

- **Order service**: Another microservice responsible for managing customer orders, packaged and deployed in a different container.

- **Payment gateway**: A service that handles payment processing, also containerized for consistency and scalability.

Each of these services is containerized and deployed to AKS, where Kubernetes manages the scaling, health monitoring, and load balancing across the microservices.

Building and running Docker containers is foundational for modern application development, allowing for the isolation, portability, and scalability required for cloud-native applications. By leveraging Docker, you can ensure that your applications run consistently across development, testing, and production environments. Deploying these containers to cloud environments such as AKS or Azure App Service allows for the efficient scaling and management of applications in production.

Next, we will explore Kubernetes orchestration and AKS, where you will learn how to manage containers at scale, ensuring that they remain reliable, scalable, and self-healing.

Setting up and managing a Kubernetes cluster using AKS

In this section, we will explore Kubernetes—the leading platform for container orchestration—and how it integrates with AKS to manage containerized applications at scale. Kubernetes automates the deployment, scaling, and operations of containers, making it ideal for complex and high-demand applications in production environments. In this section, we'll break down the key components of Kubernetes, understand how AKS simplifies Kubernetes management, and examine best practices for orchestrating containers in the cloud.

Why use Kubernetes for orchestration?

As you scale containerized applications, managing containers manually becomes inefficient and error-prone. This is where Kubernetes comes in. Kubernetes automates many of the operational tasks required to run containers at scale, such as the following:

- **Automatic scaling** of containerized applications based on load
- **Self-healing** by restarting failed containers or replacing unhealthy nodes
- **Rolling updates** and **zero-downtime deployments**
- **Load balancing** across multiple containers

Using Kubernetes, organizations can efficiently manage large-scale applications that span hundreds or thousands of containers, ensuring reliability, performance, and minimal downtime.

Core Kubernetes concepts

To fully utilize Kubernetes, it's important to understand its key components, which form the foundation for orchestrating containers. They are as follows:

- **Pods**: The smallest deployable unit in Kubernetes, a **Pod** typically contains one container, but it can run multiple tightly coupled containers that share the same resources. Pods are ephemeral and can be created, destroyed, or scaled based on demand.
- **Nodes**: A **node** is a worker machine in Kubernetes that runs Pods. A Kubernetes cluster can have many nodes, and Kubernetes distributes Pod workloads across these nodes automatically.

- **Services**: A **Service** provides a stable network endpoint for a set of Pods, ensuring that clients can access the application even if the underlying Pods are replaced or restarted. Services abstract away the details of the containers and provide load balancing.

- **Deployments**: A **Deployment** defines the desired state of your application. It tells Kubernetes how many replicas of a Pod should be running and manages updates or rollbacks to the application.

- **Ingress: Ingress** manages external access to the services in a Kubernetes cluster. It provides routing rules to define how HTTP or HTTPS traffic is forwarded to services, typically allowing multiple services to share the same IP address.

Kubernetes architecture overview

The following diagram illustrates the high-level architecture of Kubernetes:

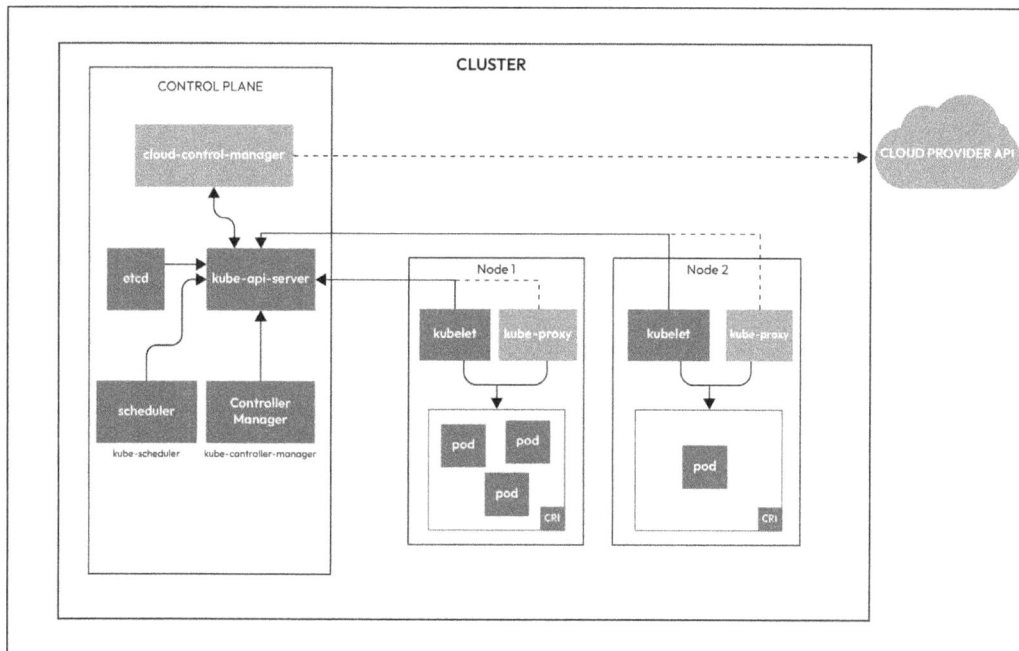

Figure 8.3 – High-level architecture view of Kubernetes

In this architecture, we have the following:

- **Pods** are the smallest units of execution and run on **nodes**.

- The **control plane** manages the overall cluster, scheduling workloads and monitoring the health of nodes.

- **Services** route traffic between Pods, while **Ingress** allows external traffic to access services in the cluster.

Azure Kubernetes Service (AKS)

AKS is a fully managed Kubernetes service that simplifies the process of running Kubernetes on Azure. AKS handles many operational tasks, such as scaling, patching, and upgrading the cluster, so that developers and operations teams can focus on deploying and managing applications.

The following are the key benefits of AKS:

- **Automated cluster management**: AKS handles the complexities of managing the Kubernetes control plane, including upgrades, scaling, and monitoring. You can focus on developing applications without worrying about the underlying infrastructure.

- **Seamless integration with Azure services**: AKS integrates with a wide range of Azure services, including **Azure Monitor** for tracking performance, **Entra ID** (formerly **Azure Active Directory**) for **role-based access control (RBAC)**, and **Azure DevOps** for CI/CD pipelines.

- **Built-in security**: AKS supports enterprise-grade security features such as network policies, Azure Policy for governance, and private cluster capabilities that isolate the Kubernetes API from the internet.

- **Cost efficiency**: AKS is cost-effective because you only pay for the worker nodes (VMs) that run your applications, while Azure manages the Kubernetes control plane for free. AKS also supports **cluster autoscaling**, automatically adjusting the number of nodes in your cluster based on demand.

Setting up an AKS cluster is a simple process using the **Azure portal**, **Azure CLI**, or an **ARM template**. The following are the essential steps to set up a fully functional AKS cluster:

1. **Creating the AKS cluster**: When creating a cluster, you can define the number of initial nodes, configure node pools, and choose the Kubernetes version. AKS provides flexible options for scaling and monitoring the cluster as needed.

2. **Networking configuration**: AKS offers two networking options—**kubenet** (basic) and **Azure CNI** (advanced). Azure CNI provides better control over Pod IP addresses by assigning each Pod an IP from the virtual network. This is ideal for enterprises requiring more advanced networking features.

3. **Integrating with Entra ID**: Integrating AKS with Entra ID enables secure RBAC for your cluster. This ensures that only authorized users can deploy applications or manage the cluster.

4. **Enabling monitoring**: You can enable **Azure Monitor** to capture logs and metrics from the cluster. This integration allows you to monitor the health and performance of your workloads, view container logs, and set up alerts for potential issues.

Some best practices for AKS

When working with AKS, it's important to follow some best practices to ensure the security, performance, and reliability of your Kubernetes applications:

- **Leverage node pools**: Use multiple node pools to separate different workloads. For example, you can use a dedicated node pool for compute-heavy applications and another for general-purpose workloads.

- **Use cluster autoscaling**: Enable **Cluster Autoscaler** to dynamically adjust the number of nodes in your AKS cluster based on application demand. This ensures that your cluster has enough capacity during peak times without over-provisioning resources when demand is low.

- **Apply resource limits**: Define resource requests and limits for each container in your Pods. This ensures that containers are allocated sufficient CPU and memory while preventing resource-hogging containers from affecting other workloads.

- **Network security**: Use **network security groups** (**NSGs**) and **network policies** to control the flow of traffic to and from your Kubernetes workloads. This can prevent unauthorized access and ensure that internal services are properly isolated from external networks.

- **Use Ingress controllers**: An Ingress controller simplifies managing external access to multiple services. For production workloads, use Azure's **Application Gateway Ingress Controller**, which integrates with AKS to manage secure HTTP(S) traffic routing and SSL termination.

- **Implement Pod Security Admission (PSA)**: Utilize PSA to enforce security policies at the namespace level. PSA helps restrict the permissions of Pods based on predefined security standards (privileged, baseline, and restricted). By implementing PSA, you can prevent potential security risks, such as running privileged containers or using unsafe volume types, thereby improving the overall security posture of your AKS cluster.

Deploying applications to AKS

Once your AKS cluster is set up, deploying containerized applications is straightforward. You'll use **Kubernetes manifests** to define how your application should run in the cluster. A Kubernetes manifest is a YAML file that describes the desired state for your application, including the container image to use, the number of replicas, and the ports to expose.

For example, consider a microservices-based e-commerce platform. You can deploy multiple microservices (such as order management, inventory, and payment processing) to AKS, with each service running in its own Pods. Kubernetes ensures that each service is independently scaled based on traffic and performance needs.

To deploy applications to AKS, follow these steps:

1. **Write Kubernetes manifests**: Define the Deployment and Service configurations in YAML files. For example, the manifest might specify that the payment processing service should run three replicas (Pods) and expose port 8080 for external access.

2. **Use Helm charts**: For more complex deployments, use **Helm charts** to manage application configurations. Helm is a package manager for Kubernetes that simplifies the deployment and management of Kubernetes applications, especially when deploying multiple services or complex configurations.

3. **Automate with CI/CD**: Integrate AKS with **Azure DevOps** or **GitHub Actions** to automate your deployment pipeline. For example, every time you push a new version of your code, the CI/CD pipeline can automatically build the new container image and deploy it to AKS.

Imagine deploying a microservices-based web application on AKS, where each microservice handles different aspects of the application:

- **User authentication**: This service manages user logins and sessions. Kubernetes ensures that multiple instances of this service are running to handle login traffic spikes.

- **Order management**: Handles order processing, and Kubernetes ensures that this service is scaled up during peak hours and scaled down during off-peak times.

- **Payment processing**: This service interacts with external payment gateways. AKS deploys multiple Pods to ensure high availability, and Kubernetes manages the load across these instances.

By deploying these services on AKS, you ensure that each microservice is isolated, scalable, and can be updated without affecting the rest of the application.

Kubernetes and AKS provide a powerful platform for managing containerized applications at scale. Kubernetes automates key operational tasks, such as deploying, scaling, and managing containers, while AKS simplifies cluster management by handling infrastructure-related tasks. By understanding core Kubernetes concepts such as Pods, Services, and Deployments, and by following best practices for security and resource management, you can build highly scalable and reliable cloud-native applications on AKS.

In the next section, we will explore how to set up an AKS cluster and deploy containerized applications, diving deeper into the practical steps of provisioning and configuring AKS.

Deploying, scaling, and updating containerized applications on AKS

The final learning objective of this chapter focuses on deploying, scaling, and updating containerized applications on AKS. Once you have your applications containerized and your AKS cluster up and running, you'll need to understand how to manage the life cycle of these applications, including deploying new versions, scaling to meet demand, and performing updates with minimal disruption.

This learning objective will guide you through the process of deploying applications on AKS using Kubernetes manifests, managing scaling policies to handle varying workloads, and ensuring that updates are rolled out smoothly while maintaining application availability.

Deploying applications on AKS

Once your AKS cluster is operational, the next step is to deploy your containerized applications. Deployment is managed using **Kubernetes manifests**—YAML files that describe the desired state of your application, such as the number of replicas, container images, resource limits, and network settings.

For example, you might have an e-commerce application with multiple microservices (user authentication, inventory management, and payment processing) that need to be deployed independently.

The following are the steps for deploying an application:

- **Create a Kubernetes manifest**: The manifest file defines how your application should run. It includes the container image, the number of Pod replicas, environment variables, and resource requirements. The following is an example manifest for deploying a simple web application:

```
apiVersion: apps/v1
kind: Deployment
metadata:
  name: web-app
spec:
  replicas: 3
  selector:
    matchLabels:
      app: web-app
  template:
    metadata:
      labels:
        app: web-app
    spec:
      containers:
      - name: web-app
        image: mycontainerregistry.azurecr.io/web-app:latest
        ports:
        - containerPort: 80
```

  This manifest creates a deployment for a web application, running three replicas of the container. It pulls the container image from ACR and exposes port 80.

- **Deploy the application**: To deploy the application, use the `kubectl` command-line tool, which communicates with your AKS cluster. Take the following example:

```
kubectl apply -f deployment.yaml
```

Kubernetes will automatically create the specified number of replicas (Pods) and manage them according to the configuration.

It is best practice to always define resource requests and limits for CPU and memory in your manifest files to ensure that containers receive sufficient resources and do not overconsume cluster resources.

Scaling applications on AKS

One of the most powerful features of Kubernetes is its ability to scale applications based on real-time demand. AKS offers several methods for scaling applications, including horizontal scaling (scaling the number of Pods) and vertical scaling (increasing the resources for individual Pods).

Horizontal Pod Autoscaling (HPA)

Horizontal Pod Autoscaling (**HPA**) automatically adjusts the number of Pod replicas based on CPU, memory, or custom metrics. For example, if your web application experiences a traffic spike, Kubernetes can automatically increase the number of running pods to handle the load.

To enable HPA, you first define a `HorizontalPodAutoscaler` resource, which tells Kubernetes when and how to scale your application based on resource utilization. The following is some example YAML:

```
apiVersion: autoscaling/v1
kind: HorizontalPodAutoscaler
metadata:
  name: web-app-hpa
spec:
  scaleTargetRef:
    apiVersion: apps/v1
    kind: Deployment
    name: web-app
  minReplicas: 3
  maxReplicas: 10
  targetCPUUtilizationPercentage: 80
```

In this example, Kubernetes will maintain a minimum of 3 and a maximum of 10 replicas for the web application, scaling up or down depending on CPU utilization. If CPU usage exceeds 80%, additional Pods will be created.

It is best practice to monitor and tune the HPA settings based on real-world usage patterns. Use Azure Monitor to collect metrics on CPU, memory, and custom metrics to ensure that the autoscaler responds appropriately to workload changes.

Cluster autoscaling

In addition to scaling Pods, you can also enable **Cluster Autoscaler**, which automatically adjusts the number of nodes in the AKS cluster based on resource demand. This ensures that the cluster can handle the increased number of Pods as workloads grow, without over-provisioning resources.

To enable cluster autoscaling in AKS, specify a minimum and maximum number of nodes for the cluster. AKS will automatically add or remove nodes based on resource requirements.

Updating applications on AKS

Kubernetes supports various strategies for updating your applications, including **rolling updates** and **blue-green deployments**. These strategies allow you to release new versions of your application without downtime or service interruption. Let's look at them next:

- **Rolling updates**: A rolling update gradually replaces old Pods with new ones. During the update, a few Pods running the old version of the application are terminated, and new Pods with the updated version are created. This ensures continuous availability during the deployment process.

- **How rolling updates work**:

  - Kubernetes gradually replaces the old Pods with new Pods

  - Traffic is routed to the new Pods as they become available

  - If any issues arise during the update, Kubernetes can automatically roll back to the previous version

- **Best practice**:

  Use rolling updates for most production workloads as they provide a smooth transition between versions without disrupting the service.

  To initiate a rolling update, you simply modify the container image in the Kubernetes manifest and reapply the deployment using `kubectl`:

  ```
  kubectl set image deployment/web-app
  web-app=mycontainerregistry.azurecr.io/web-app:v2
  ```

  This command updates the image to a new version (v2), triggering a rolling update.

Blue-green deployment

For critical workloads where zero downtime is essential, **blue-green deployment** is a strategy that deploys the new version of the application (green) alongside the existing version (blue). Traffic is routed to the blue environment until the green environment is tested and verified. Once verified, the traffic is switched to the green environment.

It is best practice to use blue-green deployment for mission-critical applications where you need full control over the deployment process and the ability to quickly roll back.

Monitoring and managing AKS deployments

Monitoring your AKS deployments is crucial to ensure that your applications run smoothly and efficiently. AKS integrates with **Azure Monitor** and **Azure Application Insights** to provide real-time data on the performance and health of your applications.

With Azure Monitor, you can do the following:

- Track metrics such as CPU and memory utilization
- Set up alerts for resource thresholds
- Visualize logs and performance metrics across your AKS cluster

It is best practice to regularly review performance data and logs from Azure Monitor to proactively identify and resolve issues before they impact users. Use Application Insights to track request times, errors, and user interactions with your applications.

Summary

In this chapter, we explored the full life cycle of containerized applications on AKS—from deploying applications using Kubernetes manifests to scaling and updating them based on real-time demand. We learned how AKS simplifies the management of Kubernetes clusters by automating tasks such as scaling, monitoring, and updating applications.

By now, you should be comfortable with deploying applications on AKS, scaling them automatically based on demand, and performing updates with minimal downtime. AKS provides the scalability and flexibility needed to run production-grade containerized applications, allowing businesses to respond to changing user demands quickly and efficiently.

In the next chapter, we will explore how to enhance security and compliance in an Azure project on Azure.

9
Enhancing Security and Compliance in an Azure Project

In today's digital landscape, organizations are increasingly reliant on the cloud for their operational needs, making security and compliance two of the most critical aspects of cloud management. This chapter is designed to help you understand the core principles and best practices for implementing robust security measures and achieving compliance within an Azure environment. Whether you're working on a small-scale Azure deployment or managing an enterprise-level cloud infrastructure, ensuring that security and compliance protocols are meticulously followed is paramount to safeguarding both data and applications from threats.

This chapter will guide you through the essential components of Azure security, covering topics such as **identity management**, **network security**, **data protection**, and **governance**. It will also provide insights into how you can leverage **Microsoft's compliance tools** to meet industry standards and regulatory requirements. Throughout the chapter, you will learn practical methods to implement policies that mitigate vulnerabilities and strengthen the security posture of your Azure infrastructure. Additionally, we will focus on creating a proactive security culture that incorporates monitoring, compliance tracking, and responding to potential threats before they become a problem.

Azure provides a wide range of tools and services that can help organizations address security needs—from configuring secure virtual networks and managing identity with **Microsoft Entra ID** to ensuring encrypted storage of data and implementing advanced threat protection. We will also delve into compliance best practices, discussing how Azure helps organizations comply with standards such as the **GDPR, ISO 27001, HIPAA**, and other relevant certifications. By the end of this chapter, you will have a comprehensive understanding of how to protect your Azure resources, monitor and respond to threats, and fulfill compliance obligations, ensuring that your cloud environment is both secure and compliant.

In this chapter, we will be covering the following learning objectives:

- Understanding the Azure Security architecture
- Implementing **identity and access management (IAM)**
- Ensuring data protection and encryption
- Configuring compliance policies with Azure Policy

Let's begin this exciting chapter!

The importance of security and compliance

As the use of cloud infrastructure continues to grow, so do the security challenges that come with it. The cloud offers unparalleled scalability and convenience, but without proper safeguards, these same characteristics can expose an organization to considerable risks. A single vulnerability can have severe consequences, including data breaches, financial losses, and reputational damage. Security in Azure involves implementing layered protections to prevent unauthorized access, ensure data confidentiality, and maintain system integrity.

Compliance, on the other hand, is about ensuring that your organization meets the legal and regulatory requirements applicable to its industry. Compliance standards, such as the **GDPR, ISO 27001**, and **PCI DSS**, provide a framework to protect data, establish operational transparency, and ensure the ethical handling of information. Meeting these standards isn't just about avoiding penalties—it's also about building trust with customers, partners, and stakeholders. In Azure, achieving compliance means taking advantage of Microsoft's compliance offerings, including compliance certifications, audit trails, and policy enforcement tools, which are specifically designed to streamline the process of meeting regulatory obligations.

Together, **security** and **compliance** are essential pillars for managing a cloud environment that is not only resilient to attacks but also aligned with industry standards. A well-implemented security strategy within Azure ensures that data is protected at every stage—from transit to storage—while compliance helps organizations operate ethically and legally. This chapter will help you understand how to build and maintain these pillars effectively, ensuring your Azure environment is ready to handle today's complex security landscape.

Understanding the Azure Security architecture

First, let me take you through the Azure Security architecture. The **Azure Security architecture** is fundamental to ensuring that your cloud infrastructure is resilient to threats while complying with industry standards. The security architecture of Azure is built on several key pillars: **identity and access management, network security, data security, monitoring, and compliance**. Each of these pillars works cohesively to provide a defense-in-depth strategy that protects resources across the entire cloud environment.

Figure 9.1 illustrates the security diagram for Azure. For now, keep these connecting dots in mind. We will be covering the mentioned dots throughout this chapter.

Figure 9.1 – Azure Security diagram

Now, let's look at each of the key pillars on which the Azure Security architecture is built.

IAM

At the core of Azure Security is **identity and access management** (**IAM**), which is primarily handled through **Microsoft Entra ID**. IAM ensures that the right people and applications have appropriate access to resources, and unauthorized users are kept out. Effective IAM starts with the implementation of **least privilege access**—granting users only the permissions they need to do their jobs and nothing more. For example, assigning a user the role of **Reader** instead of **Contributor** ensures that they can view resources but cannot modify or delete them.

Enforcing **multi-factor authentication** (**MFA**) for all users significantly enhances security by requiring additional verification, such as a phone call or an SMS code, beyond just passwords. Additionally, setting up **conditional access policies** helps ensure that users meet certain criteria, such as logging in from a trusted device or geographic location, before being granted access to sensitive information.

For example, you can configure a conditional access policy that allows only users within a particular country to access administrative tools, adding an extra layer of security for sensitive operations.

Using **privileged identity management** (**PIM**) provides just-in-time privileged access to Azure resources. This limits the risk of prolonged exposure to critical systems and prevents attackers from exploiting accounts with standing privileges.

Network security

Network security is another crucial element of the Azure Security architecture. Azure provides several tools to secure network communications, such as **Network Security Groups** (**NSGs**), **Azure Firewall**, and **Virtual Network** (**VNet**) **peering**. NSGs act as virtual firewalls that filter inbound and outbound traffic to and from Azure resources. By defining specific rules, administrators can control which traffic is allowed to communicate with resources in a subnet or **virtual machine** (**VM**).

In addition to NSGs, **Azure Firewall** provides advanced threat protection for your network by enabling centrally managed, policy-driven filtering of traffic across multiple VNets. It helps organizations secure their cloud deployments without needing complex appliance deployments or configurations. For larger deployments, implementing **Azure DDoS Protection** can help mitigate **distributed denial-of-service** (**DDoS**) attacks, ensuring that applications remain available even when under attack.

Segmenting your network using VNets and subnets is an effective way to isolate different workloads. Using VNet peering to enable secure communication between different network segments without exposing traffic to the public internet ensures that even if one segment is compromised, the attack cannot easily propagate throughout your environment.

Data security

Data security is a fundamental aspect of Azure's security architecture. Ensuring that data is protected both **at rest** and **in transit** is key to preventing unauthorized access and ensuring data integrity. Azure provides encryption options such as **Azure Disk Encryption** for VMs and **encryption at rest** for services such as **Azure Blob Storage**.

Azure Key Vault plays an essential role in managing encryption keys and secrets, offering a centralized location for storing cryptographic keys, passwords, and certificates. This service helps ensure that sensitive data is managed in a secure manner while allowing administrators to automate and control access. Azure Key Vault also integrates with other Azure services, making it easier to use encryption across your entire cloud deployment.

Regularly rotating encryption keys and using Azure Key Vault's access policies to strictly control who can manage or use these keys reduces the risk of stale or compromised keys leading to unauthorized data access.

Monitoring and threat detection

Monitoring is vital for maintaining the security of your Azure environment. Azure provides several tools for monitoring activity, including **Azure Monitor**, **Azure Sentinel**, and **Microsoft Defender for Cloud**. Together, these tools provide real-time visibility into your cloud resources, enabling you to detect and respond to suspicious activities.

Azure Sentinel is a scalable cloud-native **security information and event management** (SIEM) system that aggregates data from various sources, including Azure resources and on-premises environments. Sentinel uses artificial intelligence to correlate and analyze this data, providing actionable insights to security teams. **Microsoft Defender for Cloud** adds an additional layer of threat protection by continuously assessing your cloud environment and recommending actions to mitigate vulnerabilities.

Setting up **alerting rules** in Azure Monitor to notify administrators about unusual activities, such as failed login attempts or sudden increases in network traffic, helps with proactively identifying potential threats. Automating response actions using **Logic Apps** or **Azure Automation** can mitigate threats faster and reduce human response time.

Governance and compliance

Maintaining governance in your Azure environment is essential to ensuring that security and compliance requirements are consistently enforced. **Azure Policy** helps by setting up guardrails to enforce organizational standards and assess compliance across your environment. Policies can be applied to entire resource groups or specific resources, ensuring that configurations align with internal and external requirements.

For more comprehensive control, **Azure Blueprints** can be used to deploy a set of policies, role assignments, and resources that help ensure compliance with specific standards. For instance, if you need to comply with ISO 27001, you can create a blueprint that includes all necessary configurations and apply it to new or existing subscriptions.

Using Azure Policy to implement rules such as requiring encryption for all storage accounts or ensuring that only approved VM types are deployed helps maintain consistency and control. Regular compliance assessments using Azure's built-in tools allow you to identify any areas where your configuration deviates from compliance requirements.

In this section, we've discussed the various components of the Azure Security architecture and how they work together to provide a comprehensive security strategy for your cloud environment. By leveraging tools such as Microsoft Entra ID, NSGs, Azure Key Vault, and Azure Monitor, organizations can build a multi-layered defense that secures identity, data, and networks while maintaining compliance with industry standards.

Let's move on to the next learning objective, where we'll dive deeper into implementing IAM and explore best practices for managing identities and controlling access in an Azure environment.

Implementing IAM

IAM is a core aspect of ensuring security in Azure. The primary goal of IAM is to control who has access to resources, what actions they can perform, and under what conditions. Azure's IAM is managed primarily through Microsoft Entra ID, which acts as the control plane for identity management across all Azure services.

Figure 9.2 shows an architecture diagram from Azure's Well-Architected Framework to give us a clean perspective.

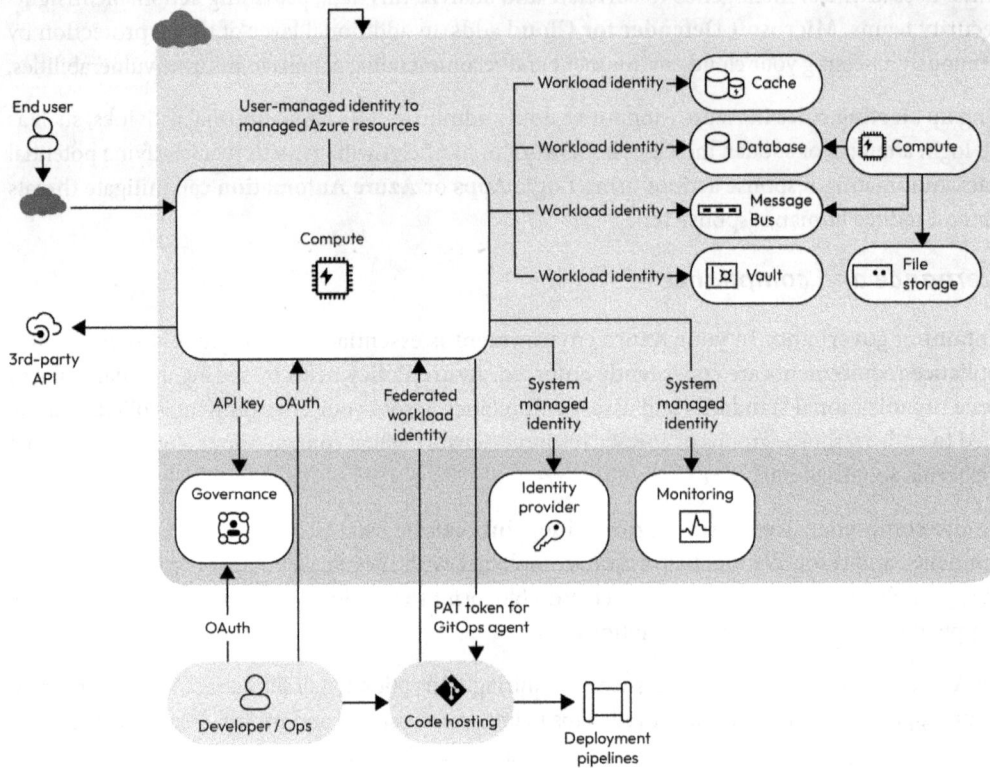

Figure 9.2 – Azure IAM from the Well-Architected Framework

Managing users and groups with Microsoft Entra ID

Effective IAM starts with managing users and groups within Microsoft Entra ID. Users are individuals who need access to Azure resources, while groups are collections of users who share similar access needs. By assigning roles to groups rather than individual users, organizations can simplify the administration of permissions. For example, instead of assigning permissions to 20 users individually, you can create a group called **Developers** and assign permissions once to the entire group.

Creating role-based groups also allows better delegation and management of user access. Assigning users to pre-defined roles such as **Reader**, **Contributor**, or **Owner** helps ensure that individuals have appropriate levels of access based on their job responsibilities. Limiting users to the lowest permission level necessary minimizes the risk of accidental or malicious changes to your cloud infrastructure.

Role-based access control (RBAC)

RBAC is a key tool for managing who has access to Azure resources. RBAC allows you to define custom roles with specific permissions that align with your organization's unique requirements. For example, you could create a custom role called **Database Operator** that has permissions to manage databases but not the underlying infrastructure. By assigning roles at different scopes—such as subscription, resource group, or individual resource level—you can ensure that users have access only to the resources they need for their work.

It is advisable to regularly review role assignments to ensure that they align with users' current responsibilities. Employees who change roles within the organization should have their permissions updated accordingly to reflect their new responsibilities. Assigning permissions dynamically by adding or removing users from groups provides a more manageable approach than directly modifying individual user permissions.

Figure 9.3 shows what the Azure RBAC model architecture looks like.

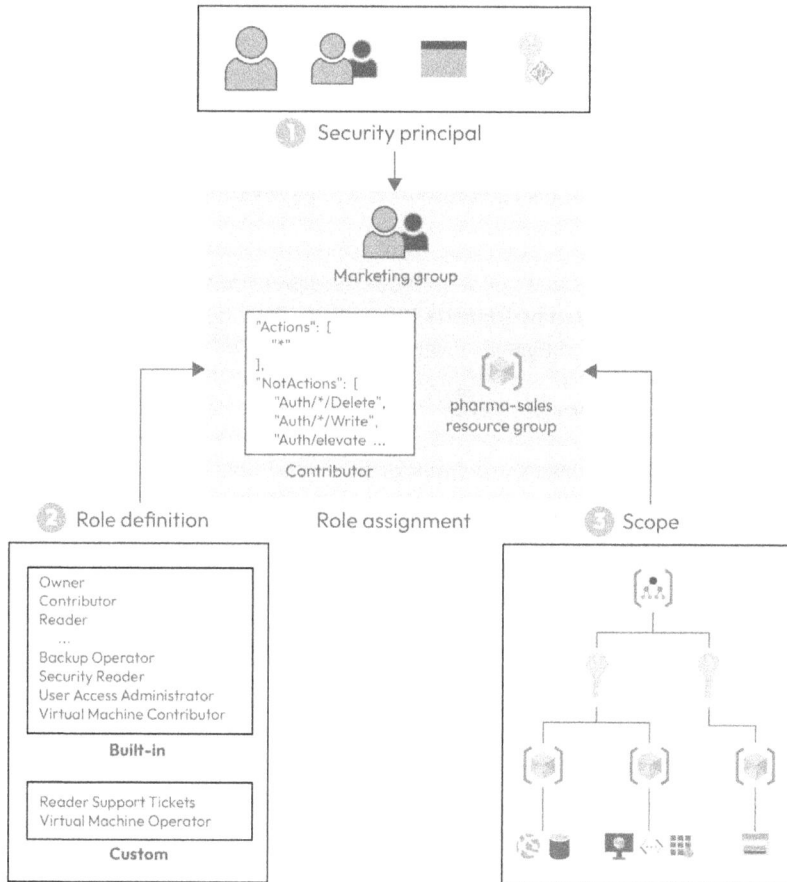

Figure 9.3 – Azure RBAC model architecture

Multi-factor authentication (MFA)

MFA adds an extra layer of security beyond passwords. Even if a user's password is compromised, MFA provides an additional factor (such as a phone number, authenticator app, or biometric verification) to authenticate their identity. Enforcing MFA for all users, especially administrators, helps protect against compromised credentials. Azure allows you to configure MFA policies to require additional authentication for specific scenarios, such as sign-ins from unfamiliar locations or devices.

For instance, conditional access policies can be created to prompt users for MFA only when certain conditions are met, such as when accessing from a location that is not listed as a trusted IP range. This ensures that security measures are balanced with user convenience, providing additional protection without overwhelming users with too many prompts.

Conditional access policies

Conditional access policies are crucial for managing access based on real-time conditions. These policies allow you to set rules that determine which users can access which resources and under what conditions. Conditional access is typically used to enforce MFA based on the user's context, such as the device they are using, their geographic location, or the application they are attempting to access.

For example, a conditional access policy can be set to grant full access only if users are signing in from within the corporate network, while those signing in from outside the network must complete MFA. This helps organizations secure their data and resources while providing flexibility to users who may need remote access.

Another effective use of conditional access is to block access entirely based on risk signals, such as suspicious login attempts detected by **Identity Protection**. For high-risk users, you can enforce restrictions until the risk has been mitigated or verified.

Privileged identity management (PIM)

PIM is a tool that helps manage, control, and monitor access to important resources. It is especially useful for managing privileged accounts, which hold permissions that could potentially affect the entire Azure environment. With PIM, users can be granted privileged roles, such as **Global Administrator** or **Subscription Owner**, on a just-in-time basis, meaning they receive elevated permissions only when needed and for a limited time.

PIM also provides alerts for suspicious or excessive use of privileged accounts, as well as detailed audit logs for tracking privileged activity. This minimizes the risks associated with prolonged elevated access and provides better accountability for privileged actions.

Figure 9.4 illustrates the Azure PIM tool.

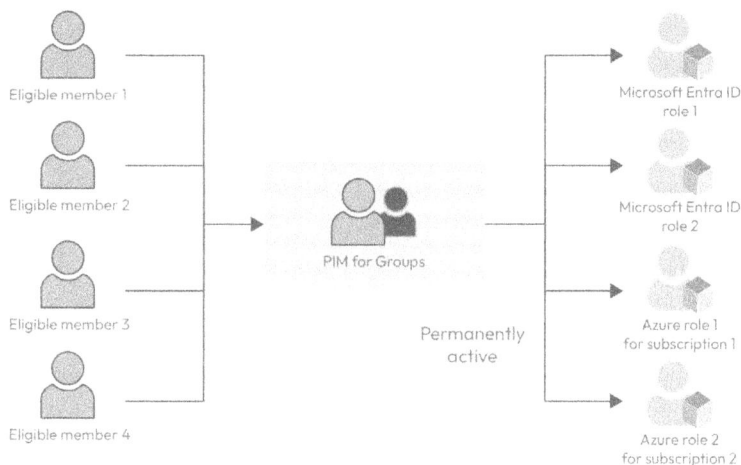

Figure 9.4 – Azure PIM

Identity Protection

Identity Protection in Azure leverages machine learning to identify potential vulnerabilities and suspicious activity related to user identities. For instance, if a user's account is detected logging in from two geographically distant locations within a short period—a phenomenon known as an **impossible travel scenario**—Identity Protection can trigger alerts or enforce risk-based conditional access policies to verify the user's identity.

Using Identity Protection, administrators can classify users or sign-in attempts by risk level—low, medium, or high—and define automated responses accordingly. For example, high-risk accounts may be required to reset their passwords immediately, while low-risk accounts could simply be flagged for review. This risk-based approach allows organizations to respond appropriately to potential security incidents without overburdening users.

In this section, we've delved into IAM and explored the critical components required to secure user identities and control access in Azure. By using Microsoft Entra ID, RBAC, MFA, conditional access, and PIM, you can establish a robust identity management strategy that protects both users and resources. In the next section, we'll examine how to ensure data protection and encryption within Azure, looking at how to secure data at rest and in transit, and manage encryption keys effectively.

Ensuring data protection and encryption

Data protection is a critical aspect of securing any cloud environment. In Azure, data can reside in multiple forms—such as databases, file shares, and object storage—and each of these requires a tailored approach to ensure that sensitive information is always safeguarded. Azure offers comprehensive data protection capabilities that address data at rest, in transit, and while in use.

Encryption for data at rest

Encryption at rest is the process of encrypting stored data to prevent unauthorized access, even if physical disks are accessed directly. Azure provides several options for encryption at rest, including Azure **Storage Service Encryption** (**SSE**) and **Azure Disk Encryption**. These encryption services use **AES-256** encryption, one of the strongest encryption standards available.

For instance, when using **Azure Blob Storage**, you can enable SSE, which automatically encrypts data as it is written to Azure and decrypts it when read. This approach requires minimal configuration and works seamlessly in the background to protect your data.

In addition, Azure Disk Encryption can be used for encrypting the operating system and data disks of VMs. This is especially important for customers with regulatory requirements that mandate that sensitive information must be encrypted when stored in the cloud. Azure Disk Encryption leverages **BitLocker** for Windows VMs and **dm-crypt** for Linux VMs, ensuring data confidentiality across different operating systems.

Encryption for data in transit

To protect data that is actively moving between systems, **encryption in transit** is implemented. This is crucial to protect data from eavesdropping or tampering during transmission. Azure enforces encryption in transit by using protocols like **Transport Layer Security** (**TLS**). For example, when users access **Azure SQL Database**, connections are encrypted using TLS to protect sensitive data transmitted between the database and client applications.

Azure also allows customers to enforce **HTTPS** over **HTTP** for web applications hosted in **Azure App Services**. By setting **HTTPS Only** to **True**, all incoming traffic is forced to use the secure HTTPS protocol, ensuring that all data transmitted between users and applications is encrypted.

Azure Key Vault

Managing encryption keys is a crucial part of ensuring the security of encrypted data. **Azure Key Vault** is a centralized cloud service for managing encryption keys, certificates, and other secrets. By storing secrets securely in Azure Key Vault, organizations can ensure that sensitive data, such as connection strings and API keys, are not hard-coded into application code or stored in less secure locations.

Consider a scenario where you are building an application that requires access to an external database. Instead of storing the database connection string in the application's configuration files, you can store it in Azure Key Vault. The application can then securely retrieve the connection string at runtime, ensuring that sensitive data remains secure and limiting the risk of exposure.

Azure Key Vault also integrates with many Azure services, enabling seamless encryption for storage accounts, VMs, and SQL databases. For example, when setting up **Azure SQL Database**, you can configure **Transparent Data Encryption** (**TDE**) and use keys managed by Azure Key Vault to further enhance security. TDE ensures that the entire database is encrypted at rest, protecting it from unauthorized access.

Data backup and recovery

Data protection also involves ensuring that data is available when needed. **Backup and recovery** solutions in Azure help protect against data loss due to accidental deletion, corruption, or hardware failure. Azure provides **Azure Backup**, a service that allows organizations to back up their data to Azure storage. This service supports backups for Azure VMs, on-premises servers, and Azure workloads such as SQL databases.

For example, an organization running an Azure VM hosting an important web application can set up Azure Backup to create point-in-time snapshots of the VM's data. In case of accidental deletion or a malware attack, the organization can restore the VM to a previous state, minimizing downtime and data loss.

Access control for data protection

Access control plays a significant role in protecting data within Azure. By leveraging RBAC, organizations can enforce strict policies on who has permission to read, write, or delete data. For example, you can create a role that grants permission to view storage account data but does not allow deleting or modifying it. Assigning this role to a specific user or group ensures that only authorized personnel have the ability to interact with sensitive data.

Using **Shared Access Signatures** (**SAS**) is another effective way to grant temporary access to Azure Storage resources without sharing the storage account keys. SAS tokens can be configured with granular permissions, including expiration dates and allowed IP addresses, providing more flexibility and control over data access.

Consider a scenario where you need to provide a third-party vendor with access to specific files stored in **Azure Blob Storage** for a limited period. Instead of sharing your account keys, you can generate a SAS token that grants read-only access to the specific files and set an expiration date to ensure the vendor's access is automatically revoked after a certain period.

Data masking and classification

Another important aspect of data protection is **data masking and classification**. Azure provides **SQL Data Discovery and Classification**, a feature of **Azure SQL Database** that identifies and classifies sensitive data. By classifying sensitive columns, such as **personally identifiable information** (**PII**), organizations can ensure that the most critical data is given additional protections and controls.

Dynamic Data Masking (**DDM**) is also available in Azure SQL Database to obfuscate sensitive data at the database level. For example, if you have a table containing customer credit card information, you can configure DDM to mask the credit card number so users only see the last four digits. This ensures that even if unauthorized access occurs, the sensitive data remains protected.

In this section, we explored the various methods and tools available in Azure for ensuring data protection and encryption. These tools, including Azure Key Vault, Azure Disk Encryption, and backup solutions, enable organizations to secure data at rest and in transit, manage encryption keys effectively, and implement robust access control measures. In the next section, we will move on to configuring compliance policies with Azure Policy and discuss how to enforce standards and maintain governance across your cloud environment.

Configuring compliance policies with Azure Policy

To ensure your Azure environment meets the required standards and best practices, it is crucial to implement governance and compliance measures using Azure Policy. Azure Policy is a service in Azure that enables you to create, assign, and manage policies that enforce organizational standards and assess compliance across your entire environment. By using Azure Policy, you can make sure that resources within your Azure subscription are compliant with both internal and external standards, such as the GDPR, ISO 27001, and PCI DSS.

Figure 9.5 is an Azure Policy diagram:

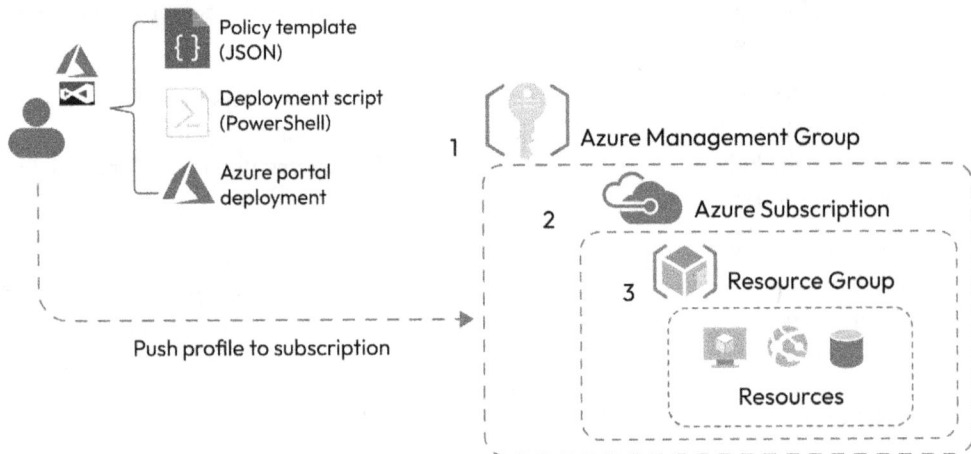

Figure 9.5 – Azure Policy diagram

What is Azure Policy?

Azure Policy is a governance tool that provides a way to define rules and enforce behaviors for your Azure resources. For instance, you can create a policy that mandates that all storage accounts must use secure transfer protocols, or that only specific VM sizes can be deployed. By setting these rules, you can ensure that your cloud environment adheres to your organization's standards, preventing misconfigurations that could lead to security vulnerabilities.

Azure Policy can be used to audit and enforce compliance, either by providing alerts when non-compliant resources are detected or by taking automatic action to bring them back into compliance. For example, if a user creates a storage account without encryption enabled, Azure Policy can automatically apply encryption settings to that storage account. This makes Azure Policy a powerful tool for proactively managing compliance and ensuring a consistent security posture across all resources.

Defining and assigning policies

To use Azure Policy effectively, you start by defining a **policy definition** that specifies what to enforce. Policy definitions are written in JSON and can include conditions such as resource types, properties, and tags. For example, you can write a policy that checks if a VM has an attached monitoring agent, and if not, flags it as non-compliant.

Once a policy is defined, it can be assigned to a scope, such as a **subscription**, **resource group**, or **specific resource**. This allows you to apply policies at different levels of your Azure hierarchy. Assigning a policy at the subscription level means all resources created within that subscription must adhere to the policy, whereas assigning it at the resource group level limits its enforcement to only the resources within that group.

Azure also provides **built-in policies** that cover many common scenarios, such as ensuring storage account encryption, enforcing tag requirements, or restricting public IP access. Using these built-in policies can accelerate the process of ensuring compliance with industry standards.

Policy initiatives

Policy initiatives are collections of policy definitions grouped together to achieve a specific goal. For example, an initiative to comply with ISO 27001 might include multiple policies, such as encryption requirements, tag governance, and resource location restrictions. Initiatives help streamline compliance efforts by packaging all the necessary policies in a single entity, making it easier to assign and manage.

By using initiatives, you can ensure a more comprehensive and structured approach to achieving compliance. When new resources are created or existing ones are modified, Azure Policy automatically evaluates them against the policies in the initiative and flags non-compliance. This approach helps organizations maintain a high standard of governance and simplifies the process of meeting multiple regulatory requirements simultaneously.

Monitoring and compliance reporting

Azure provides detailed **compliance reporting** through the **Azure Policy compliance dashboard**, allowing you to monitor the state of compliance for your resources. The dashboard provides insights into how well your environment aligns with assigned policies, highlighting non-compliant resources and enabling you to take corrective action.

Consider a scenario where your organization must comply with PCI DSS standards. By assigning a set of policies to enforce encryption, secure configurations, and monitoring, you can use the compliance dashboard to quickly determine which resources are compliant and which require attention. This proactive approach helps identify vulnerabilities early, ensuring compliance with security standards.

Azure Policy also integrates with other monitoring and security services, such as **Azure Security Center**. The integration provides an end-to-end view of compliance, enabling security teams to prioritize and address non-compliance issues more effectively.

Summary

In this chapter, we explored how to strengthen the security and compliance posture of your Azure environment through the application of best practices and Azure-native tools. This chapter provided an in-depth look at the Azure Security architecture, encompassing identity and access management, network security, data protection, and monitoring.

We also covered IAM in Azure, highlighting the importance of Microsoft Entra ID, MFA, and PIM to safeguard access to resources. Additionally, we examined network security and the role of NSGs, Azure Firewall, and VNet peering in securing communications within your Azure infrastructure.

The section on data protection and encryption explained how to protect sensitive information at rest and in transit, using tools such as Azure Disk Encryption, Azure Key Vault, and Azure Backup. We also discussed the importance of data masking and classification in ensuring that sensitive data is properly protected.

Finally, we discussed how to configure compliance policies with Azure Policy to enforce organizational standards and ensure adherence to regulatory requirements. Azure Policy helps organizations proactively maintain compliance, leveraging policy definitions, initiatives, and compliance reporting to track and manage the compliance state of all Azure resources.

With the knowledge gained in this chapter, you should now be able to effectively implement security measures and compliance policies in Azure, ensuring that your cloud environment is both resilient and aligned with regulatory standards. By using Azure's comprehensive security and compliance tools, you can build a robust cloud infrastructure that not only meets business needs but also mitigates the risks associated with modern cloud deployments.

In the next and final chapter, we will delve into developing a cloud cost optimization strategy.

10

Developing a Cloud Cost Optimization Strategy

Here we go—the final chapter, and one of the most critical chapters in your Azure journey! As cloud adoption accelerates, organizations of all sizes are looking to maximize the value of their cloud investments while ensuring operational excellence. Achieving the right balance between performance, scalability, innovation, and cost-efficiency is paramount.

In this chapter, we focus on developing a cloud cost optimization strategy. It's not just about reducing expenses; it's about continually aligning cloud spending with business goals, performance needs, and future growth. Cost optimization is an ongoing process—one that requires regular monitoring, governance, and adaptation to evolving workloads.

In this chapter, we will explore the following topics:

- Azure pricing models and cost management tools

- Resource monitoring, scaling strategies, and best practices

- Leveraging Reserved Instances, Spot Instances, and Azure Hybrid Benefits

- Implementing governance policies for effective cost control

By the end of this chapter, you will be able to design, implement, and maintain a cost optimization strategy that meets both your technical and financial objectives.

Why cloud cost optimization matters

Cloud technology continues to revolutionize how organizations deploy and manage workloads, yet this revolution can lead to unforeseen challenges in financial oversight. Azure's instant scalability and on-demand provisioning make it remarkably simple to spin up new **virtual machines** (**VMs**), services, and databases. Left unregulated, however, the costs associated with these resources can escalate rapidly.

When a business invests in the cloud, each dollar spent should ideally map to a tangible outcome, such as higher revenue, faster innovation, or better customer experiences. Unchecked cloud spending often results in overspending on idle services, over-provisioned compute, or excessive data storage. Teams might run development environments continuously, even when they remain unused for extended periods, or they might choose compute tiers that far exceed actual usage requirements. In both scenarios, the result is an accumulation of unnecessary fees that eat into operating budgets.

Cost optimization ensures that technical priorities align with business objectives. It begins by establishing full visibility into resource consumption. For example, a company that has not tagged its Azure resources or set up a clear reporting structure will struggle to determine which department or project contributes to the largest share of the monthly invoice. Lack of insight can lead to arbitrary cost-cutting measures that hamper innovation. Conversely, organizations that track resource usage at a granular level can make strategic decisions. They might discover that customer-facing services legitimately require higher-performance VMs, while certain internal tools or testing workflows can safely run on smaller configurations or at off-peak hours.

Another central reason to refine cloud spending is **sustainability**. Although the cloud is often seen as an infinite pool of resources, data centers still consume significant energy. Running large clusters of VMs that rarely see full CPU utilization has a tangible impact on an organization's carbon footprint. By scaling services appropriately, switching off underused resources, or adopting serverless functions for event-driven workloads, businesses can reduce both operational costs and environmental impact.

Real-world examples highlight the breadth of these challenges. An e-commerce retailer might prepare for seasonal traffic surges by deploying far more instances than necessary, leading to high costs even in off-peak seasons. A healthcare provider might move all patient management systems to the cloud but fail to establish automated shutdown or archiving policies for test environments. Over time, the growing cluster of idle test databases inflates their monthly invoice. A fast-scaling startup might encourage each team to create its own subscriptions without a centralized process for monitoring costs, eventually discovering that some teams pay for resources that replicate existing environments elsewhere.

Continuous improvement is at the heart of effective cloud cost management. Azure's pay-as-you-go model can be a double-edged sword: it allows teams to innovate rapidly, yet also invites resource sprawl if the environment lacks standard governance. Organizations that regularly review usage reports, analyze scaling patterns, and adjust resource allocations are far more likely to keep budgets under control. This review process could involve weekly or monthly meetings where engineering leads evaluate the cost impact of their recent deployments. Over time, this habit fosters a culture of accountability and encourages teams to think creatively about achieving business objectives within sustainable financial limits.

In short, cloud cost optimization matters because it ensures a healthy equilibrium between innovation, performance, and fiscal responsibility. It promotes responsible usage of shared computing resources, helps organizations align their technology investments with strategic outcomes, and reduces the chance that mounting bills will disrupt essential services. As we move forward to explore Azure's specific pricing models and cost management features, remember that these tools and techniques exist not to stifle growth, but to support it in a sustainable and targeted way.

Azure pricing models and cost management tools

Managing cloud costs effectively begins with understanding how to align resource spending with business needs. Microsoft Azure provides flexible pricing models and powerful cost management tools to ensure you only pay for what you use, but using them effectively requires a strategic approach. From dynamic pay-as-you-go billing to long-term **Reserved Instances** (**RIs**) and the cost-saving Azure Hybrid Benefit, Azure offers options to meet every workload's unique requirements. In this section, we'll explore these models in depth and show how they integrate with tools such as Azure Cost Management + Billing to give you full visibility and control over your cloud expenses.

Azure pricing models

Azure provides various pricing models tailored to different business needs, balancing flexibility, cost efficiency, and commitment levels.

Pay-As-You-Go – Flexibility at a premium

The **Pay-As-You-Go** (**PAYG**) model is Azure's most flexible pricing option and is typically the starting point for many organizations. With PAYG, you are billed based on the exact usage of your resources. This is ideal for unpredictable workloads, such as a start-up launching a new app or an e-commerce store handling holiday traffic spikes.

PAYG is particularly beneficial for short-term projects or experimental deployments. For example, a marketing firm running a pilot analytics campaign might choose PAYG to avoid committing to long-term capacity. The pricing model ensures they only pay for what they use, whether it's CPU cycles, storage, or API calls.

However, while PAYG excels in flexibility, it can become expensive over time if used for workloads that run continuously. Imagine an analytics platform running 24/7 on PAYG—its cost over a year might far exceed what an RI would offer for the same workload.

Reserved Instances – Long-term stability with savings

When workloads stabilize, RIs are the go-to option. They allow you to reserve capacity for one or three years, significantly reducing costs compared to PAYG. RIs are particularly useful for always-on workloads, such as databases or enterprise applications.

For example, a manufacturing firm running predictive maintenance software that continuously processes sensor data could reserve VM capacity. This ensures predictable performance while cutting costs by up to 72%. RIs provide budget predictability, enabling organizations to plan their cloud expenditures confidently.

The main drawback of RIs is the need for careful forecasting. Overcommitting to resources that go underutilized can erode the savings. However, Azure allows flexibility to modify or exchange reservations, mitigating this risk to some extent.

> **Important Note**
>
> Azure Savings Plans allow customers to commit to hourly spending instead of specific VM sizes, providing savings with more flexibility than RIs.

Spot Instances – Cost-efficient for intermittent workloads

Spot Instances (SIs) provide a unique opportunity for savings by allowing organizations to purchase unused Azure capacity at steep discounts. However, these resources can be reclaimed by Azure with little notice when demand for standard instances increases.

Spot pricing is perfect for batch jobs, rendering tasks, and machine learning training—workloads that can tolerate interruptions. A film production company, for instance, might use SIs to render CGI for a movie. If the job is interrupted, it resumes seamlessly when capacity becomes available again.

While SIs require applications to handle interruptions gracefully, the cost savings—often exceeding 60%—are well worth the effort for non-critical workloads.

Azure Hybrid Benefit – Maximize existing investments

Azure Hybrid Benefit allows organizations to reuse their existing licenses for Windows Server or SQL Server in Azure, dramatically reducing costs for these workloads.

By bringing these licenses into Azure, organizations avoid paying duplicate licensing fees. For example, a financial institution migrating its core transaction system to Azure could apply Azure Hybrid Benefit to its Windows-based VMs, cutting compute costs significantly. When combined with RIs, this benefit amplifies savings even further, making it one of the most compelling choices for enterprises with established Microsoft licenses.

This pricing model is particularly attractive for enterprises transitioning from on-premises environments as it enables them to maximize their prior investments while modernizing their infrastructure.

Now that we have had a good overview of Azure's pricing models, let's dive into Cost Management and Billing with Azure.

Azure Cost Management and Billing: a comprehensive overview

Azure Cost Management and Billing is a powerful suite of tools designed to help organizations monitor, manage, and optimize their cloud spending effectively. By providing deep insights into resource usage and costs, it enables businesses to maintain control over their budgets while ensuring operational efficiency. Whether you're managing a small Azure environment or a large-scale enterprise deployment, these tools are integral to aligning cloud spending with organizational objectives.

Key features of Azure Cost Management and Billing

Keeping cloud costs under control is a top priority for organizations using Azure. Azure Cost Management and Billing provide a set of powerful tools to help businesses track, optimize, and manage their cloud spending more effectively. Here are some key features that make it easier to stay on top of costs, set budgets, and maximize efficiency.

Cost Analysis

Cost Analysis provides a detailed view of your Azure spending, helping you understand how resources are being consumed. This feature enables granular tracking of costs across multiple dimensions, such as resource type, subscription, resource group, or tags.

Cost data is visualized in charts and reports, allowing you to identify spending patterns and high-cost resources. For example, you can analyze which services or regions are consuming the most budget.

Example use case: An organization managing multiple environments (production, development, and testing) can use Cost Analysis to identify which environment is driving up costs and take corrective action, such as shutting down idle resources. Also, Azure offers dev/test pricing for non-production environments, helping organizations cut costs for development workloads.

Budgeting and alerts

Setting budgets in Azure Cost Management helps you define spending thresholds for subscriptions, resource groups, or specific services. Alerts can be configured to notify stakeholders when spending approaches, exceeds, or deviates from these budgets:

- **Budget creation**: You can create monthly, quarterly, or annual budgets based on historical usage or projected costs
- **Alerts and notifications**: Notifications can be sent via email or integrated with tools such as Microsoft Teams, ensuring that relevant teams are aware of potential overspending

Example use case: A retail company sets a monthly budget for its Azure e-commerce platform. When costs reach 90% of the budget, an alert is triggered, prompting the team to investigate and optimize resource usage.

Cost allocation with tags

Azure allows tagging of resources with metadata such as department, project, or environment (for example, HR, Finance, or Development). Tags enable cost allocation by associating expenses with specific business units or projects. Tags simplify cost tracking, making it easier to identify which department or project is driving expenses.

Example use case: A software company tags resources based on projects (for example, Mobile App Development) and uses Cost Management to calculate the total expenditure for each project.

Cost optimization recommendations with Azure Advisor

Azure Advisor integrates with Cost Management to provide actionable recommendations for reducing costs. These recommendations may include the following:

- Identifying and resizing underutilized VMs

- Suggesting reserved instances for long-running workloads

- Highlighting idle resources that can be shut down or deleted

Example use case: A healthcare provider using Azure discovers that a set of VMs is running at only 20% capacity. Azure Advisor recommends resizing these instances to smaller configurations, reducing costs by 30%.

Forecasting and cost prediction

Azure Cost Management includes forecasting tools that predict future spending based on historical usage trends. These predictions allow organizations to plan budgets more accurately and make informed decisions about scaling or resource allocation.

Example use case: A logistics company uses cost forecasting to estimate expenses for the holiday season, ensuring they allocate sufficient budget for increased cloud usage during peak demand.

Benefits of Azure Cost Management and Billing

The following points are related to the Azure Cost Management and Billing benefits of Azure Cost Management:

- **Enhanced financial visibility**: With real-time cost tracking, organizations gain clear visibility into their Azure spending, helping them identify inefficiency and avoid surprises

- **Actionable insights**: The tool provides detailed reports and recommendations, enabling teams to take proactive steps to optimize costs and allocate budgets more effectively

- **Alignment with business goals**: By enabling cost allocation and forecasting, Azure Cost Management ensures that spending aligns with organizational priorities and supports strategic initiatives

- **Improved accountability**: Budgeting and tagging features promote accountability by linking costs to specific teams, projects, or departments, fostering a culture of financial responsibility

In *Figure 10.1*, Azure Cost Management pillars are illustrated:

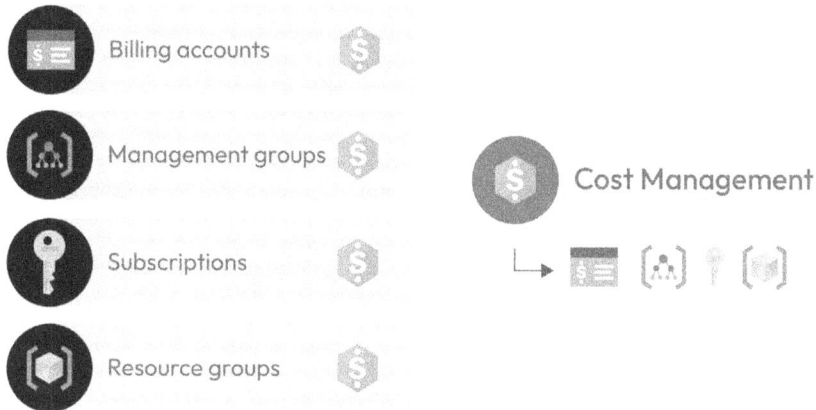

Figure 10.1 – Azure Cost Management overview

Azure Cost Management and Billing is an essential toolset for organizations aiming to achieve financial efficiency in the cloud. By providing deep insights, actionable recommendations, and robust controls, it empowers businesses to make informed decisions, reduce waste, and align spending with strategic goals. In the next section, we'll explore *resource monitoring and scaling for cost efficiency*, focusing on dynamic resource management to further optimize cloud operations.

Implementing resource monitoring and scaling for cost efficiency

Efficient resource monitoring and scaling are essential for optimizing costs while maintaining performance in the cloud. Azure provides powerful tools to monitor resource usage, track performance, and dynamically scale services based on demand. By implementing these practices, organizations can reduce waste, prevent over-provisioning, and ensure that their cloud infrastructure operates within budget without compromising service delivery.

Resource monitoring focuses on tracking real-time usage metrics and identifying inefficiency, while scaling ensures that resources adapt to workload demands. This section will explore the key Azure services and techniques for monitoring and scaling, emphasizing how these practices lead to cost-efficient cloud operations.

Monitoring Resources with Azure Monitor

Azure Monitor is the central hub for monitoring Azure resources. It provides a comprehensive set of tools to collect, analyze, and act on telemetry data, enabling organizations to maintain visibility into their cloud infrastructure.

Key features of Azure Monitor

Azure Monitor provides deep insights into the performance and health of your cloud resources, helping organizations optimize efficiency and quickly respond to potential issues. Here are some of its key features and how they help in real-world scenarios:

- **Metric collection**: Azure Monitor collects metrics such as CPU usage, memory consumption, network traffic, and disk performance. These metrics provide insights into resource utilization and help identify bottlenecks or underutilized assets.

  Example use case: A VM running a web application shows consistently low CPU utilization (below 20%). This indicates that the VM is over-provisioned and can be resized to a smaller instance, reducing costs.

- **Log Analytics**: With Azure Monitor, you can enable **Log Analytics** to track and analyze logs generated by Azure resources. This helps with troubleshooting performance issues and understanding resource usage patterns.

  Example use cases: An e-commerce platform tracks request logs from its web servers. By analyzing these logs, the team identifies a specific API endpoint with high response times, leading to targeted optimizations.

- **Alerts and notifications**: Azure Monitor allows you to set up alerts based on predefined conditions, such as high CPU usage or unexpected spikes in network traffic. These alerts can be integrated with tools such as Microsoft Teams or Slack to ensure timely responses.

  Example use cases: A development team configures alerts to notify them when database performance drops below a certain threshold, ensuring they can act quickly to resolve issues.

Scaling resources dynamically

Dynamic scaling is a cornerstone of cost efficiency in the cloud. Azure supports multiple scaling mechanisms, allowing organizations to match resource capacity with workload demands.

Auto-scaling for VMs

Azure's **Virtual Machine Scale Sets** (**VMSS**) enables automatic scaling of VMs based on demand. VMSS adjusts the number of VMs in a set by monitoring performance metrics such as CPU usage or incoming requests:

- **Example use cases**: A streaming service experiences peak traffic during the evening. With VMSS, the service automatically adds more VMs to handle the load and scales down during off-peak hours, saving costs during periods of low usage.

- **How it works**: You can define auto-scaling rules, such as increasing VM instances when CPU usage exceeds 70% for more than 5 minutes, ensuring that resources adapt dynamically to workload changes.

Scaling web applications with Azure App Service

Azure App Service provides built-in auto-scaling capabilities for web applications, ensuring optimal performance without manual intervention. Applications can scale horizontally (by adding more instances) or vertically (by upgrading to larger instances):

- **Example use case**: A retail website scales out to handle increased traffic during a flash sale. After the sale ends, the application scales back to its original configuration, minimizing costs.

- **Key benefit**: Auto-scaling ensures that applications remain responsive while avoiding over-provisioning, which leads to unnecessary expenses.

Scaling databases with Azure SQL Database

Azure SQL Database offers **hyperscale** and **elastic pool** features to scale databases based on workload requirements:

- **Key scaling options**:
  - **Hyperscale**: Suitable for large, unpredictable workloads that require rapid scaling
  - **Elastic Pools**: Allow multiple databases to share resources, optimizing costs for varying usage patterns
- **Example use case**: A **software-as-a-service** (**SaaS**) company hosts hundreds of client databases. By using elastic pools, the company reduces costs by sharing resources among databases with fluctuating demands.

Best practices for scaling

Here are some best practices that organizations should follow to maximize efficiency and optimize scaling strategies:

- **Define scaling rules**: Use metrics such as CPU usage, memory consumption, and request rates to create scaling thresholds that align with application needs

- **Test scaling scenarios**: Perform load testing to validate that scaling rules effectively handle spikes in demand without over-allocating resources.

- **Enable burst capacity**: For critical workloads, configure burst capacity to handle unexpected traffic without downtime

Example: optimizing costs with resource monitoring and scaling

A fintech company running a trading platform on Azure faces challenges with performance and costs during market opening hours. It implements the following strategies:

- **Monitor performance**: Using Azure Monitor, the company tracks real-time metrics such as API latency and transaction rates. It identifies a surge in CPU usage during market hours, indicating the need for scaling.

- **Scale resources dynamically**:

  - Configure auto-scaling rules for their API servers based on incoming request rates

  - Use Azure SQL Database's hyperscale feature to handle large volumes of financial transactions

- **Outcome**: By combining monitoring and scaling, the company maintains seamless platform performance during peak hours while reducing costs during off-peak periods. This approach results in a 30% reduction in monthly infrastructure expenses.

Resource monitoring and dynamic scaling are critical components of a cost-efficient cloud strategy. Tools such as Azure Monitor provide the visibility needed to optimize resource utilization, while Azure's scaling capabilities ensure that workloads adapt to demand without over-provisioning. Together, these practices enable organizations to achieve cost savings, enhance performance, and deliver exceptional user experiences.

In the next section, we'll explore how to leverage RIs and Azure Hybrid Benefit, focusing on how long-term commitments and license optimizations can further reduce costs in Azure.

Leveraging RIs, SIs, and Azure Hybrid Benefits

While Azure's PAYG pricing model provides flexibility for unpredictable workloads, organizations with consistent or long-term resource needs can achieve significant cost savings by leveraging RIs, SIs, and Azure Hybrid Benefit. These options provide predictable pricing, reduce operational expenses, and maximize the value of existing investments in on-premises software licenses.

This section will explore how RIs, SIs, and Azure Hybrid Benefit work, when to use them, and how they align with business goals to optimize cloud spending. Through real-world scenarios and practical insights, you'll understand how these features can lead to substantial cost reductions.

Understanding RIs

RIs enable organizations to commit to using specific Azure resources—such as VMs—for a period of one or three years. In return, Azure offers significant discounts compared to PAYG pricing.

How RIs work

RIs are purchased for specific VM configurations, including **size**, **region**, and **operating system**. Unlike SIs, which are suitable for interruptible workloads, RIs guarantee resource availability and are ideal for stable, predictable workloads:

- **Key benefits**:

  - **Cost savings**: Discounts of up to 72% compared to PAYG pricing

- **Predictable costs**: Simplifies budget planning with consistent monthly or upfront payments

- **Flexibility**: Azure allows modifications to RI attributes (e.g., region or VM size) to adapt to changing needs

- **Example use case**: A healthcare provider operates an always-on patient records application using VMs with consistent performance requirements. By purchasing RIs, they lock in discounted rates, reducing costs by 60% over three years while maintaining 24/7 service availability.

Understanding Azure SIs

Azure SIs allow organizations to purchase unused Azure compute capacity at significantly reduced costs. These instances are ideal for workloads that can tolerate interruptions, such as batch processing, testing, and non-critical applications:

- **How Azure SIs work**: Azure SIs are offered at a discounted rate compared to standard PAYG prices. However, they come with the condition that they can be evicted (terminated) by Azure if the capacity is needed for other users. Pricing for SIs fluctuates based on supply and demand, and users can set a maximum price they are willing to pay per hour. Unlike RIs, which provide guaranteed availability for stable workloads, SIs are best suited for transient or flexible workloads.

- **Key benefits**:

  - **Significant cost savings**: SIs offer discounts of up to 90% compared to PAYG pricing, making them highly cost-effective for suitable workloads

  - **Flexibility for non-critical tasks**: Ideal for tasks such as batch processing, CI/CD pipelines, or running large-scale simulations where interruptions are acceptable

  - **Efficient resource utilization**: Leverages unused Azure capacity, allowing organizations to achieve their goals at a fraction of the cost

- **Example use case**: A data analytics company runs periodic simulations to optimize supply chain logistics. These simulations, while computationally intensive, do not require uninterrupted operation. By using Azure SIs, the company reduces compute costs by 85%. If a simulation is interrupted, the workload simply resumes from the last checkpoint, ensuring minimal disruption at a fraction of the expense of standard instances.

Azure Hybrid Benefit

The Azure Hybrid Benefit allows organizations to use their existing on-premises software licenses for Windows Server and SQL Server on Azure, significantly lowering cloud costs. This benefit is particularly useful for organizations transitioning to the cloud or maintaining hybrid environments:

- **How Azure Hybrid Benefit works**: Organizations with active **Software Assurance** (**SA**) on their licenses can apply these licenses to Azure resources, avoiding the cost of buying new licenses.

- **Key benefits:**

  - **Cost reduction:** Save up to 85% on VM and database costs

  - **Flexibility:** Combine with RIs for even greater savings

  - **Alignment with hybrid strategies:** Enables seamless integration of on-premises and cloud environments

- **Example use case:** A financial services firm migrating their SQL Server database to Azure SQL Managed Instance applies the Azure Hybrid Benefit to reuse their on-premises licenses. This reduces their database costs by nearly 50%, allowing them to reinvest the savings into other innovation projects.

Combining RIs and Azure Hybrid Benefit

Organizations can combine RIs and Azure Hybrid Benefit to maximize cost savings. This approach is especially effective for long-term workloads that require licensed resources.

Example use case: A manufacturing company running a global ERP system on Azure VMs purchases RIs for their always-on workloads and applies the Azure Hybrid Benefit to reuse existing Windows Server licenses. By doing so, they achieve a 70% reduction in their cloud compute costs over three years.

Best practices for leveraging RIs and Azure Hybrid Benefit

To get the most out of RIs and Azure Hybrid Benefit, follow these best practices:

- **Analyze workload patterns:** Use Azure Cost Management to identify stable workloads that are suitable for RIs. Focus on VMs or databases with consistent utilization over time.

- **Optimize commitment levels:** Choose between one-year or three-year terms based on budget flexibility and workload predictability. Longer commitments yield higher discounts but require more certainty about future needs.

- **Review license eligibility:** Ensure on-premises licenses are eligible for Azure Hybrid Benefit by verifying SA status. Use the Azure Pricing Calculator to estimate potential savings.

- **Monitor and adjust:** Regularly review RIs and Hybrid Benefit allocations to ensure they align with evolving workloads. Azure allows modifications to RIs (e.g., changing region or VM family), enabling you to adapt to changing requirements.

By leveraging RIs, SIs, and Azure Hybrid Benefit, organizations can dramatically reduce cloud costs while ensuring resource availability and operational efficiency. These strategies are particularly beneficial for predictable, long-term workloads, enabling businesses to allocate budgets more effectively.

In the next and final section of this chapter and this book, we will delve into how to establish governance policies for cloud spending, focusing on enforcing cost control measures and aligning spending with organizational priorities.

Implementing governance policies for effective cost control

Cloud governance is a critical component of managing cloud environments effectively, ensuring that resources are used responsibly, and costs are controlled. Without proper governance, organizations risk overspending, non-compliance with policies, and inefficient resource allocation. Azure offers powerful tools, such as **Azure Policy** and **Management Groups**, to help enforce governance policies across cloud environments.

In this section, we will explore how to establish governance frameworks to maintain control over cloud spending, align expenditures with business priorities, and ensure adherence to organizational standards. By implementing these governance practices, organizations can foster a culture of accountability while optimizing cloud costs.

Why governance policies matter in Cost Management

Governance policies provide guardrails for cloud usage, ensuring that resources are deployed, managed, and decommissioned according to organizational guidelines. These policies help to do the following:

- **Control costs**: Prevent the creation of unnecessary or oversized resources
- **Ensure accountability**: Track spending across teams and projects using tagging and reporting
- **Enhance compliance**: Enforce regulatory and internal standards to meet business requirements
- **Improve resource utilization**: Streamline the provisioning and lifecycle management of cloud assets

Example use case: A software development company deploys governance policies to prevent the creation of premium VMs in non-production environments, ensuring cost control without compromising performance in critical areas.

Key tools and techniques for governance in Azure

Azure provides several governance tools to help organizations enforce cost-control policies and maintain compliance across their cloud environments:

- **Azure Policy**: Azure Policy allows you to define and enforce rules that govern the configuration and usage of resources to ensure compliance with organizational standards.

  - Policies are defined using JSON and can be applied at the management group, subscription, resource group, or resource level. For example, you can enforce encryption for all storage accounts.

- *Cost Control Example*: Restrict the deployment of high-cost VM SKUs to prevent over-provisioning.

- **Azure Cost Management + Billing**: This tool provides insights into cloud spending and enables budgeting, cost tracking, and optimization.

  - Offers dashboards, reports, forecasts, and alerting tools to help manage and control costs across Azure and other cloud providers.

  - *Cost Control Example*: Set spending budgets and receive alerts when usage exceeds predefined thresholds.

- **Management Groups**: Management Groups allow you to organize subscriptions into a hierarchy for centralized governance.

  - Apply policies and access controls across multiple subscriptions consistently by grouping them under a common management group.

  - *Cost Control Example*: Apply standardized cost-related policies, such as restricting allowed regions or VM sizes, across all business unit subscriptions.

- **Role-Based Access Control (RBAC)**: RBAC helps ensure that users have only the permissions they need to perform their tasks—nothing more.

  - Assign built-in or custom roles to users, groups, or service principals at various scopes (for example, subscription or resource group).

  - *Cost Control Example*: Limit access to cost-impacting operations, such as provisioning large VMs or scaling resources, to specific roles.

Azure Management Groups

Azure Management Groups allow organizations to structure and organize subscriptions hierarchically. Policies and **role-based access control** (RBAC) can be applied at the management group level for consistent enforcement:

- **How it works**: Subscriptions are grouped into logical categories (e.g., production, development, testing), and policies can be assigned at the group level to standardize settings across multiple subscriptions

- **Example use case**: A global enterprise with multiple Azure subscriptions uses management groups to enforce cost limits and resource tagging policies for all development environments

Governance for a multi-team organization

A technology company with multiple teams working on separate Azure projects faces challenges in managing costs and ensuring accountability:

- **Challenge**: Teams deploy resources without standardized guidelines, leading to unused assets and inconsistent spending
- **Solution**: The company establishes governance policies using Azure tools:
  - Implements tagging policies to categorize resources by project and department
  - Creates management groups to enforce cost limits for development and testing environments
  - Uses Azure Policy to restrict premium resource types to critical workloads only
- **Outcome**: The company reduces unnecessary spending by 30% and improves visibility into cloud expenditures across teams

Best practices for establishing governance policies

The following best practices ensure governance policies are effective, enforce compliance, and optimize cloud costs:

- **Define clear guidelines**: Establish policies that align with organizational goals, such as restricting certain resource types or setting budgets for specific environments
- **Implement resource tagging**: Use consistent tagging conventions to track resource ownership, purpose, and environment
- **Monitor compliance**: Use Azure Policy to audit resource configurations and enforce corrective actions for non-compliance
- **Automate governance**: Leverage Azure Automation and streamline policy enforcement and resource provisioning

Establishing governance policies is essential for maintaining control over cloud spending and ensuring that resources are used efficiently and responsibly. By leveraging Azure tools such as Policy and Management Groups, organizations can implement robust governance frameworks that align with business objectives, reduce costs, and foster accountability.

Summary

With this learning objective, we conclude this chapter. Together, we have explored how to optimize costs through pricing models, monitoring, scaling, and governance. These practices empower organizations to achieve financial efficiency while maintaining a scalable and performant cloud infrastructure.

I truly hope you enjoyed this chapter and the entire journey through Azure Cloud Projects. My goal was to share valuable insights and practical knowledge that you can apply in your cloud journey. If this book added even a small spark of learning or inspiration, then it has fulfilled its purpose. I'd love to hear your thoughts, feedback, and experiences, let's connect and continue exploring the endless possibilities of Azure together. Wishing you success in all your cloud endeavors!

Get This Book's PDF Version and Exclusive Extras

UNLOCK NOW

Scan the QR code (or go to `packtpub.com/unlock`). Search for this book by name, confirm the edition, and then follow the steps on the page.

Note: Keep your invoice handly. Purchase made directly from packt don't require one.

Stay Sharp in Cloud and DevOps – Join 44,000+ Subscribers of CloudPro

CloudPro is a weekly newsletter for cloud professionals who want to stay current on the fast-evolving world of cloud computing, DevOps, and infrastructure engineering.

Every issue delivers focused, high-signal content on topics like:

- AWS, GCP & multi-cloud architecture
- Containers, Kubernetes & orchestration
- Infrastructure as Code (IaC) with Terraform, Pulumi, etc.
- Platform engineering & automation workflows
- Observability, performance tuning, and reliability best practices

Whether you're a cloud engineer, SRE, DevOps practitioner, or platform lead, CloudPro helps you stay on top of what matters, without the noise.

Scan the QR code to join for free and get weekly insights straight to your inbox:

`https://packt.link/cloudpro`

Unlock Your Exclusive Benefits

Your copy of this book includes the following exclusive benefit:

- ⟳ Next-gen Packt Reader
- 📄 DRM-free PDF/ePub downloads

Follow the guide below to unlock them. The process takes only a few minutes and needs to be completed once.

Unlock this Book's Free Benefits in 3 Easy Steps

Step 1

Keep your purchase invoice ready for *Step 3*. If you have a physical copy, scan it using your phone and save it as a PDF, JPG, or PNG.

For more help on finding your invoice, visit `https://www.packtpub.com/unlock-benefits/help`.

> **Note**
>
> If you bought this book directly from Packt, no invoice is required. After *Step 2*, you can access your exclusive content right away.

Step 2

Scan the QR code or go to `packtpub.com/unlock`.

On the page that opens (similar to *Figure 11.1* on desktop), search for this book by name and select the correct edition.

Figure 11.1: Packt unlock landing page on desktop

Step 3

After selecting your book, sign in to your Packt account or create one for free. Then upload your invoice (PDF, PNG, or JPG, up to 10 MB). Follow the on-screen instructions to finish the process.

Need help?

If you get stuck and need help, visit
`https://www.packtpub.com/unlock-benefits/help`
for a detailed FAQ on how to find your invoices and more. This QR
code will take you to the help page.

> **Note**
>
> If you are still facing issues, reach out to `customercare@packt.com`.

Index

‹packt›

packtpub.com

Subscribe to our online digital library for full access to over 7,000 books and videos, as well as industry leading tools to help you plan your personal development and advance your career. For more information, please visit our website.

Why subscribe?

- Spend less time learning and more time coding with practical eBooks and Videos from over 4,000 industry professionals

- Improve your learning with Skill Plans built especially for you

- Get a free eBook or video every month

- Fully searchable for easy access to vital information

- Copy and paste, print, and bookmark content

Did you know that Packt offers eBook versions of every book published, with PDF and ePub files available? You can upgrade to the eBook version at packtpub.com and as a print book customer, you are entitled to a discount on the eBook copy. Get in touch with us at customercare@packtpub.com for more details.

At www.packtpub.com, you can also read a collection of free technical articles, sign up for a range of free newsletters, and receive exclusive discounts and offers on Packt books and eBooks.

Other Books You May Enjoy

If you enjoyed this book, you may be interested in these other books by Packt:

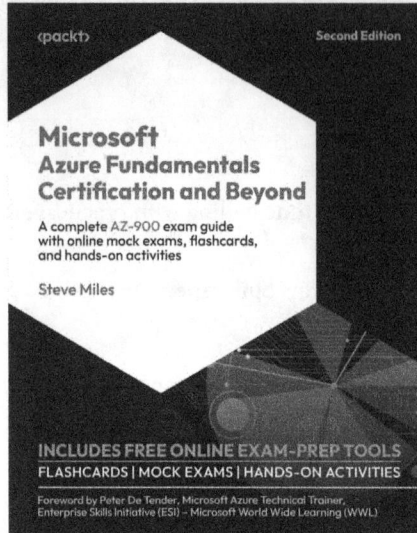

Microsoft Azure Fundamentals Certification and Beyond

Steve Miles

ISBN: 978-1-83763-059-2

- Core cloud computing concepts and how they apply to Azure
- Azure's key services, deployment methods, and management tools
- Implementation of security concepts, identity management, and governance features
- Resource deployment, monitoring, and compliance best practices
- Skills to manage and optimize Azure environments effectively

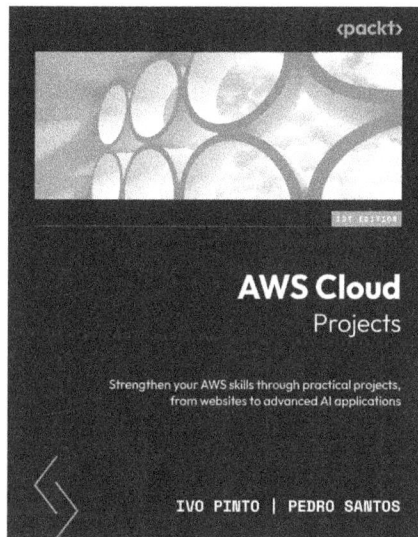

AWS Cloud Projects

Ivo Pinto, Pedro Santos

ISBN: 978-1-83588-928-2

- Develop a professional CV website while learning AWS fundamentals
- Build a recipe-sharing application using AWS's serverless toolkit
- Leverage AWS AI services to create a photo friendliness analyzer for professional profiles
- Implement a CI/CD pipeline to automate content translation across languages
- Develop an AI-powered Q&A chatbot using Amazon Lex and cutting-edge LLMs
- Build a business intelligence application to analyze website clickstream data and understand user behavior with AWS

Packt is searching for authors like you

If you're interested in becoming an author for Packt, please visit `authors.packtpub.com` and apply today. We have worked with thousands of developers and tech professionals, just like you, to help them share their insight with the global tech community. You can make a general application, apply for a specific hot topic that we are recruiting an author for, or submit your own idea.

Share Your Thoughts

Now you've finished *Azure Cloud Projects*, we'd love to hear your thoughts! Scan the QR code below to go straight to the Amazon review page for this book and share your feedback or leave a review on the site that you purchased it from.

`https://packt.link/r/1-836-20423-X`

Your review is important to us and the tech community and will help us make sure we're delivering excellent quality content.